Democracy under Fire

Democracy under Fire

Donald Trump and the Breaking of American History

LAWRENCE R. JACOBS

OXFORD

UNIVERSITY PRESS

Oxford University Press is a department of the University of Oxford. It furthers
the University's objective of excellence in research, scholarship, and education
by publishing worldwide. Oxford is a registered trade mark of Oxford University
Press in the UK and certain other countries.

Published in the United States of America by Oxford University Press
198 Madison Avenue, New York, NY 10016, United States of America.

CIP data is on file at the Library of Congress

ISBN 978–0–19–087724–8

DOI: 10.1093/oso/9780190877248.001.0001

1 3 5 7 9 8 6 4 2

Printed by LSC communications, United States of America

For Julie Schumacher—
My soulmate who lifts me with her grace, intelligence, humor,
and tenacity

Table of Contents

Acknowledgments

I have accumulated many debts of gratitude. The University of Minnesota's Humphrey School of Public Affairs and Walter F. and Joan Mondale Chair provided generous support. My Visiting Fellow year at All Souls College at Oxford University created a remarkably stimulating environment.

Graduate students at the University of Minnesota's Department of Political Science and Humphrey School have been energetic and diligent in tracking down my many questions and requests over a number of years. In particular, I thank Jonathan Spiegler and Carissa Kemp. I am most grateful to Penny Thomas, who toiled on this project for four years with good cheer and terrific research skills. I wrote this book while balancing other responsibilities; directing the Center for the Study of Politics and Governance was infinitely more manageable due to the calm and brilliant leadership of Lea Chittenden.

David McBride at Oxford University Press read an early chapter and then the entire manuscript with a keen eye. Emily Mackenzie Benitez skippered the manuscript through the production process with efficiency and attention to detail and Bob Land copy edited this book with skill.

Barbara Mikulski and Walter Mondale generously talked with me about Democratic Party politics in the 1960s and 1970s. Vin Weber was a valuable sounding board about the Republican primary system and the hurdles facing significant reform of either party's primaries.

Democracy under Fire delivers a stinging diagnosis of contemporary American politics that is rooted in more than 250 years of contentious history. Conversations and written feedback from many colleagues were enormously helpful in sparking thought-provoking questions and bracing challenges. Rob Mickey, Bob Shapiro, and Michael Minta offered sharp observations after reading sections of the manuscript. Lisa Disch inspired me to re-think democratic theory, and Suzanne Mettler fed my alarm about the threats to American democracy. Steve Skowronek invigorated my thinking about the Progressive Era. I am particularly grateful to Theda Skocpol's collaborations and feedback over a number of years, stimulating my thinking about macrohistory, contemporary American politics, and their linkages. Desmond King generously contributed to this project through years of back-and-forth exchanges on its themes and a meticulous reading of the entire draft manuscript.

1

The Making of
Democratic Vulnerability

"January 6 was a disgrace," Senate Republican Leader Mitch McConnell solemnly intoned at the end of Donald Trump's second impeachment trial on February 13, 2021. "American citizens attacked their own government . . . to try to stop a specific piece of democratic business they did not like." As to the culprit, the US Senate's Republican leader declared that "there is no question that President Trump is practically and morally responsible . . . [by unleashing] the growing crescendo of false statements, conspiracy theories, and reckless hyperbole which the defeated president kept shouting into the largest megaphone on planet Earth."

Trump's "disgraceful dereliction of duty" on January 6 was a singular threat to American democracy, but his disdain for the rules, procedures, and norms of representative governance was well known before he even ran for president. In the third debate with Hillary Clinton, he refused—as he would four years later—to commit to conceding the election if he lost. He spewed unconstitutional and illegal threats—taking away citizenship or imprisoning flag-burners, reopening the closed investigation of his Democratic opponent's use of a private email server, and suing the media for news reports he disliked.[1] His disdain for America's rule of law was accompanied by racist and vulgar comments including his boast during an *Access Hollywood* tape about "grabbing [women] by the pussy" and pressuring married women into having sex.

Anticipating Trump's disregard for American law and the Constitution, prominent Republicans in Congress as well as former senior government officials and governors repudiated candidate Trump as "unfit" as the GOP nominee.[2] The serious misgivings of Republican leaders were confirmed after he entered the Oval Office, though most Republicans planning on a future in politics remained silent or fell in line behind him. President Trump disregarded the norms of self-restraint that undergird democratic governance: he spread 30,573 false or misleading claims; declared the media "the enemy of the people," even though it was a bulwark of the First Amendment; and interfered with the legal process by pressuring Attorney General Jeff Sessions, FBI director James Comey, and White House counsel Donald McGahn to take inappropriate or illegal actions.[3] He launched shady efforts to pressure foreign governments—notably Ukraine—to smear his political rival, Joe Biden, and reward allies with clemency.[4] Trump also accelerated the accretion of presidential power at the expense of Congress by defying its oversight and subpoenas and ignoring its power of the purse by unilaterally spending money to build a southern wall. Even after losing the election and Biden's inauguration, Trump's unfounded charges of vote fraud soiled the legitimacy of elections and spurred misguided Republican efforts to tamper with state election procedures and laws.

Given the clear-eyed assessment of candidate Trump by Republican leaders, why did the party nominate him as its presidential candidate in 2016? Why did his contempt for democratic rules, procedures, and norms fail to disqualify him as its presidential candidate? Is there no "filter" in America's representative system of government to block a dangerous renegade from seeking entry to the Oval Office?

Much of the attention paid to Trump's rise to power has focused on his corrosive personality and divisive style of governing. Missing has been an examination of the structure of politics that acquiesced in his rise.

The ascendance of Trump is not an aberration but a predicted—indeed, recurrent—result of a nomination process that sidelined party officials and senior officials and deferred to a relatively small number of ideologically motivated party activists, interest groups, and donors. Worse, the system that handcuffed party leaders from stopping a known renegade is considered "democratic."

Will "government of the people, by the people, for the people, . . . not perish from the earth," as Abraham Lincoln intoned on the blood-drenched soil of Gettysburg? It is vulnerable and there are few, if any, reliable protections against the future nomination of dangerous candidates by either major political party. The "scheme of representation"—as James Madison put it in Federalist Paper 10—does not extend to party nominations to filter out candidates who threaten the Constitution. It must be erected if democratic political representation is to endure.

How did genuine democracy become so vulnerable? Researchers and informed observers frequently point to the Democratic Party reforms in 1969–1970 that triggered the adoption of presidential primary elections to select candidates.[5] This episode is important, but the changes were structured by three prior political clashes over the form of American democracy since the late eighteenth century. The Declaration of Independence laid a cornerstone in 1776 for democratic governance by proclaiming the principle that all male citizens are created equal. While the framers of the US Constitution initially disdained political parties as sources of faction, Thomas Jefferson was motivated by his loss to John Adams in the 1796 presidential contest to weaponize nascent parties to create a "revolution" in mass voting that elected him in 1800. In the 1820s and 1830s, the infamous frontier General Andrew Jackson extended the mobilizing capacity of political parties and added a critical new form of American democracy—the national party convention to choose the presidential candidates—in order to realize the Declaration's promise of political equality. The fourth critical juncture was the quixotic push during the early twentieth century's Progressive Era to restore democracy by establishing direct primaries to end boss control over the party convention.

The four critical junctures in the development of democratic rules and procedures differed in their immediate contexts but each confronted the organizing principles of political equality and government authority. James Madison engineered the Constitutional Convention to establish the authority and legitimacy of government—including representative institutions—and contain the "strong democracy" that erupted in states during the 1780s as farmers, laborers, and other "ordinary" citizens converted the Declaration's call for political equality into a reality. Madison's double-sided strategy—control the expression of political equality and lay a foundation for representative rules and procedures—was extended by Jackson's political strategist Martin Van Buren, who anchored representative institutions in the political party nomination process in the 1830s. The Progressive Era is often touted for launching the direct primary but the fierce and effective opposition to its wide adoption stands out as do the prophetic warnings by Herbert Croly—one of the intellectual trailblazers of the Progressive movement—about its threat to the authority and legitimacy of representative institutions. The tension posed by equality and authority that explicitly preoccupied state builders during America's first 180 years was ignored—or unknown—to the reformers of the Democratic Party in 1969–1970; their embrace of primary elections undermined the authority and legitimacy of the established party structure.

The enduring hold of white supremacy tested America's commitment to the principle of political equality. The soaring promises of the Declaration of Independence coexisted with slavery and the Jim Crow state and local laws that remained well into the twentieth century. Reformers promised to expand representative democracy by establishing the direct primary but ended up reconstituting America's racial orders first by creating "white primaries" that kept the Jim Crow South in power until the mid- twentieth century and later by dissipating the votes of Blacks, Indigenous, and other people of color.[6]

The critical junctures that changed democratic institutions were accompanied by loud and, at times, well-organized popular campaigns, but it was elite politics that consistently generated tangible reform. Protesters and the "police riot" at the 1968 Democratic Convention lit up Chicago; ambitious politicians seized on these events as a pretext to exploit cracks in the party's establishment, in an effort to covertly transform the nomination process and advance their presidential aspirations.

If American democracy is going to fend off the next Donald Trump, attention must be focused on restraining governing and political elites within the confines of representative rules and procedures. Elites—not citizens—are chiefly responsible for diminishing the authority and legitimacy of democratic institutions.[7] *Democracy under Fire*'s history of the origins of direct primaries and its enveloping of American politics opens a window onto broader themes about the nature and limits of American democracy and economic and racial inequality in political representation.

The following three sections set the stage for tracing the development of democratic rules and procedures in the coming chapters. We begin by discussing the enormous—often, decisive—influence of the candidate nomination process on American democracy today. The following section explores the exaggerated criticisms of citizens in representative democracy and underappreciated threats of governing and political elites. The third section outlines the chapters on each of the four historical junctures and the closing chapters on the consequences of the primary system and reforms to curb its most damaging effects. We close with a word about connecting research on history to contemporary politics.

American Democracy Held Hostage
by Primaries

Representative democracy rests on the bedrock principles of political equality and civil liberties to participate in the rough-and-tumble world of debating public controversies and making laws.[8] The US Constitution and Bill of Rights laid the institutional foundation for political equality to vote and participate in a range of additional political activities including organizing and speaking out against government officials and policies. Equal political participation by citizens is essential in a system of representation that considers the wishes and wants of all citizens. "Equal activity," Sidney Verba reasons, "is crucial for equal consideration since political activity is the means by which citizens make their needs and preferences known to governing elites and induce them to be responsive."[9]

American politics as it currently stands violates the foundational principles of political equality and consent of the governed.

The Hijacking of Elections

Primary elections have become gatekeepers that reproduce or multiply political advantage. Some states exclude citizens from voting in primary elections for a party's nominee if they are not members of that party. Even among citizens eligible to participate in primary elections, most abstain. Only a quarter or third of eligible voters participate during presidential election years and far less during off-election years and less prominent races.[10] Even in the lively 2016 battle to select the Democratic and Republican nominees, only 25.7 percent of eligible voters participated, which is considerably less than half of the general election turnout of 59.2 percent. In the election two years later, only about 20 percent turned out, which was a substantial

increase over the previous midterm election in 2014. Turnout
was also modest in the closely fought 2020 Democratic nomination. Only 13.9 percent turned out in the decisive South Carolina
primary that propelled Biden to winning the nomination.
Turnout in the big states of Florida, Ohio, and Texas was about
10 percent.[11] Bernie Sanders targeted Michigan and its working
class to reignite his campaign but turnout remained low; it was
more than threefold higher in the general election. Exclusion
and abstention are racially concentrated. Participation by
people of color in primaries is lower than for whites. In recent
primary elections, Black turnout has been 15 percent on average
compared to 25 percent for whites.[12]

The Power of the Few

E. E. Schattschneider wrote a slender (and initially ignored) mas-
terpiece on the tilted pattern of American politics and its source—
the limited and biased scope of conflict.[13] Political conflict, he
concludes, tends to be privatized among relatively small and unrepresentative factions instead of socialized to engage the mass of citizens in the political fights that impact their lives. The institutions of
American elections bias participation toward the better established
and organized.

Unrepresentativeness is a consistent pattern in American politics: voting, contacting government representatives, and a host of
other forms of political activities are disproportionately pursued by
the white, affluent, and better-educated citizens and those in organized groups.[14] The process of primaries contributes by advantaging
organized special interests and ideological factions committed
to establishing and entrenching their privileged influence on
American politics. While the originators of the primary envisioned
more inclusive representation, it shifted power over candidate
nominations from party officials to relatively small cliques of

advocates on the left and right, special interests pleading for their clients, and deep-pocketed donors and their networks.[15]

The Republican Party shifted in a sharply conservative direction, as apparent by the composition of its national presidential conventions. Since the primary system settled in, Republican convention delegates have become far more conservative (rising from 48 percent of delegates in 1976 to 72 percent in 2008) and far less moderate (dropping from 45 percent to 26 percent during the same period). By comparison, liberals became more present at Democratic National Conventions, though only modestly: rising from 40 percent in 1976 to 43 percent in 2008. The presence of moderates rose—rather than declined—from 47 percent to 50 percent during the same period.[16]

Attentive to the incentive structure that guides their careers, candidates concentrate on securing the support of the party activists, interest groups, and donors who serve as convention delegates that choose nominees and fuel their campaigns.[17] Instead of promising patronage as was common in the old system, the political currency for contemporary candidates to win nomination is to promise unflinching policy commitments. Pro-life advocates search for GOP candidates who commit to appointing social conservative judges while pro-choice and single-payer healthcare supporters insist that Democratic nominees embrace their agendas. In the 1972 presidential nomination battle, George McGovern was unable to secure the support of the old New Deal coalition with labor and, instead, mobilized backing where he could get it—"the most extreme of the peace groups and the young of the campus," even though the majority did not share their views.[18] After Ronald Reagan was denied the nomination in 1976, he succeeded in 1980 by mobilizing a "New Right" coalition of economic and social conservatives.[19] George H. W. Bush engaged in a particularly striking makeover: after running as a pro-choice candidate during the 1980 presidential nomination contest and losing, he opted for a pro-life position in 1988 and won the nomination and general election.

Once elected, Democrats or Republicans who refuse to abide by the policy demands of networks of activists, organized groups, and donors face a stark choice: retire in anticipation of a dismal future or prepare to be "primaried" by groups who recruit and bankroll challengers.[20] Even politicians who devoted years to advancing the agendas of activists have been unceremoniously tossed by Club for Growth, FreedomWorks, MoveOn.org, and other ideological activists and donors if they compromise on a single salient issue. The name "Bob Bennett" brings shivers among his colleagues in the US Senate. Senator Bennett represented Utah in the US Senate for three terms as a staunch Republican conservative, earning high ratings from the National Rifle Association, US Chamber of Commerce, and American Conservative Union. His bid for the Republican nomination was unceremoniously defeated in 2010 by the Tea Party. His political felony? He had the temerity to follow the pleas of President George W. Bush to vote to rescue the banking system during the 2008 financial crisis and avoid "Herbert Hoover time," as Vice President Richard Cheney put it.

Why did Republicans who despised Donald Trump in private vote against his impeachment? Answer: the incentive structure that the primary created. Meet the new Robert Bennett: Liz Cheney who is a conservative US House leader and daughter of the former vice president. Her offense was to vote in Congress to impeach Trump following the January 6, 2021, insurrection and call out his seditious conduct: "Trump is seeking to unravel critical elements of our constitutional structure that make our democracy work—confidence in the results of elections and the rule of law." She challenged Republicans to "choose truth and fidelity to the Constitution." The GOP's response to Trump's fury and that of GOP activists was swift. Rep. Cheney's defeated opponent in 2016 summed up her home state's reaction: "She gave the state of Wyoming the middle finger."[21] She faces the dreary prospect in 2022 of a well-funded primary challenger and defeat in a state that is heavily Republican and voted for Trump by over forty points.[22] Even before she gets to an election, House Republicans demoted her from their leadership.

Members of Congress and presidents who seek a successful career in politics have received a clear message: follow party activists and their coalition. If elected officials find themselves out of step with party activists, many change their policy positions to align with them. Politicians, however, are rarely out of step: activists recruit many of the Republican and Democratic candidates in the first place based on shared policy commitments and activism.[23]

Take note of what is missing: the views of most Americans. The activists within the Democratic and, especially Republican Parties hold extreme policy preferences compared to those of most Americans. Polls show that the views of GOP activists toward abortion, Obamacare, and other issues are far more conservative than those of most Americans. Polls also show liberals more progressive on abortion and single-payer health reform. Also missing are encompassing debates and large-scale organizations—epitomized by mass organizing political parties—that make the stakes plain and attract the interest and participation of the broad public and the marginalized citizens who often remain on the sidelines (youth, people of color, and lower-income people).

American Democracy in Retreat

A two-step process narrows American democracy. *Step 1*: Small cliques of advocates who are more liberal and far more conservative than most Americans use low-turnout primaries to dictate the candidates that each party nominates. In 2010, for instance, the Tea Party's takeover of the Republican Party was aided by candidates who won primaries with turnout of 12 to 15 percent. On the Democratic side, the progressive firebrand Alexandria Ocasio-Cortez won her 2018 primary against the moderate incumbent Joe

Crowley with only 12 percent turnout of registered Democrats in New York's 14th Congressional District.[24]

Step 2 amplifies the power of party activists and their coalitions. Voter evaluations of the nominee's traits and qualifications during the fall general election are often short-circuited by partisan sorting. Three out of four voters affiliate as Democrat or Republican, which automatically delivers large blocks of ballots to each major party's nominee. The tractor beam of partisanship secures reelection for legislators in heavily partisan legislative districts and boosts even candidates facing competitive contests. The outsized significance of party activists in general elections is conditioned, in part, by economic circumstances: the relatively few unaffiliated voters reward candidates in the incumbent party during good times and punish them in bad times. The merits and messages of each party's candidates may matter, but the single best predictor of general election results is partisanship at a time when nearly all Democrats and Republicans mechanically rally behind their tribe's nominee.

In short, nomination contests—and not general elections—are decisive decision points for selecting government officials. Most voters are forced on Election Day to choose between candidates who are more liberal or conservative than themselves.[25] That pivotal choice is set by relatively small numbers of ideological party activists, groups, and donors. Worse still, once in office, politicians cater to that party clique to keep their positions.

This two-step process opened the door to Donald Trump's nomination and then election in 2016 despite the widespread opposition of Republican leaders and indications that he would threaten the US Constitution and legal system.

Step 1: He fashioned his 2016 campaign to win narrow factions and voting segments to secure the nomination even though it made him the most unpopular nominee in modern history. While Trump was perceived as a moderate conservative according to the American National Election Studies, he stood out in a crowded primary field of seventeen candidates for his fiery antiestablishment screed that appealed to the economic unease and social resentment of white Americans. "The governing elite are wrong," he railed, on "every major issue affecting this country" because the political system is undemocratic. "Members of the club—the consultants, the pollsters, the politicians, the pundits and the special interests—grow rich and powerful... [by] substitut[ing] their will for America's will." He melded his race-infused populist appeal to "Make America Great Again" and deport immigrants with a promise to an influential GOP faction: Trump's nomination of judges would be approved by born-again evangelical groups. Despite Trump's sinful personal life, state exit polls consistently showed Trump besting his primary competitors among evangelicals (including the authentic social conservative Ted Cruz). He also won primary voters who identified immigrants as a major national problem and favored their deportation, along with those who expressed anger at the federal government.

Trump secured a modest but consistent plurality of the primary vote in state contests. A majority of Republican primary voters opposed Trump but split their votes among his rivals. The result is that Trump won all three February primaries with only 34 percent of the primary vote and nearly all the March primaries with under 38 percent. Even with most candidates dropping out by April, Trump only won 40 percent of the primary vote by the end of the primary battle.[26] Put more broadly, the nearly 129 million voters in the 2016 general elections were compelled to consider a Republican candidate who received support from 6.1 percent of the U.S. electorate.

Step 2: Once he secured the GOP nomination, much of his support came from predictable sources. He drew votes from nearly all Republicans who chose him over Hillary Clinton. He added to this base by picking up just enough support from disaffected Americans who blamed the "in" party for the economic doldrums, were hostile toward immigration, and fueled by racial resentment.[27] He won independents 48-42 as well as 79 percent reporting that the national economy was poor and 69 percent declaring that the country was seriously off track. These forces drew 63 million voters to Trump and allowed him to eke out an Electoral College victory even though Clinton won the popular vote, with nearly 66 million supporting her.

While the primary system was initially heralded for fulfilling the Declaration's promise of political equality and popular consent, it equipped Trump's relatively small number of primary supporters to steer the will of the majority. He strode onto the uniquely visible stages afforded by the primary, locked in his nomination despite the opposition of GOP leaders, and cleared the barriers to put his name on the ballot in states across the country. Each of these steps biased the scope of conflict toward the organized and well-resourced.[28] That's not all. After the 2016 elections, Trump and Republican members of Congress remained focused on catering to the insiders who secured their nominations, as was evident in the policies and appointments they approved. Trump converted the dependence of GOP lawmakers on party activists who supported him into a weapon to block two impeachment trials and launch an extraordinary challenge to the Electoral College after the 2020 elections.

Trump's march to the pinnacle of power is closely tied to race—the tensions he openly fanned and the process he used. The primary process is stained by its deep roots in the South and the establishment of Jim Crow discrimination. Borrowing a page from segregationists who used the primary to solidify the white vote, Trump's vicious attacks on Blacks and Mexican Americans as a candidate and president coalesced frustrated less-well-educated white voters into a loyal following. There's more. Since the 1970s, the primary has contributed, in certain circumstances, to depressing the election of candidates of color despite America's egalitarian claims to empower "the people."

Who Is to Blame?

Political elites are mainly responsible for the vulnerability of
American democratic institutions to well-organized activists and
groups and the disruption that Donald Trump provoked on January
6. The pattern of elite misjudgment and expediency contradicts the
longstanding habit of blaming citizens for the ills of democracy.

Doubters of Democracy

Soon after the 2016 election, a writer for the *New Yorker*—a gathering ground for refined liberal opinion—revealed that he had spent
the fall "staying up late, reading polls in terror" and wondering if
the culprit is the "flawed and faulty nature of democracy."[29] This
doubter of democracy joins a broad and enduring tradition of citizen blaming.

Here are the particulars lodged against citizens since Plato about
twenty-four hundred years ago (yes, democracy doubting is literally an ancient undertaking):

> *First up: Citizens are ignorant.* "Democracy is the rule of the
> people," one critic insisted, "but the people are in many
> ways unfit to rule." An icon to democracy doubters, Joseph
> Schumpeter bitingly described the "mental performance"
> of citizens as "infantile" and "primitive."[30] The problem,
> critics of democracy claim, is that the voters are "ignorant,
> irrational, [and] misinformed" and stumble into a "dance of
> dunces."[31]
>
> *Second charge: Citizens lack a serious and steady tempera-
> ment.* Since the framing of the US Constitution, democracy
> doubters warned that gusts of "passion" would fan impul-
> sive action by citizens, which would trample on the rights of
> individuals and produce rash decisions. Slothful and quick to

anger are traits that result from the "lazy citizenship habits of many Americans."[32]

Third charge: Citizens and their advocates expect too much and are insufficiently deferential to governing elites—the senior government officials and policy experts who should do the deciding. The problem is "excess democracy" stemming from voters demanding too much and overloading the governing process.[33] The remedy, we are lectured, is to "minimiz[e] the democratic distortion" or, as Jason Brennan proposes, restrict voting to citizens who pass a test.[34]

Criticism of citizens is a familiar back alley to lauding elites and experts as governors.[35] A former governor of the Federal Reserve Bank boasted in 1997 that its reliance on expert bankers and economists worked so well that more areas of policy decisions (from taxes to spending) should be delegated to "technocratic policy making." "Highly skilled technical staff" reliably identify expert answers.[36] A decade after this celebration of expert rule, America's 2008 financial crisis ravaged the global economy due to missteps by the Federal Reserve, which subsequently became a lightning rod for economic inequality and racial disparities.[37]

Designing Institutions for Citizens

The knowledge and attitudes of individuals are uneven, yet the assault on democracy exaggerates both the limitations of citizens as a whole and the superiority of experts and governing elites.

Citizens Are Competent Enough

The mass of Americans may fail a professor's quiz about the names of political figures. But they consistently form rational, stable policy preferences based on available information.[38]

Where Americans are not well informed about matters of salience, they use cognitive cues to gain workable information. They routinely rely on trusted sources or "civic educators"—friends, parents, co-workers, teachers, faith leaders, and community leaders.[39] Community groups regularly organize citizen-to-citizen conversations that boost knowledge about public issues and competing perspectives.[40]

Citizens are not, however, sequestered. Their attitudes toward salient issues are rarely autonomous products of their own reasoning. Instead, they are influenced by new events as well as elite manipulation.[41]

The knowledge and preferences of citizens are impacted more broadly by the operation of democratic institutions. When the political system is unresponsive, citizens have little motivation to invest in participation, acquire knowledge, and commit to engagement. Sustained failure of government to address issues of urgency to communities of color and other marginalized groups depresses their interest, knowledge, and participation.[42] A series of experiments found that people who are given access to talk to members of Congress about serious public policy invest the time and effort to become more informed and engaged. Public opinion surveys echo this finding: supermajorities of Americans welcome the opportunity for deeper political participation in a political system that is responsive and not rigged by insiders and special interests.[43]

Why Would We Want to Hand More Power to Elites?

Elites are not benign "guardians" but rather highly motivated actors seeking to advance their careers and interests. Democracy doubters are quick to dismiss citizens but rarely scrutinize the knowledge, judicious temperament, and commitment of elites to the rule of law and broad public good. Expertise is required in a robust system of political representation, but lopsided dependence on specialization can bring potentially damaging narrowness.[44] The failure to prevent the September 11, 2001, attacks and the Federal Reserve's failure to head off the 2008 financial crisis are examples of specialists concentrating on discrete problems and missing the consequences of their interaction in a larger system.[45] While champions of expert rule laud authoritative officials and specialists, they are wrong on a regular basis: the launching of the Iraq War in 2003 on the false premise that Saddam Hussein possessed weapons of mass destruction,[46] the initial collapse of Obamacare's online enrollment system, and Trump's botched responses to containing the Coronavirus pandemic during 2020.[47]

Political elites are the culprits responsible for Donald Trump's rise to power. The rapacious ambition of elected officials and political candidates who developed and sold the primary left American democracy exposed, as Madison most feared, to politicians with "factious tempers . . . [or] sinister designs" who advance their interests at the expense of the broader public well-being. Rather than delivering on the much-heralded promise to serve "the people," political elites damaged public trust in democratic government by accelerating the pattern of backroom dealing by lawmakers, special interests, and obscure agencies looking to please the insiders.[48]

The Vulnerability of Democratic Legitimacy and Authority

Primaries contribute to the dangerous weakening of the legitimacy and authority of democratic rules and procedures.[49] Legitimacy is the mortar on which contemporary government depends. It justifies the exercise of authority and the inclination of citizens to follow official laws and regulations.

Democratic rules and procedures are an important source of legitimacy. Popular consent and political equality—and the rights of speech, assembly, and voting—supply the ballast for the moral claims of government officials to rule in the name of "the people."[50]

Trump was able to circumvent the opposition of Republican leaders because of four damaging impacts of primaries on democratic legitimacy and authority. First, primaries reinforce and deepen political inequality. Candidates who have long defended the Constitution and rule of law were defeated in the 2016 GOP primaries. Republican members of Congress intent on staying in office were at the mercy of the party activist coalition, which positioned Trump to intimidate them from challenging him. Primaries not only silenced most Republicans but also reinforced the power of the insiders and thereby political distrust, which may dampen another source of resistance.

Second, primaries invited persistent recriminations about unfair and rigged elections, subjecting everyday people to a steady stream of criticism about the integrity of American democracy. Dueling politicians now boost their careers—as Trump and Bernie Sanders did in 2016—by denigrating the Republican and Democratic Parties' nominations as corrupt.[51] Political distrust is an understandable reaction by everyday Americans to this near constant attacks on democratic institutions. The contemporary feeding of public distrust intensifies a centuries-long pattern: Americans have been bombarded with charges of party dishonesty, reformers lifted their hopes with promises of much-touted solutions, and then the persistence of the system's flaws have drawn a new round of charges of undemocratic practices. Democratic institutions are under nearly unceasing assault by Democrats and Republicans.

Third, the primary created a mechanism for Trump to capitalize on racial resentment to build a loyal following to win the GOP nomination in 2016 and supply a foundation of support afterward.[52] The media attention to the presidential primary competition—along with the efforts of the Trump's campaign organization—created a nearly unparalleled launching pad for his racist attacks and recruitment of supporters. The political press widely covered his denigration of Mexican immigrants as criminals and rapists, his claim that a judge's Mexican heritage should rule him out from handling his case, and his persistent promotion of malicious falsehoods about African Americans—that President Barack Obama was Muslim and born in Kenya and that Black teenagers were responsible for a 1989 rape of a white woman in Central Park in New York City. White supremacist groups gleefully welcomed Trump's messages, with the leader of the Virginia KKK explaining that "[a] lot of Klan members like Donald Trump because a lot of what he believes, we believe in."[53] Trump exploited a system with broader effects; it sustained racial disparities in running and winning elections.[54]

Fourth, primaries do not filter out demagogues and authoritarians. Republican officials who were certain of Trump's inappropriateness for the presidency were unable to stop his nomination and eventual election in 2016. Once in the seat of power, congressional Republicans calculated they were unable to prevent Trump's violations of Constitutional and legal rules and norms—including his inciting of the January 6 insurrection. His assaults on the legitimacy of elections after the 2020 elections were supported by many state Republicans, further damaging the authority and credibility of democratic institutions. The primary failed to block this political deviant, and its incentive system deterred Republicans from performing the much-touted role of elites—doing the right thing for the country.

Looking Back to Move Forward

Two hundred years of battling over political parties and their nomination systems preceded the Republican Party's acquiescence to Trump's 2016 nomination. This history produced an understanding of democracy as dependent on a party nomination process controlled by relatively small, unrepresentative factions. The perverse result is that what is described as "democratic" widens economic and racial inequality and undercuts popular consent.

Trump's rise to power is the culmination of a retreat from democratic political representation with grand historic proportions. His January 6, 2021, call to invade Congress broke from a tradition in American history dating to 1800: the peaceful transfer of power. Even before this fateful day, Trump's conduct fit a broader pattern of spewing racial venom, falsely alleging election fraud, and undercutting or rupturing the rules and procedures of the US Constitution. There would be no Trump, however, without the history of democratic decay. Making sense of Trump requires scrutiny of American political history.

The Plan of the Book

The next two sections examine seminal historic junctures in the formation of democratic institutions that cleared a path for Donald Trump and stand in the way of reforms to repel the next assault. The first section follows the formation of a new governing synthesis to control political participation and channel it through a system of political representation. Chapter 2 traverses the period from the rule of gentry in Colonial America through the ratification of the US Constitution. After the Declaration of Independence in 1776, new citizen activism arose that approached a form of "strong democracy"; everyday laborers and farmers ran for office, organized to elect slates of candidates and instructed them to deliver on specific community needs, and educated their neighbors about community challenges and legislative actions.[55] Madison and a small circle reacted with alarm by secretly planning the Constitutional Convention in 1787 to close down this "Robinhood Society." Faced with the practical need for popular appeal, Madison and his collaborators charted a new synthesis to contain what they considered excessive democracy while retaining sufficient elements of political representation to secure ratification.

Chapter 3 traces the formative contributions of Thomas Jefferson and Andrew Jackson to a uniquely American coupling of political representation and political parties, setting the parameters for future political reforms. The fissuring of the Constitution's framers mixed with Jefferson's and Jackson's ambition to avenge controversial losses, motivating each to breach the prior stigma associated with political parties to mobilize new voters while also taking steps to protect the authority and legitimacy of democratic institutions.

The second section examines the unraveling of the early-nineteenth-century synthesis. Chapter 4 connects the early designs of democratic institutions to the stunted introduction of the direct primary during the Progressive Era. Elite divisions and the frustrated ambitions of Progressive-Era politicians provoked upstarts led by Wisconsin's Robert La Follette to promote primary reform to catapult him to the ranks of governor, US senator, and leading presidential candidate. The contested development of primaries merged with battles over the franchise and America's racial orders; these critical dynamics are incorporated in this and later chapters.

Chapter 5 links the widespread adoption of primaries to George McGovern's covert toppling of national and state Democratic parties as impactful organizations. Grasping for the bona fides as a reformer to propel his presidential campaign, McGovern seized on La Follette's design to herald a new democratic era and borrowed from the rhetoric of protesters at the chaotic and violent 1968 Democratic Convention in Chicago.

Why has America—a country once lauded for its civic culture—taken a turn toward instability and ideological tribalism? The third section assesses the damage of primary elections and looks to the future by identifying meaningful reforms of America's democratic institutions. Chapter 6 assesses the transformational consequences for contemporary American politics of the primary system adopted in the 1970s. Primaries created a process that fostered partisan polarization by enabling new electoral alignments to form and intimidating elected officials to kowtow to activist coalitions on the left and especially the right; increased political inequality by shifting power to a complex, inner-facing process that favored the affluent and better organized; and weakened the authority and legitimacy of democratic procedures and rules by fueling continual attacks on the process and opening the door to candidates hostile to the US Constitution.

What can be done to address the fragility of American democratic institutions? Chapter 7 chases off fanciful reform proposals that ignore severe constraints and instead outlines feasible steps for fortifying the democratic process in the form of political representation. The most urgent priorities are restraining the ambition of elected officials and political candidates and improving the conditions of political equality within a system of political representation.

The Structure of History

Properly understanding Trump's rise (and the potential responses to it) requires a grasp of American history—particularly the central tendencies of macrohistorical development.[56] Three tendencies stand out and appear in the coming chapters.

Convergence

The conjuncture of three processes triggered the timing and direction of democratic reforms. The first is competition among political and economic elites and the stymieing of political entrepreneurs seeking elected office. Jefferson, Jackson, La Follette, and McGovern each clashed with established powers and turned to reforming political parties, which in turn deepened divisions among elites. Second, the politically ambitious deployed populist calls to "the people" as a strategic device to advance their personal interests by mobilizing support against a political system hostile to them.

Third, institutions pattern politics, exerting an independent and decisive influence by creating the roles, rules, and norms that circumscribe the behavior of political actors and their perception of feasible options.[57] When McGovern searched in 1969–1970 for familiar and available reforms of the party establishment, he latched onto La Follette's innovation of a direct primary to select national convention delegates, which itself was a legacy of Jefferson's creation of mass mobilizing political parties and Jackson's embrace of party conventions to empower "the people" in candidate selection. At each juncture, prior change structured the parameters for subsequent change in democratic institutions and influenced "downstream politics" by altering the allocation of political resources and changing the meaning of democracy.[58]

Political elites and reformers fought sustained battles over the forms of American democracy but not on the terms they chose. At each critical juncture, the past invaded the judgments of government elites and reformers as they assessed what was rational for them and politically feasible.

Contingency

The history of democratic rules and procedures is contingent within the parameters of institutional development. When institutional forms were malleable in the first half of the 1780s, the precedents of strong democracy in the 1780s introduced opportunities for the marrying of community organizing with effective engagement with government policy making; this moment of possibility was intentionally stymied—rather than tolerated and nurtured—by the Constitution's design and governing elites. At a later juncture, Progressive reformers and intellectuals—including Herbert Croly—blunted the widespread adoption of primaries by rejecting La Follette's framing of them as the only alternative to corrupt party machines, instead proposing a "republican" approach to party nominations that channeled Madison.[59] What form of democracy could have taken shape if the direction of Croly and other

Progressives had been embraced instead of the wrecking ball of primaries?

Strains and Breakdowns

The development of political institutions generates patterns of regularity but also strains, breakdowns, and pitches conflict. The practice of American democracy has long ground against the founding principles of political equality and popular consent; the resulting frustration and backlashes create propitious conditions for skilled entrepreneurs.

The Making of Democratic Institutions

Tracing the arc of American democracy requires both a search for generalizations about the form and content of change and attention to the uniqueness of distinct historical periods. This middle level of abstraction draws on both broad theories of democracy and institutional change as well as detailed histories of critical junctures in American political history.[60]

Democracy under Fire has relied on original research as well as prior studies by historians of particular eras, empirical findings by social scientists of specific political patterns, and the probing analysis of democratic theory. Similarly, I have relied on critical concepts such as populism and racial orders as tools for prying into the maneuvering of governing elites and the formation of political institutions rather than as subjects of study in themselves.[61] My debt to prior research is evident in my extensive endnotes.

Donald Trump is the product of not simply the particular features of twenty-first-century politics. He is an expression of accumulating deformations of political representation and understanding of democracy. We begin with the rapid transformations of the early republic in the last third of eighteenth-century America. Within a few decades, a democratic culture formed and knocked the gentry from their perch atop the social hierarchy. Madison and his allies secretly responded to the era's turbulence by designing a system of political representation that acknowledged popular consent and substantially restored elite control.

PART I

A NEW SYNTHESIS: DEMOCRACY AND ORDER

Everyday Americans in 1776 read the Declaration of Independence and took it to heart, as a clarion call for active citizenship. The dawn of a new era of "strong democracy" brought laborers and farmers into governance and stirred James Madison and a small circle to rein these newcomers in. The result was a Constitutional Convention in 1787 to contain "excessive" democracy, while preserving sufficient elements of political representation to win the Constitution's ratification. With George Washington's departure in 1796, the ambition and institutional innovations of Thomas Jefferson and Andrew Jackson coupled political representation and political parties, setting the parameters for future reforms.

2

Strong Democracy and Political Representation, 1776–1787

Broadway celebrates Alexander Hamilton, but historians hail James Madison as the "Father of the Constitution."[1] Madison's "finest hour" was organizing the small private convention that drafted the US Constitution during the steamy Philadelphia summer of 1787. As for Hamilton, he too was a brilliant and young delegate at the Constitutional Convention but was often missing in action.

Following the Declaration of Independence in 1776, the Articles of Confederation created a loose affiliation of states that became hotbeds of collective political action.[2] Many state legislatures opened their doors to everyday people as representatives, which in turn created political opportunities for voters to pressure lawmakers through instructions to support bills that reduced economic duress; state and community associations created the organizational resources to recruit everyday people as candidates and elect them; and the new states' leaders framed high family debt and foreclosure as "unjust" attacks by the gentry and wealthy against farmers and Revolutionary War veterans. The flourishing of political activism following the Declaration demonstrated, in certain respects, "strong democracy" in which citizens exercised democratic procedural rights to speak out, vote, and assemble both to move legislation and to act outside the halls of government.[3]

Madison and a small circle took aim at the jealously guarded independence of individual states for an overriding reason: the state legislatures responded to debtors and farmers facing foreclosure with significant economic assistance. Madison's group secretly launched a radical plan: replace the independent state legislatures with an insulated national government designed to protect wealth and reinstall the "better sort" who enjoyed social status and power before the Declaration. Madison's view faced resistance from fellow framers of the Constitution—and later from citizens. From Benjamin Franklin's front-row seat in the debates of the 1780s, he ardently defended robust democracy and was not shy about firing barbs at the elite backlash for "debas[ing] the spirit of the common people." "[S]ome of the greatest rogues," he quipped, "were the richest rogues."[4] By contrast, everyday citizens, in Franklin's view, were the foundation of the new country: "It is of great consequence that we should not depress the virtue and public spirit of our common people."[5] (Franklin's outspoken defense of the Declaration's egalitarianism earned him the ridicule of the gentry and some of the Constitution's designers.)

The Constitutional Convention (May 25–September 17, 1787) started out to reduce the degree of citizen influence. Defeats at the Constitutional Convention coaxed Madison, however, to change his original plans to respond to the mass expectation of political equality and accept the practical challenges of winning ratification of the new Constitution. As a result, the new government authority that the Constitution birthed in 1787 both restricted the vibrant democracy in the states and laid the foundation for representative democracy in a concession to public expectations and political necessity. Madison left Philadelphia disappointed.

The debate over ratifying the Constitution was acrimonious on many topics but largely bypassed a fundamental issue: the continuation of slavery. At the Constitutional Convention, southern states insisted on allowing slavery as their price for joining the union; the northern states accepted the immorality of human bondage as the cost of a political bargain.[6] The process of seeking state ratification of the Constitution after its public release in September 1787 precipitated loud debate over the rights and liberties of whites but was largely silent about the failure to extend political freedom to people of color, indigenous people, and women.[7]

For future generations of Americans, the Constitution's racial exclusion and dual approach to democracy sparked struggle over the shortchanging of the Declaration's embrace of political equality and popular sovereignty. The resulting frustration and upsurges would, over time, both challenge Madison's democratic restraints and build on the Constitution's institutional framework for political representation and citizenship rights. This chapter tells the story of Madison's evolution from throttling the vibrant expression of political equality in states to establishing the rules and procedures for representative democracy.

Why Madison Led a Conservative Restoration

A long line of astute observers have been struck by America's "paternal love" and "fetish-worship" of the US Constitution.[8] The adoration of the Constitution has cast an "aurora of divinity" upon George Washington, Madison, Hamilton, and others for their courage, intelligence, and worldliness in drafting the Constitution and forming its first government. They are, we are regularly reminded, an "incomparable generation."[9]

The Constitution's drafters take credit for rescuing what they—and many historians—describe as a floundering confederation of states, which was failing to conduct the basic functions of government.[10] In the year prior to the Constitutional Convention, Madison catalogued the "vices" of the Confederation. His dour diagnosis: failure to control commerce, build canals, and establish adequate military defense, among other shortfalls.[11] The states compounded these deficiencies by failing to abide by treaties and trampling on the rights of other states. While the Declaration of Independence soared with the optimism of breaking from Britain and starting anew, Madison and his clique portrayed the dysfunction of the subsequent years as consumed by disorder and chaos.[12]

This account is not wrong as much as it is overblown and incomplete. Its singular focus on diagnosing the Confederation and lauding the personal qualities of the Constitution's framers distracts from their tangible motives to redistribute power and resources.[13]

Madison's private writings make clear that his primary concern was as much about what state legislations were failing to do as what they were doing and who was doing it. Madison is celebrated for erecting "checks and balances" to encumber government abuse of power, but autocrats were not his principal target. Rather, Madison and his allies were alarmed by state legislatures passing laws to issue paper money and deliver relief to debtors in response to citizen demands. As "commoners" replaced the gentry as elected officials in state government, Madison's optimism in 1776 soured to "dark foreboding about the America yet to come" and "skepticism about the people and popular majorities." Hamilton similarly concluded that democracy was "our real disease."[14] Prominent political contemporaries agreed that the "evils . . . from the excess of democracy" in state legislatures were the "chief danger" to the survival of the states.[15]

The Problem

The Constitution's framers were motivated to retain, even in diminished form, the social status that the gentry enjoyed before the Revolution and stop the threats to wealth by diminishing government responsiveness.

Toppling the Gentry

Historian Gordon Wood documents a distinction in eighteenth-century America between two groups—commoners and the gentry, who claimed to possess "different psyches, different emotional makeups, different natures." Into the 1760s, men in power—including Madison, Washington, Hamilton, and Adams—described ordinary people as "the grazing multitude" and the "unthinking," "vulgar" "common herd" who were easily excited and lacked intelligence. Their "place" in society, according to the "better sort," followed a grim cycle—they are "born and eat and sleep and die."[16] By contrast, "gentlemen" placed themselves at the apex of the social hierarchy because of their family, education, and refinement.

The gentry dominated government through the mid-eighteenth century, and governing elites—including the Constitution's drafters—were comfortable talking openly about their superiority to "ordinary people."[17] The president of Dickinson College (Charles Nisbet) assuredly reported that "men of learning, leisure and easy circumstances . . . are much fitter for every part of the business of government than the ordinary class of people."[18] For the gentry, serving in government was a social expectation tied to prominence, learning, duty, and what was presented as a unique grasp of virtue untarnished by private interests.[19] In turn, social standing—and the connections and privileges associated with it—were tools for conducting government affairs in a period of minimal administrative capacity. The "identification between social and political authority [and] private and public leadership [helps to explain]," Gordon Wood writes, why "most ordinary folk were not deeply involved in provincial or imperial politics [and] . . . [few] regarded government as a means by which economic and social power might be redistributed or problems of their lives resolved."[20] Colonial politics were often limited to contests among the gentry, with everyday voters acquiescing to those with wealth and social prominence. It was not unusual, for instance, that towns in Massachusetts did not send representatives to provincial government.

The 1760s, however, witnessed the downfall of the Colonial Era's social hierarchy. The revolt against British rule under the banner "No taxation without representation" rallied colonists not only for independence but also gave life to the idea of "democratick" government. The Declaration of Independence crystallized these expectations by embracing the democratic principles that "all men are created equal" and that government should rest on the "consent of the governed." Shortly after signing the Declaration, Benjamin Franklin presided over Pennsylvania's state constitutional convention, which adopted stronger egalitarian positions and earned him the reputation as among America's most forceful advocates of democracy. It pronounced that "all men are born equally free and equal," approved a unicameral legislature to facilitate responsiveness to citizens, and declared that the state government would work for the "common benefits . . . and not for the particular emolument or advantage of any . . . set of men who are only part of [the] community."[21]

While ordinary people often abstained from seeking seats in government during the Colonial Era, everyday laborers denounced barriers to their representation in the 1770s as resulting from the "selfish views . . . of oligarchy."[22] Citizen committees, conventions, and other associations formed to propel into politics the "plain folks"—artisans, mechanics, carpenters, butchers, shoemakers, and others without money or "respectable" family lineages. They won elections, entered government, and made decisions.[23] In Philadelphia, artisans, laborers, and other socially marginalized groups elected their own representatives to four out of ten city offices in 1770. The composition of the New Hampshire House of Representatives flipped from mostly gentlemen in 1765 to mostly farmers within two decades. In the plantation-led South, the proportion of legislators who were everyday farmers doubled from one-eighth before the Revolution to a quarter in the 1780s. A qualitative change occurred among citizens during the 1770s: the old view of government as unconcerned with their lives was replaced with a new recognition of it as a potential force to redistribute economic resources and improve their life circumstances.[24]

The new democratic culture ushered in the then novel idea that the wealthy, better dressed, and more educated were no better than anyone else. The social standing of "gentlemen" no longer produced automatic deference, and ambitious politicians (including those who were "well born") shed the outward pretense of superiority and defined themselves as democrats. Thomas Paine's scathing 1776 pamphlet, *Common Sense*, eviscerated the older social order: "Male and female are the distinctions of nature, good and bad the distinctions of heaven, but how a race of men came into the world so exalted above the rest . . . is worth inquiring into." By the 1770s, the titles of "Citizen" and "Mr." replaced the Colonial Era's stigmatized monikers for commoners: "yeoman" and "husbandman."

Newspapers and state legislatures rang out with tirades against the aristocrats. Up-and-comers like John Adams turned his invective from ordinary people to the "Airs of Wisdom and Superiority" associated with aristocrats. Looking back, a prominent southern politician marveled at the change in society and the crumbling of older rankings: "a revolution has taken place in the whole structure of society."[25]

The gentry and the affluent deeply resented their loss of status and power. Gentlemen fumed at the popularizing of their lifestyle because it "allow[ed] . . . the lowest of people to try to make themselves equal with better people."[26]

One "cause of the evils," according to the gentry and Madison, was the surge of everyday people into state governments. This produced a "defect of adequate statesmen." Madison and his allies, Gordon Wood reports, "were not as much opposed to the governmental power of the states as to the character of the people who were wielding it."[27] "The majority who rule," Madison observed, "[are not] the safest Guardians both of public Good and of private rights."[28] They were "base and selfish" and committed to "securing their own interest to the ruin of the commonwealth."[29] The commoners who entered government possessed "neither their property, their virtue, nor their abilities"; they were merely "plain, illiterate husbandmen."[30] State officials were elected by voters who support "provincial perspectives and [were] vulnerable to demagogues with partisan agendas." The result, according to the president of Yale University Ezra Stiles, is that state representatives harbor "mean, interested or capricious motive[s]" and stooped to "vot[ing] for a new town or a new county."[31] State governments, Hamilton concluded, "can be nothing but temporary, expedient, fickle, and [engaged in] folly."[32]

Madison and his allies stressed what was missing: the gentry's performance as "disinterested and dispassionate umpires" who were "restrained from the pursuit of interests adverse to those of the whole society."[33] Where everyday people slavishly attended to their self-interests, the gentry (according to Madison) were "the purest and noblest characters." Unlike the commoners, they "possess [the] most wisdom to discern and most virtue to pursue the common good of society" and "best serve the long-term public interest."[34]

For Madison, the toppling of the gentry and affluent was not an abstract proposition. He personally felt the sting of the social transformation. Before the Revolution, he followed the pattern of a prominent Virginia plantation family: educated at what became Princeton University, affluent, and engaged in government service. In his 1777 campaign for the new Virginia legislature, however, he lost to a tavern owner who offended Madison's sense of etiquette by making "personal solicitations" of voters and using the "corrupting influence of spirituous liquors."[35]

Contending Interests

The gentry's battle in the 1780s to restore their social status and political power was part of a broader conflict over the distributional effects of democratic state legislatures. The new era of "acutely actual" representation occurred during the economic downturn of the 1780s that threatened the land on which many Americans depended. Farmers struggled to recover from the theft of crops by American and British soldiers; the British destruction of ships and trade barriers negatively impacted agricultural markets; and decisions of American officials in the states were ruinous—namely, the imposition of unaffordable taxes to pay off wartime loans and a court system that favored politically connected gentry who controlled large tracts of land. The struggle for economic survival flowed into the battle for stronger democracy (wider suffrage, equal representation, and unicameral legislatures to improve responsiveness to citizens) and tangible government assistance for farmers.[36]

The form and degree of citizen activism in legislative and community politics during the 1780s exhibited three features of strong democracy that are unusual in the history of American politics.[37] First, white male citizens seized on the Declaration's proclamation of equality and democratic rights to organize sustained political activism that encompassed a broad range of interests.[38] Everyday people who had been on the margins of Colonial Era politics developed the skills and networks to recruit and motivate their neighbors and strengthen their collective capacities. In Philadelphia in the 1770s, for instance, mechanics and other laborers comprising half of the city's males joined the Patriotic Society, debated policies, and coordinated pressure on government officials. Similar encompassing associations formed and regularly met in New York and other cities. Their coherence, encompassing scope, and ability to marshal resources were, in part, evident in the meeting halls they built or purchased.[39]

Citizens and emerging voices of opposition formed hundreds of "committees of correspondence" across the colonies during the 1760s and 1770s to share criticisms of British taxes and regulations, articulate demands, and coordinate collective strategies of resistance across towns and regions.[40] The committees of correspondence articulated emerging notions of citizenship rights. These committees created networks to share a stream of printed pamphlets and hand-written letters, which were passed hand-to-hand among neighbors and read aloud at town hall meetings.

Citizens also organized outside government to voice frustration and press for change on a regular basis during the Colonial and post-Declaration eras.[41] One common extragovernmental activity came in the form of public disturbances over land and exorbitant taxes. The desperate scramble by farmers to get and hold titles to land fueled public protests in the 1760s and 1770s against local landlords and the courts that favored them in New Jersey, Pennsylvania, North Carolina, South Carolina, and elsewhere. After the Revolution, farmer disturbances continued in Maine, Vermont, and Massachusetts, among other states.

Servants, sailors, and everyday people also turned to raucous public gatherings as a form of political expression and means to temporarily assert power when official channels were blocked or unresponsive. The Whig and Republican Society of Philadelphia, the Marine Anti-Britannic Society of Charleston, and similar bodies in Massachusetts and elsewhere organized networks, met (on occasion in conventions), and at times took to the street to stop the collection of taxes and debts.[42] The community groups, according to Sean Wilentz, "articulated a coherent egalitarian politics ... [that was] insistent on equal legislative representation for all parts of the state."[43]

Daniel Shays and his neighbors organized a particularly infamous public disturbance during the 1780s across five Massachusetts counties. They protested the state legislature's steep tax increases during a depressed economy, which threatened widespread foreclosures, including possibly half of the farms in one county. One citizen petition warned of the dismal consequences of "the driving of the [tax] collectors"—farms were "seized for tax[es] [and] some children are destitute of milk and other necessities of life." The first steps by Shays and his neighbors were to organize popular conventions to make the case for debt relief; when their protests fell on deaf ears, they took up arms and interfered with the courts.

Madison and governing elites seized on the taking up of arms by the ragtag group of Massachusetts farmers to claim that "crisis" and "the horrors of anarchy and licentiousness" were overtaking the states. They found in Shays the "new proofs of the necessity" for their conservative counterrevolution to restrict the highly active and influential organizing of common people.[44]

In reality, Shays and his collaborators were hardly a lawless band of renegades who threatened rampant disorder. They were veterans of the Revolutionary War; Shays was a captain in the fight for independence. Many participants in the uprising were community leaders, well off before the economic downturn removed them from the top quintile of local taxpayers. Nor did their revolt pose a dire threat. A larger and better-armed military force readily crushed them, imprisoning 150 and sentencing some to death. Ratcheting down Madison's hyperbole, his ally Thomas Jefferson described them as launching a "little rebellion."[45]

Shays and those he inspired do stand out, though, as gifted political organizers. At a time when communications and travel were challenging, they created and sustained a collective understanding of their grievances and the culprits, brought people together, and recruited new members to address common concerns (as opposed to business or pecuniary ends).

The second distinctive feature of the political activism after the Declaration is that "commoners" responded to new political opportunities in state politics by recruiting candidates from their ranks (instead of deferring to the gentry); forming large, disciplined voting blocs; and directing lawmakers after elections.[46] They had begun, in the horrified estimation of conservative politician Gouverneur Morris, "to think and reason" as they inserted themselves into political affairs. Citizen associations recruited candidates among mechanics, laborers, and other everyday citizens to run and win appointments and elections to city and state bodies.[47]

One of the most effective tools developed by citizen associations was to instruct candidates once elected. They dismissed the concept that elected officials should exercise independence as "trustees" and instead treated legislators as agents to follow their specific instructions. Some legislators resisted the limitation on their discretion. In Maryland, for instance, three delegates resigned their posts in 1776 after associations of local voters sent them instructions about the writing of the state constitution.[48] In a sign, though, of the influence of citizen associations, instructions were widely adopted in the 1780s and representatives appeared to generally follow them.

Political activism became a means for redistributing wealth and creating a "Robinhood Society" that aided less-well-off voters at the expense of the better off.[49] Citizen associations recruited and elected candidates to state legislatures and then insisted they follow instructions to print paper money and pass laws that reduced debt and taxes. Most states took these steps before the 1787 Convention to draft the US Constitution. The provision of economic assistance helped the ailing and motivated further political activism: it confirmed the influence of citizen associations, which in turn contributed to recruiting new members and expanding their resources and power.

Economic and political elites reacted, however, with alarm. Noah Webster echoed the views of the gentry and affluent who were accustomed to exercising power: "Most of the destructive measures which have been pursued by the states . . . originated in [the] . . . instructions to representatives."[50] Madison derided the "sinister designs" and "schemes of injustice" by impoverished farmers and Revolutionary War veterans who used their rights as citizens to organize politically to pressure elected representatives.[51]

Shays' Rebellion supplied Madison with a visceral illustration of the skill and impact of mass political participation. The threat was not a band of farmers violently taking over but the effectiveness of Shays and his allies using elections and lobbying legislators to push back against elite efforts to curb the right to vote based on property restrictions. Indeed, the government's unnecessarily heavy-handed response stirred a broad public backlash among farmers and other everyday people who peacefully exercised their democratic rights through the "auspices of Constitutional forms."[52] In Massachusetts, they won new legislation, defeated the governor who had organized the repression, and received concessions from the new governor to expand economic assistance. Most of the rebels were eventually treated with leniency, including Shays, who was granted a pardon.

Madison exploded. He was alarmed not only at the "violence of faction" as he would later report but also the new reality that everyday citizens felt a sense of agency to use their democratic rights to pressure government to secure economic relief. In a telling report, Madison condemned the opponents of tax and debt collection in Massachusetts for organizing "strength in the field of electioneering" to enact "their wicked measures . . . *under the forms of the constitution*."[53]

The third feature of political activism in the 1780s was the strategic framing of interests.[54] Where Madison and his allies contrasted the gentry's disinterested "virtue" with the narrow selfishness of "commoners," citizen associations during the 1780s flipped the framing: they portrayed high taxes and debt and the seizing of property as assaults by the gentry and wealthy against Revolutionary War veterans and laborers. Artisans—often in opposition to merchants—formed an awareness of their own specific political interest.[55] Citizens in associations of laborers and others advanced a notion of interest that equated economic redistribution with fairness for those who sacrificed for the country and were gripped by poverty.[56]

One of the purposes of citizen activists was to frame their agenda and methods to inspire political activism.[57] Madison's conclusions are self-serving, but his reports capture the political potency of laborers, mechanics, and farmers forming "a majority having common interests." A consistent theme in the 1780s is the organizing of everyday citizens to pursue concerted agendas on economic issues and democratic rights instead of splintering into isolated factions preoccupied with their narrow interests.[58]

Skepticism toward Madison's self-serving framing of interests is shared by independent researchers: they question Madison's derisive view of citizen activism and his praise of the better educated and well established as "disinterested and dispassionate umpires."[59] Gordon Wood's documentation of the battle over social status challenges Madison's notion of impartiality.[60] After all, Madison's allies were determined to dislodge "commoners" and revive the gentry to the top of the social hierarchy. Charles Beard's interpretation of the Constitution emphasizes the "cohesive" economic interests of creditors and speculators in government securities who promoted a crackdown on the leniency of state legislators toward debtors.[61] Although historians generally refute Beard's account as inaccurate or overly narrow, Michael Klarman agrees that "calculations of material interests were a vitally important factor" in the Constitution's design.[62] He modifies Beard by identifying a wider spectrum of "clashing interests": creditors versus debtors but also urban merchants and shippers versus rural farmers and backwoodsmen, and the conflicts between states and regions (especially the South). Race and gender were critical dimensions of Madison's definition of interests and rights, excluding most of the population from citizen activism.

The Solution

Madison, Washington, Hamilton, and their collaborators quietly devised a far-reaching scheme to recover the gentry's elevated status in government and to encumber responsive government to the point where it could not redistribute wealth. The plotting of this ascendant elite to restrain new citizen activism confronted a sober realization at the Constitutional Convention: a full rolling back of strong democracy was not feasible after a decade of intense citizen activism and instead would require an institutional form that gave meaning to the Declaration's promise of "consent of the governed."

Madison, in particular, took the lead, though delegates revised his plans at crucial junctures. More than a year before the Constitutional Convention, he prepared a series of reports based on his studies of ancient and contemporary political theory and history. Because books were rare, he relied on Jefferson's "literary cargo" from Paris—amounting to over two hundred books.[63] One delegate described Madison as "manag[ing] every great question [at the Convention]" and standing out as "the best-informed man at any point in the debates."[64]

Madison's "second American Revolution" to terminate the Confederation and design a new system required secrecy to avoid unleashing a backlash by state legislatures and enraged citizens.[65] Step 1 was to catalogue what they saw as the Confederation's fundamental flaws—the election of everyday people and the excessive responsiveness of state government to them, especially on economic redistribution.[66] Step 2 was quietly maneuvering state legislatures to authorize a convention on the false pretense of "render[ing] the constitution . . . adequate to the exigencies of the Union." With legislators and citizen associations disarmed, Madison's cabal guided state officials to select Convention delegates who were predisposed to their agenda. The result: none of the Constitution's drafters favored the decision of states to issue paper money and reduce debts even though most states had adopted these laws.

Step 3 of the "coup" was to agree—well before the Convention—to hijack the Philadelphia meeting from its ostensibly mundane purpose to implement the fundamental new direction promoted by Madison: severely restraining state legislatures and creating a new national government run by a partially insulated elite of rulers. State legislatures neither authorized this sweeping agenda nor imagined it as a possibility.[67]

Madison and his allies tailored the Constitutional Convention to remedy what they saw as the fundamental defects of the Articles of Confederation. The Constitution was, in the first instance, a "political device designed to control the social forces the Revolution had released," and in particular, to recoup as much of the old, gentry-based social hierarchy as feasible.[68] Its second remedial action was to "change . . . the principle and proportion of representation," according to Madison, by creating "filtration" to insulate, as much as possible, government officials from the citizen instructions to enact economic redistribution.[69]

Muting Democracy and Economic Redistribution

The Constitutional Convention designed four features to tame the new citizen habit of practicing "consent" to improve their life circumstances and substantially restore elite control to forestall economic redistribution.

The Constitutional Convention's most radical step was to puncture the independence of states and erect a national government armed with "supreme" authority. It fashioned Article VI (section 2) to establish the Constitution and its statutes and treaties as "the law of the land."

In addition to establishing the general supremacy of the national government, the Convention specifically barred states from continuing to pursue economic redistribution by issuing paper money and debtor relief laws. The Constitution's Article I (section 10) states, "No state shall . . . coin money; emit bills of credit; make anything but gold and silver coin a tender of payment of debates; or pass any law impairing the obligation of contracts." This unilateral revocation of powers exercised by states during the Confederation hurt farmers; they served the interests of creditors who held government securities and bonds and resided in northeastern cities.[70]

Rewiring democratic representation was the second Constitutional design feature. Madison deceptively described the Constitution in Federalist Paper 10 as rejecting "pure democracy" in favor of a "system of representation." The reality, however, is that state legislatures were representative bodies; Madison's concern was with representation itself, specifically its use to produce high responsiveness in passing economic redistribution. The Constitutional

Convention muted the "scheme of representation" by inserting the "filtration" of indirect elections (an independent Electoral College was expected to select presidents) and selection of US senators by state legislatures, which Madison privately described as "a check on democracy."[71] (The Seventeenth Amendment later created the direct election of US senators). Even the right to vote—the gas for the "consent of the governed" engine—was not recognized by the Constitutional Convention in order to leave states the option to blunt it through property qualifications.[72] These design features echo in debates in our own time over ballot access for Americans of color by leaving voting rights in limbo and at the discretion of states.[73]

Even as Madison and his collaborators designed features to tamp down strong democracy, they anchored citizen representation in the authority and legitimacy of the new national government as a concession to the anticipated debate over ratifying the Constitution. The significance of this dual-track approach would grow over time: they decidedly weakened the "acutely actual" citizen engagement in the states while also laying an enduring foundation for representative rules and procedures that subsequent generations would leverage to improve the rights and conditions of citizens.

The third design feature was to create a powerful insulated executive to filter citizen demands for economic redistribution. The Constitutional Convention equipped the executive with the authority to veto congressional actions and serve as commander in chief to put down Shays-like rebellions as well as fend off foreign threats.[74] These stated powers were augmented by a large reservoir of what Hamilton later declared to be "implied" authority to take unilateral action.[75]

At a time when suspicion about executive power remained high after the colonial experience with the hated British king, the delegates also "contriv[ed] the interior structure of the government" to prevent autocracy (as explained in Federalist Paper 51) while also establishing additional institutional obstacles to citizen pressure. The creation of "checks and balances" armed the three government branches, Madison explained in Federalist Papers 51 and 10, with the "necessary constitutional means and personal motives to resist encroachments of the others." Just as important, divided authority set up another barrier to organized citizens: breaking with the popular demands for responsive unicameral legislature, the Constitutional Convention split legislative power to equip the appointed Senate to block the popularly elected House from pursuing economic redistribution on its own.[76]

Over time, progressives seeking economic redistribution have been slowed or frustrated by the design features of a separate legislative chamber or an independent president. Yet the Constitution also created the gears of representation that progressives used (with encumbrances) during the presidencies of Franklin Roosevelt, Lyndon Johnson, Barack Obama, and Joe Biden.

The fourth design feature sought to impede the formation of collective political action in the first place. Madison offered a two-part recipe in Federalist Paper 10 and his letters to Jefferson: in the first place, states covered large, extended areas "where people are broken into . . . many interests"; second, republican government would give voice and influence to these factions. He reasoned that "extending the sphere of government to include a multitude of factions and interests . . . would constantly check each other" within the government.[77] If "united we stand" animated the organized political activism of the 1780s, the Constitutional Convention rallied behind the principle of "divided we rule."

Restoring the Gentry

The Constitutional Convention devised what they hoped would spur a partial remedy for the second fundamental flaw of the 1780s: the erosion of social hierarchy and replacement of the gentry in government with "commoners." Madison privately expected the new government to introduce the stability he associated with the British king; Hamilton pushed to go further toward European monarchies.[78] He devoted one of his longest Convention speeches to granting extensive power to an elective monarch who would serve for life unless impeached. In a telling private exchange with Hamilton, Jefferson shared portraits of "my trinity of the greatest men"—Francis Bacon, Sir Isaac Newton, and John Locke; Hamilton retorted, "The greatest man that ever lived was Julius Caesar."[79]

The Senate was explicitly modeled on the British House of Lords. Delegates expected the selection of senators by state legislators to retain the "aristocratic part of our government" and to "represent the wealth of the country."[80]

The mechanism for selecting presidents was also expected to incorporate the gentry. Delegates spoke of the knowledge and independence of those selected for the Electoral College, which they assumed would include the "well-born."[81]

The hopes of the Constitution's framers to restore the old social hierarchy remained aspirational. Formal steps to embrace elements of European monarchies—including royal titles and references—were struck down as out of step with popular sentiment in the 1780s.

Madison Favored Stronger Conservative Counterrevolution

The degree to which the Constitution retained citizen rights and influences—even as it established significant elite filters and latitude—disappointed Madison and Hamilton. They left Philadelphia frustrated that the Constitution had not gone further to empower the national government and constrain citizens.[82] Madison's most significant and disappointing defeat was his proposal to empower the new national government with a "veto" over state legislatures to ensure that they could not continue to reduce taxes and debt and issue paper money. The Constitution's explicit language barring states from these policies in Article I (section 10) were insufficient in Madison's view; he doubted that the judiciary would enforce it.[83]

Delegates explored—but defeated—other steps to further erode democracy. The Constitution established direct popular election of the House but only after overriding delegates who attempted to block it. Elbridge Gerry argued to drop the election of House members because citizens were, in his view, "dupes of preten[d] patriots" and "daily misled into baneful measures."[84] Most Convention delegates also wanted to bar citizens who lacked adequate property from voting in federal elections. Philadelphia lawyer and politician John Dickinson insisted that property qualifications to voting were a "necessary defense against the dangerous influence of those multitudes without property." Practical and political considerations led to this measure's defeat.[85]

The structure of representation that the Convention approved was outlined by Madison, but critical alterations by delegates shrewdly anticipated the opposition to ratifying the Constitution. More than a few delegates to the Convention agreed with Elbridge Gerry that it was unlikely that "the people will ever agree [to the Constitution due to its] aristocratic [tendencies]."[86]

The attentiveness of the delegates to incorporating political equality and popular sovereignty did not slow their exclusion of blacks, Indians, and in certain respects, women. The Convention accepted the states' deep and enduring racial orders.[87] Northern delegates accepted slavery in exchange for the South's backing of the union.[88] The result of this immoral trade is that the slave population grew more than fivefold between 1790 and 1860, and attitudes of racial subjugation became deeply set in American political development.[89]

Constitutional Design, Clever Communications, Strong Democracy's Demise

One of the mysteries of the Constitution is its ratification in eleven states by the summer of 1788 after the beginning of the process in November 1787. Madison and his allies restricted state democracies and defied the preferences of many citizens. Yet state conventions met, public debate occurred (raucously at times), and votes to ratify the Constitution won majorities of state delegates at a time when political activism was intense and well organized.

Anti-Federalists Fight Back

The trepidation by Convention delegates about the opposition to ratifying the Constitution was confirmed by the sharp backlash that verged in some states on an organized social movement.[90] Critics of the Constitution—miscast as Anti-Federalists—decried the far-reaching transformation proposed by the document's drafters.[91] The Constitution launched, according to Patrick Henry (one of the most articulate speakers in Virginia's ratifying convention), a "revolution as radical as that which separated us from Great Britain."[92] Enough of the state ratification conventions were contested that the Constitution's adoption was precarious. In the pivotal state of New York, two-thirds of delegates initially opposed its approval.[93]

The Anti-Federalist attacks on the Constitution echoed, in part, earlier arguments developed by political activists and citizen associations.

The Attack on "Virtue"

Opponents of the Constitution disputed Madison's claims that the well-educated and well-born set aside their own interests to serve the public interest and abide by a code of virtue. Anti-Federalists insisted that the "gentlemen" Madison praised would promote their own interests by blocking steps that shifted some of the wealth of a few to aid struggling farmers and laborers.[94]

Anti-Federalists blasted the motives of the Constitution's drafters who misleadingly described themselves as the Federalists. "What crisis?" was the sharp rejoinder to Madison and others who claimed that they were honorable statesmen wrestling with dire circumstances. Patrick Henry goaded them, "I wish to hear the real actual existing danger, which should lead us to take those steps so dangerous [to the Confederation]." The Federalists, he concluded, "exceeded their power" and used the ruse of a crisis to propose radical change: "[They] tell us of dangers to terrify us into an adoption of this new Government" and intimidate citizens with "imaginary dangers."[95]

One of the Constitution's astute critics who published under the pseudonym "Brutus Junior" in northeastern states echoed Patrick's doubts about the "immediate danger of anarchy and commotions." "The governments of the respective states," he reported, "are in the full exercise of their powers; and the lives, the liberty, and property of individuals are protected. . . . [The challenges in] the regulation of trade and . . . payment of the interest of the public debt . . . may be taken [care of with] calm discussion and deliberate conclusions." He proceeded to condemn the Federalists: "Tyrants have always made use of this plea [of dire crisis and danger]; but nothing in our circumstances can justify it."[96] Even Madison's mentor, Thomas Jefferson, also reached similar conclusions: "Our Convention has been too much impressed by the [Shays] insurrection in Massachusetts."[97]

Rejecting "Oligarchic" Government and Defending Economic Redistribution

A persistent criticism of the Constitution was that its centralization of power in a national government weakened the "Spirit of 1776" and the Declaration's promise of "consent of the governed."[98] "Highly and dangerously oligarchic" was how an Anti-Federalist summed up the new national government.[99] Patrick Henry warned that "our rights and privileges are endangered" by the imposition of a "distant" national government with "supreme" authority over taxing, borrowing money, currency, commerce, and war.[100] While Anti-Federalists were not reticent about acknowledging the risks of ill-informed or misled majorities, they tended to agree that "harm is more often done by the tyranny of the rulers than by the licentiousness of the people."[101]

The Anti-Federalist known as "Martin Luther" insisted on "just principles of representation." "Representatives," he contended, "ought to speak the sentiments of his constituents and ought to vote in the same manner that his constituents would do." Questioning Madison's use of "filtration" to insulate government officials from citizens, Martin Luther made the case for representatives to be "dependent on his constituents and answerable to them. . . . [His connection] ought to be as near and as close as possible."[102]

The Anti-Federalists cautioned in newspaper columns that the Constitution proposed a limited form of representation—it merely "offered" what the British monarchy held out and pulled back from the "Spirit of 1776." The Constitution proposed a framework of representation, Patrick Henry charged, that was "grossly inadequate" and can "only nominally . . . be found."[103] The Old Whig observed that distancing "common people" from government in deference to "their superiors . . . isn't the language of the Revolution." He ridiculed the claim that "common people have no right to judge of the affairs of government; that they are not fit for it; that they should leave these matters to their superiors." Turning to satire to draw the attention of late-eighteenth-century newspaper readers, he mocked the Federalists as "very kind gentlemen who insist upon doing so much good for us." After all, he continues, "idiots and maniacs ought certainly to be restrained from doing themselves mischief, and ought to be compelled to that which is for their own good."[104]

With acute accuracy, Anti-Federalists publicly itemized the Constitutional Convention's private calculations to block direct citizen election of government officials. A common target was the selection of presidents by the Electoral College. "The president cannot represent you," reasoned "Letters of Cato," "because he is not your own immediate choice."[105] The Electoral College, "A Columbia Patriot" pointed out, was "nearly tantamount to the exclusion of the voice of the people."[106] The selection of senators by state legislatures was identified as another mechanism to blunt direct popular consent.[107]

Although it was not a consistent theme among Anti-Federalists, some connected the Constitution's scaling back of representation with the termination of economic redistribution by state legislatures.[108] The Constitution's opponents understood that the Federalists "calculated . . . to abolish and annihilate the State government" to sharply reduce the "attachments" of representatives with the "specific and particular needs" of their constituents. Where state legislators were "near and close" to their constituents and responded to their circumstances, the new national government was not expected to "sympathetically [appreciate] the wants of the people" and improve their "circumstances and interests."[109]

"The rich men," the American explained, favored the revolt against the British during the Revolution because "it was for their interest . . . as long as they could stay at home and send the common people into the field to fight their battles." "After the war," he continued, "the rich men . . . offe[r] you a plan of a new Federal Government, contrived with great art and shaded with obscurity, [to fix] . . . the yoke. . . on your necks [until]. . . your boasted liberty is but a sound."[110]

The Constitution's efforts to block state legislatures from aiding the vulnerable registered in the ratification conventions. Towns that benefited from tax and debt relief and the issuing of paper money during the 1780s often produced delegates who voted against ratification and were allies of the Anti-Federalists. Their ranks were joined by westerners, southerners, and small farmers saddled with debt-heavy land.[111]

Resisting the Gentry's Restoration

Divining the Federalists' private aim to restore the gentry's status and position, Anti-Federalists warned that the Constitution was designed to "form an aristocratic body."[112] Brutus Junior shared with his readers that "many [of the Constitutional Convention delegates] possessed . . . high aristocratic ideas."[113] Letter of Cato agreed that the Constitution will usher in an "aristocracy bordering on a monarchy."[114]

Old Whig and other Anti-Federalists linked the Constitution's aristocratic inclination to festooning presidents with a "fountain of all honors in the United States" and enormous powers that create "in reality . . . a king."[115] The Columbian Patriot equated the Electoral College with an "aristocratic junto."[116]

The Federalists' Counterrevolution Prevailed

If American citizens voted on whether to adopt the US Constitution in the late 1780s, it may well have been defeated because of its affront to state sovereignty and responsive lawmaking. The Federalists, however, overcame the opposition to the Constitution to secure ratification by outmaneuvering the Anti-Federalists, exploiting biases in the process, and perhaps most decisively, retaining (muted) representative government.

The Federalists strategically calibrated communications to dampen the potential for intense public opposition to the Constitution. From the beginning, they were secretive about their plan to hijack the Convention's purpose from improving the Confederation to replacing it. They also kept a tight lid on the discussions in Philadelphia. The result: The Constitution was unexpected and, indeed, shocking in its scope and radical design. When the Constitution was first presented to the Confederation's Congress, some members responded by attempting to censure the delegates to the Constitutional Convention for ignoring their guidelines to work on improvements. It took two days of debate to defeat it.

During the ratification process, the Federalists undercut potent criticisms through misdirection to distract attention from its most radical and unpopular feature—curtailing the powers of what had previously been independent states. One of their most effective contrivances was to label themselves the "Federalists," even though they were nationalists, while branding the advocates of state sovereignty the "Anti-Federalists." Friendly newspaper coverage aided the Federalists' crafted communications: it was more extensive than what was available to the Anti-Federalists and amplified the deceptive framing of the Constitution.[117]

In addition to the Federalists' crafted public communications, they aggressively orchestrated the process of ratification in ways that outmaneuvered the Constitution's critics. In comparison to the Anti-Federalists, the Constitution's advocates included more professionals (lawyers, merchants, and creditors) with experience operating within government and jiggering the government process to their benefit. In particular, they worked within state legislatures to authorize the Constitutional Convention and designed an advantageous procedure of requiring the approval of only nine states instead of all thirteen. The Federalists' network also coordinated their strategies across state ratifying conventions; their opponents often lacked this level of networking.[118] In the decisive campaign in New York State, Hamilton and other Federalists coordinated their campaign to confront the initial opposition to ratifying the Constitution with a communications blitz through friendly newspapers and strategic compromises that peeled off critics. In the end, the New York convention narrowly approved ratification with 52.6 percent of the votes.[119]

The Anti-Federalists struggled to overcome the advantages of the Constitution's advocates. The Anti-Federalists lacked reliable newspaper coverage. They also could not match the professional training and capacity of the Federalists to coordinate and turn out its supporters to the state ratifying conventions—especially the critical events in large coastal cities.

The Anti-Federalists lacked the strategic experience and skill to blunt their opponents. One of their most damaging mistakes was boycotting the Convention, which enabled Madison and his allies to shroud the Constitution in secrecy. Prominent figures—such as Virginia's powerful Patrick Henry—chose not to attend, handing the Federalists an enormous advantage. By not showing up in Philadelphia or keeping their reservations private (as was the case with the delegates who refused to sign the Constitution), the critics ceded the capacity to sound the public alarm about the emerging nationalist plan and build broad opposition well before the ratification process. Instead, the Anti-Federalists gave the Constitution's drafters a free pass to construct an insulated national government with less time to inform citizen associations, publicly pose questions, and build resistance.

The Federalists possessed another advantage: one of their primary motivations—stopping economic redistribution—was not a consistent priority for the Anti-Federalists. Although some spoke up for the economic stakes of citizens active in local and state governments, the ranks of Anti-Federalists included owners of land and businesses as well as conservatives leery of government altering the distribution of resources. The most visible Anti-Federalists tended to be relatively well educated and affluent; many were doubtful about debt relief and the issuing of paper money and refrained from making economic leveling a priority.[120]

Perhaps the most significant step taken by the Federalists was to preempt a clear referendum on representation and aristocracy. During the Constitution's drafting, delegates voted down and omitted antidemocratic features that threatened to intensify opposition during the impending ratification process. While most delegates privately shared misgivings about democratic rights and welcomed "the vigor of monarchy and the stability of aristocracy," they also accepted that they could not publicly back this agenda without being seen as abandoning the Declaration's promise of equality and public consent.[121] Anticipation of a political firestorm contributed to voting down proposals for property qualifications to vote and hold office as well rejecting the opposition to direct elections to the US House of Representatives.

The Framers' calculated concessions to political feasibility equipped them with flexibility during the ratification process. They responded to Anti-Federalists by spotlighting features of citizen representation and popular sovereignty and obscured the effect of the controversial overall structure to revive the gentry and roll back the strong democracy in states. When faced with charges of proposing "a system destructive to liberty"—as Patrick Henry and many other Anti-Federalists charged—Madison and his allies committed to adopting the Bill of Rights during the first Congress.[122]

In short, the Federalists used advantages in resources and organization to marginalize Anti-Federalist arguments and overcome expressed and latent public resistance.

A Legacy of Populist Backlash

In relatively quick succession following the Declaration of Independence in 1776, the British were defeated, the Articles of Confederation unleashed organized citizen engagement in state politics and economic redistribution, and the Constitutional Convention reacted by containing and institutionalizing new (though restrained) democratic practices.

Generic accounts of the Constitution's separation of powers and checks and balances often focus on abstract philosophical debates and ignore the pitched social battles that defined its institutional and political origins. The clash between the old and newly emerging social orders defined the contradictory impulses of the Constitutional Convention. On the one hand, delegates were transfixed by newly engaged citizens pressing to wrest control over government and society. Associations of laborers and farmers set out in the decade after the Declaration to organize citizens who had typically stayed away from politics during the Colonial Era to exercise their political rights through elections and assembly and to pressure state legislatures to respond to their instructions and dire economic needs. Madison's private communications voiced the alarm of many who were affluent and among the gentry. The Constitution's answer was to replace responsive state legislatures with a national government designed to filter and slow the effects of citizen activism.

On the other hand, the shrewdest among the Constitution's delegates appreciated that their effectiveness depended on acknowledging in some form the new sense of agency among citizens who were inspired by the Declaration and their experiences in the states. Returning to the Colonial social and political orders was not an option. The result is that the framers of the Constitution founded democratic rules, procedures, and rights that became an arsenal for future generations seeking to expand political representation.

The momentous years of the early republic left two contradictory legacies. First, the strong democracy of the 1780s demonstrates that political representation in America is neither monolithic nor necessarily defined by the "foreclosing" of authentic citizen participation and political influence.[123] While the feasibility of reviving this model is uncertain, there is a vibrant precedent for the contemporary linking of citizen activism and political effectiveness.[124]

The second legacy contributed to impeding coherent citizen activism and erecting the contemporary model of constrained political representation. Madison's constitutional framework fostered over time a style of factional politics that atomized citizens and concentrated power among the few.

3

The American Form of Democracy, 1796–1836

Thomas Jefferson and Andrew Jackson were bookends in the development of a distinctively American form of democracy during the first third of the nineteenth century. While they share seminal roles in American political history, their personal demeanors and backgrounds differ starkly. Jefferson was an urbane international man of letters and astute political figure who drafted the Declaration of Independence and served as third president (1801–1809). Jackson rode to the presidency (1829–1837) on the glory of defeating the British in New Orleans during the War of 1812. Unlike the well-mannered and affluent presidents before him, Jackson's ascent earned him a reputation as a brutal killer who defied orders, a vulgar frontiersman, and a "dangerous man," as Jefferson put it. The reception among Washington, DC officialdom to Jefferson's first inaugural speech—"conciliatory . . . without any species of distraction or disorder"—contrasted markedly with its horror at the "King Mob" that Jackson welcomed to his swearing-in.[1]

Jefferson and Jackson capitalized on the convergence of three dynamics to precipitate enduring changes in democratic institutions. First, the alliance of the Constitution's framers fractured, creating space for significant institutional innovation. President George Washington enjoyed unusually broad support; his departure gave way to intense political rivalry and competition that revealed a significant flaw with the Constitution. The closely contested presidential elections in 1796 and 1824 produced deadlocks that required resolution by the US House of Representatives. The outcomes were contentious and, from the perspectives of the vanquished (Jefferson and Jackson), illegitimate because political maneuvering replaced the "will of the people."

Second, Jefferson and Jackson advanced their ambition with populist calls to "the people" to muster masses of voters against a political system closed to them. Although the democratic upsurge in the 1780s lingered in the minds of governing elites, both targeted the egalitarian rights of white males to swell their vote totals and overtake insiders. Third, the Declaration's promise of democratic rights and the Constitution's representative system created a structure and incentives for innovation to reach new voters while protecting the authority and legitimacy of democratic institutions.

Jefferson and Jackson pioneered changes that generated two challenges. First, how could they reliably harvest votes from putative supporters? Success in moving new voters to the ballot box was one steep hurdle, but the other was steering support at the ballot box to the right candidate in an era without a history of strong loyalty to a political party. Second, would Jefferson's and Jackson's marshaling of mass participation trigger—as political and economic elites anticipated—a relapse to the excessive democracy of the 1780s and its "Robinhood Society" in which rising numbers of less-well-off voters used their ballots at the expense of creditors and wealthy landowners? Their disruption of the prevailing norms by mobilizing voters required—according to Jefferson and Jackson and their allies—countermeasures to contain mass democracy and protect the authority of democratic institutions from demagogues posing as the voice of the people.

The new forms of politics in the early Republic—the selection of presidential nominees by political parties and their national nominating conventions—would have enduring effects. They initiated democratic rules and incentives that structured the pursuit of power for generations. They also became a target of political conflict. In the wake of Jefferson and Jackson, American democracy would, over time, come to be equated with battles over how political parties nominate candidates. White supremacy and its clash with America's founding commitments was another front of future conflict: egalitarianism played out in party organizations and national conventions in ways that, at times, facilitated the perpetuation of racial orders and, at other times, disrupted them.

Thomas Jefferson: The Breakdown of the Constitution and the Search for Order

Uncertainty hung over America's future after the Constitution's ratification provoked fiery debate in the late 1780s. Would the Constitutional Convention's institutional constructions take hold or remain intensely contested, struggle to gain authority and legitimacy, and invite public disturbances? Without a tradition of peacefully transferring power, would losing candidates in the new constitutional system dispute the results or accept their outcome despite personal and policy disagreements? If it avoided the pitfalls of disorder, what form would political struggles for power and position take?

Abstract speculation quickly gave way to dueling verdicts of lasting significance. The basic structure sketched in Philadelphia in 1787 was rapidly accepted. The Constitution's critics—the Anti-Federalists—traded their barbed attacks on the document's legitimacy for participation within the new framework to advocate for liberty and fairness as well as tangible considerations. Elite agreement among elected politicians and government officials to support George Washington as the country's first president soothed animosity and created a cooling-off period following the acrimony that accompanied the Constitution's ratification.

Even as the explicit challenges to the Constitution dissipated, however, its lofty designs collided with unanticipated practical problems that threatened to undermine the new political system.

Washington's decision not to run for reelection following his second term tested the operation of the Electoral College in the 1796 and 1800 presidential elections. Its operation both rewarded personal ambition in place of the "republican values" the Constitution's framers lauded (virtue, individual liberty, and the public good) and fueled corrosive doubts about the integrity of the process among political elites.

The bitter 1796 presidential contest between Washington's vice president, John Adams, and his former secretary of state, Thomas Jefferson, produced a peculiar outcome: both won even though they hailed from rival political parties. Adams became president and Jefferson was selected his vice president. This anomaly of a cross-party executive resulted from a miscalculation by the Constitutional Convention: members of the Electoral College, which were selected by state legislatures, were each granted two votes to cast for president; the majority winner became president and the runner-up was vice president. In the 1796 election, Adams received a majority of the electoral votes (seventy-one) while Jefferson received the second-most (sixty-eight).

In the absence of George Washington's unifying influence, Adams and Jefferson and their supporters inaugurated political parties to improve their prospects despite the earlier warnings of the Constitution's framers that parties would foster factions, ambition, and self-interest over the public good. Policy disagreements over the size and scope of government—Jefferson and later Jackson favored minimal interventions—intensified electoral motivations. Jefferson and Madison teamed up to found the Democratic-Republican Party in the early 1790s and strengthened it during Washington's second term in order to oppose Hamilton's nationalist agenda, promote republicanism, and organize against Adams. They built a base in the South, which broadened into a national party over the coming decades. By contrast, Adams and his supporters affiliated with the Federalist Party and marshalled a base of support in New England.

The 1800 presidential election—as well as the 1824 contest—laid bare a further flaw with the Constitutional Convention's design of the Electoral College. The first election of the nineteenth century started as a rematch of Adams and Jefferson but ended with another anomaly: Jefferson and Aaron Burr (the former US senator who ran as Jefferson's vice presidential candidate) received identical Electoral College totals and faced off in the US House of Representatives. (Each received the Electoral College votes of the states they won, and the Constitution's rules prevented electoral voters from distinguishing between their presidential and vice presidential choices.) Jefferson and others expected Burr to defer to his senior running mate, but instead he contested the race through two months and thirty-six ballots in the US House of Representatives until Jefferson prevailed.

The pattern of the US House (and not voters) deciding the outcome of elections was unpopular, corrosive of founding principles, and an infuriating hurdle for dueling politicians. It undermined one of the nation's founding principles—popular sovereignty. In place of voters determining the outcome of elections, the US House decided the outcome after months of unseemly dealmaking. It also undermined the principle of separating the distinct branches of government. Congressional selection of the president would, in the words of Gouveneur Morris at the Constitutional Convention, make the president "the tool of a faction of some leading demagogue in the Legislature."[2]

Jefferson and his ambitious campaign supporters responded to the Constitution's election fiasco by developing novel strategies to capitalize on the mostly dormant pool of eligible voters while also containing the potentially disruptive consequences of citizen activism that stirred elite misgivings. The confluence of political entrepreneurship with elite divisions created an opening to introduce new political institutions to sharply increase voter turnout while safeguarding the authority of government institutions and political representation.

Elite Mobilization and Voter Resurgence

Jefferson's determined campaign invested resources in reaping the electoral benefits of white men gaining access to democratic rights to vote and speak critically in public about government policies and officials (including the president). Jefferson's campaigns—especially his 1800 race—produced an "unprecedent democratic revolution."[3]

By the late eighteenth century, property requirements were in place and, indeed, expanded (as in Massachusetts) to block universal suffrage for white men in more than half of the thirteen original states. States took other steps to favor the better off—including malapportionment of seats and bicameral legislatures. In 1800, five of the eleven governors were selected not by popular vote but by state legislatures.[4]

Jefferson's supporters and their allies pushed forward, however, to make the egalitarian rights of white men a reality and contest the Colonial Era's aristocracy. By the nineteenth century, the earlier pretentions of the wealthy and the habit of "deference" to the "better born" among everyday people was in retreat, surviving only in scattered enclaves, including the stubbornly feudal Connecticut.[5] A writer in Massachusetts complained in 1786 that the "wealthy men [who follow 'aristocratic principles' hoped to] . . . drive out that hardy and independent spirit from among us and forge chains for our liberties."[6] But these vestiges of the gentry were bombarded— with encouragement by Jefferson's allies—by a sustained and growing assault of formal petitions and newspaper articles insisting on wider voting rights and fairer representation. "Poor ragged democrats," a Jefferson supporter insisted, no longer deferred to "ye well-fed, well-dressed, chariot-lolling, caucus-keeping, levee-reveling federalists."[7]

Jefferson's supporters built alliances with older community groups active in politics as well as newer arrivals. The Revolutionary Era committees of correspondence lingered in some parts of the country as a means of responding to misinformation by the Adams administration, filling gaps in public knowledge, and coordinating criticism of national policy.

Of more significance were about thirty-five Democratic-Republican societies that drew in journeymen artisans and master craftsmen after the 1790s to confront political elites and the gentry and insist on the "equal rights of man."[8] They stoutly challenged the custom of public deference to those in power, who "laughed at and ridiculed [common people and] consider . . . government to belong naturally only to a few families [who] ought to be obeyed and supported."[9] The Democratic-Republican societies—also referenced as "True Republican," "Constitutional," "United Freeman," and "Patriotic"—were particularly aggressive in exercising what had been abstract Constitutional rights to free speech. Their targets were the Federalist Party and, in particular, Alexander Hamilton's activist agenda as the first US Treasury secretary that they derided as the "prescriptions of Aristocracy, under the masque of Federalism."[10]

Particular venom was targeted at Hamilton's push—with Washington's support—to float government securities, impose an excise tax on distilled liquor, and establish a national bank to pay down the mammoth federal and state debt accumulated during the Revolutionary War and Confederation. These policies were necessary, Hamilton and Washington insisted, to create pools of capital for economic development and restore the confidence of financial markets. The Democratic-Republican societies and other critics vigorously objected, however. They charged, as a Georgia representative in the US House put it, that the policies were "calculated to benefit a small part of the country." Indeed, there were winners and losers. Speculators in the North cashed in on the government securities they purchased at low rates in the 1780s; it also bailed out debt-laden states like Massachusetts. The losers included southern states that had mostly retired their debts and those burdened by the excise tax on liquor. The anger erupted in Pennsylvania where rural societies launched the 1794 Whiskey Rebellion, blocking a federal tax collector in defiance of Hamilton's excise tax, and flouting the new government's authority.[11]

The Federalists confirmed criticisms of their arrogance and ultimately invigorated opposition by attempting to squash the dissent in the 1790s. President Washington was joined by the Senate and House in formally censuring Democratic-Republican societies for challenging government policy and inciting disorder. By 1798, John Adams signed the Alien and Sedition Acts to suppress criticisms of the federal government that it claimed were false. Instead of terminating public opposition, the Democratic-Republican societies—as well as Jefferson and Madison— seized on the acts as targets of political attack for violating the First Amendment and the values of the Revolution.[12] Jefferson protested the "attack[s on] . . . the freedom of discussion [and] the freedom of writing, printing, and publishing."[13]

The maneuvering by Jefferson and his allies produced a "democratic outpouring" and smashing electoral victory in the 1800 election.[14] Jefferson's campaign walloped Adams by more than a twenty-two-percentage-point margin—61.4 percent to 38.6 percent.[15]

It also expanded the electorate and set a precedent for mass electoral mobilization on which Jackson would build. While only a small portion of the population voted during George Washington's two elections, national voter turnout increased from 20.1 percent of the eligible population to 32.3 percent between 1796 and 1800.[16] As many as seven out of ten eligible voters cast ballots in some counties during the 1800 contest. By the end of Jefferson's presidency, the proportion of white male turnout for certain elections doubled to 70 percent in Massachusetts and nearly tripled in Pennsylvania. This pattern of sharply higher turnout swept New England and the Middle Atlantic states.[17]

Searching for a New Synthesis of Egalitarianism and Order

A priority of the Washington and Adams administrations was strengthening the central government's resources and administrative tools to project economic and military power.[18] The search for new government capacity was paralleled by the Jefferson campaign's construction of new organizational practices and techniques to reach and turn out voters reliably. Jefferson's dependence on his party organization was reinforced by norms against direct personal campaign appeals, which were equated at the time with demagoguery.[19]

Political ambition to avenge Jefferson's 1796 defeat drove his campaign to build the political party into an instrument for mass mobilization by drawing on the techniques and strategies of the Democratic-Republican societies and other community groups. Under the watchful eye of Aaron Burr and Philadelphia's John Beckley, they repurposed existing publications and political groups to stage public events, recruit loyal campaign workers, and create an infrastructure of loyal newspapers to spread their campaign messages in 1800. Election committees and networkers operated in Massachusetts, Virginia, Maryland, New Jersey, Pennsylvania, and New York (with a particular focus on Manhattan). In Massachusetts, for instance, Republicans deployed county and town committees to distribute campaign messages, build voter support, and turn out the vote on Election Day. Most of these activities flouted the Sedition Law that Adams passed. In the case of Democratic-Republican societies, the Jefferson forces shifted them from criticizing government to election work. They redirected existing local committees and networks—including urban activists—to convey a coherent message through partisan newspapers and other types of communications as well as to introduce methods for reaching more voters and getting more of them to the ballot box.[20]

Jefferson coupled his campaign's institutional turn with a form of "nascent populism," in Michael Kazin's artful phrase, that would develop more fully under Andrew Jackson and, especially, late-nineteenth-century reformers.[21] Jefferson's campaign message attacked the hold of urban speculators over a distant powerful government and charged that the Federalists leached off the labor of others, corruptly lined their pockets, and prosecuted those who spoke up. Jefferson promised to take on corruption to protect republican values and ensure that rewards result "not from birth, but from our actions," as he proclaimed in his inaugural address.

Jefferson exercised another populist strategy—promising to restore power to "the people" and championing the value of equality. He connected the national unity with a reverence of "those who labor in the earth"—the free planters and yeomen who were moral, hardworking, and independent.

Jefferson and his campaign deftly summoned public frustration and resentment to advance their own ambitions. Jefferson himself candidly attributed his power to his pastoral populism that would deliver a "mighty wave of public opinion" to support him and his reforms.[22] Elite manipulation of populism to serve their own interest is a consistent pattern, as future chapters show.

Adams and the Federalist Party lost a landslide election in 1800 after failing to "square their politics with the democratic ideas unleashed in the 1790s."[23] The new political reality of an expanding electorate and the imperative of organization to compete did not register—as it did for Jefferson's supporters—in its planning and campaigning. Adams and his supporters remained in the hold of eighteenth-century elite orthodoxy: the expectation that citizens defer to their betters and the fear that activism by the "common man" threatens property and order.

Elite Trepidations about "the Mob"

The successful use of party organization and populist appeals by Jefferson's campaign forged new forms of politics that modified the incentives initially introduced by the Constitution and, over time, defined the options, interests, and challenges for future political figures. Their renewal of egalitarian commitments created, however, tensions by appearing to erode the authority of government and jeopardize the social order.

The unease of political and community leaders with rapidly expanding political participation was, in part, driven by partisan opposition to Jefferson and his allies. Federalists equated the mobilization of citizens to vote and publicly protest policies with the "ungovernable passions of a simple democracy" and warned that an impending uprising would create a "land of groans, tears, and blood." Federalists were particularly unsettled by the danger posed by Democratic-Republican societies. Their formation for the "avowed purpose of a general influence and control upon the measures of government" was declared "unlawful" by prominent Federalist Oliver Wolcott Jr. A conservative English émigré agreed that they were "butchers, tinkers, broken hucksters, and trans-Atlantic traitors."[24] Jefferson was vilified for this democratic surge by landowners and the wealthy who derided him as a traitor to his class.[25]

Jefferson and the elites who supported him were not immune, though, to the apprehension about the democratic outpouring after Washington's departure. Jefferson was initially leery of the Democratic-Republican societies and only came to accept them as an expediency to overcome the deadlock with the Federalists that the Electoral College reinforced. His own unease was reinforced by other Republicans who favored restraining what they described as a frightening arousal of the masses into a popular political force. This unease with democratic outpourings was harbored by his ally James Madison even as he benefited from it.[26] Jefferson was also mindful that a reputation for excessive populism would harm his search for tactical alliances with other elites in a time of deadlock—most notably with his rival Hamilton, who tilted the 1800 election in his favor.[27]

Jefferson and his campaign searched for a particular form of representational politics that simultaneously enabled them to benefit from mass political participation and addressed elite trepidations about the danger of "mob" rule. In several steps, Jefferson and his supporters designed and protected the authority and legitimacy of representative institutions.

Before the 1796 election, Jefferson and his inner circle imposed limits on the participation of Democratic-Republican societies and other community groups in order to safeguard and restrict political representation. In particular, the citizen groups that Jefferson rallied were blocked from managing candidate nominations and campaigns. Insulating the selection of candidates helps to account for Jefferson's acceptance of the Congressional Caucus—or "King Caucus"—to control the nomination of candidates during the eighteenth and early nineteenth centuries. "Members of Congress," nineteenth-century political sociologist Moisei Ostrogorski explained, believed they "have better opportunities of knowing the character and talents of the several candidates than those who have never seen them and never acted with them."[28]

In addition to acquiescing to the selection of candidates by the Congressional Caucus, Jefferson's cautious approach to containing citizen activism was also evident in his use of electoral politics as a mechanism to channel and contain citizens—including the most engaged. Later in his life, Jefferson identified his contribution as advancing America's form of government "not . . . by the sword but by the rational and peaceable instrument of reform."[29]

As for Jefferson's populism, it too was characterized by ambiguity: he preached the virtues of the yeoman farmer and sins of distant government, but he also enlarged national and presidential power once in the White House.[30] Jefferson's innovation was not to threaten the Republic but rather to find a new synthesis of so-cial control and the exercise of political equality. Jefferson's mod-eration and devotion to the authority and legitimacy of democratic institutions permeated his inaugural address, where he famously cautioned that "every difference of opinion is not a difference of principle."[31] In the decades following Washington's retirement from politics, Jackson and Van Buren joined Jefferson in searching for a new political synthesis that would equip them to win the White House by rousing citizens to exercise their rights to vote while con-tinuing to channel and contain mass political participation within safe boundaries.

Andrew Jackson and the Institutional Turn

Before 1824, when Andrew Jackson emerged in national politics, the combination of war, economic panic, and elite competition renewed scrutiny of the limits on the exercise of egalitarian citizen rights. The War of 1812 was precipitated by Britain's enforcement of a blockade that restricted American trade with Napoleon's France as well as its arming of Native Americans to impede President James Madison's plans for western expansion. The war was initially unpopular due to its costs. The Americans suffered military defeats that included the burning of the Capitol; the British raids along the East Coast were quite effective in interrupting trade. The tide turned, however, with America's victories, the stymieing of Britain's invasion, and the negotiation of the Treaty of Gent (1814) that left US boundaries unchanged. The conclusion of the War of 1812 unleashed triumphant celebrations and what became known as the "Era of Good Feelings."[32] It also catapulted Jackson into national fame as a general who repelled Britain's invasion of New Orleans and sapped its fighting spirit.

In the eyes of many Americans at the time, the War of 1812 was a victory for the country's budding democracy that everyday people fought and died to defend. During and after the war, reformers and newspapers seized on the opportunity to demand that wartime service and sacrifices be rewarded by continuing the Jeffersonian wave of expanding the right to vote and equitable political representation. A supporter of New York political titan DeWitt Clinton (an early-nineteenth-century mayor of New York City and governor of the state) explained the necessary political calculus: "We must be on the side of the people. . . . If our adversaries are republicans, we must be democratic; if they are democratic, we must be Jacobinal."[33] For a nineteenth-century audience, the point was clear: better to give the pretense of favoring the French Revolution and its radical push to dismantle barriers to equality than be seen as tolerating the privileges of the old order.

As politicians competed to promote the widening of egalitarian rights to broader circles of white men, property qualifications to vote were mostly rolled back: many of the state restrictions at the war's start were abolished or weakened. This pattern of broadening suffrage occurred in New Jersey, Ohio, New England states, and recently admitted western states (including Indiana and Illinois), which were eager to attract new settlers and satisfy statehood requirements. New York continued a process of rolling back restrictions that started a dozen years earlier when Federalists limited voting in New York City to merely 5 percent of the qualified electorate. In addition, Pennsylvania was part of a group of eighteen states that would put the selection of presidential electors in the hands of voters by 1824. (Voters directly chose presidential electors in all but two states by 1828.) Connecticut and Rhode Island continued to stand out as exceptions in this wave of reform, but after 1815, reformers pushed through wider suffrage and lowered barriers to voting by white males.[34]

The incentives of ambitious politicians to compete for the swelling number of eligible voters increased as labor associations continued to grow in northern cities. Philadelphia's Mechanics'

Union of Trade Associations was part of a movement in cities that combined electoral politics with the mobilizing of men working in artisan trades—dock workers, cartmen, shop clerks, and other laborers.[35]

Andrew Jackson strode into this moment of exceptional turmoil as a brash and ruthless frontiersman bathed in national glory from his victory during the War of 1812. Entering national politics for the first time can be a handicap, but not during this period when the rising attention of political elites to citizens collided with a devastating economic crisis that began in 1819. The targets of popular blame were those in power. The Democratic-Republican Party won the White House and majorities in Congress for more than two decades after the Federalist Party crested with John Adams's 1796 presidential election. As the Federalist Party dissolved, a large group rebranded themselves as "New Republicans" and followed the lead of Henry Clay, the Speaker of the House of Representatives. Clay pushed through Congress a package of initiatives he labeled the "American System" that continued Hamilton's agenda of using the central government to promote the economy: tariffs were imposed to shield domestic manufacturing from the competition of cheaper British goods; public lands were sold; the Bank of the US was rechartered; and new spending was approved for transportation—roads, canals, and bridges—as well as favors for friends and supporters.

The Panic of 1819 impoverished legions of Americans and ignited a political backlash against Washington, DC, and the activist policies it had pursued. Although the economic crisis was precipitated by global and domestic financial markets, it set the stage for Jackson to ride in from the frontier as a populist outsider ready to blame the established order.[36]

The convergence of political ambition, intense elite competition, and Jefferson's elevating of political parties as an avatar of democracy guided Jackson's strategies for election and reform.

Elite Mobilization: Jackson Targets Voters

Jackson ran for president three times. The first run was in 1824 and was built on his national reputation as a war hero and outsider unsullied by the culpability of Washington, DC, in the economic devastation. Turning a potential weakness into an asset, Jackson and his supporters promoted his lack of connections to the founding generation or to a well-known family name as a political advantage.

Jackson's personal journey from the margins of early America granted him authenticity, but it was inadequate to prevail in 1824. He won in the East, South, and West and secured the most popular votes (152,901) and electoral votes (99). As in 1796, the Constitution's Electoral College intervened despite the Twelfth Amendment that separated the vote for president and vice president: Jackson failed to satisfy its requirement of a majority of 131 electoral votes. Meeting in January 1825, the House of Representatives selected the second-place finisher—John Quincy Adams (114,023 votes and 84 electoral votes)—as the sixth president after he reportedly cut a deal with the third-place finisher, Henry Clay.[37] Jackson refused to bargain and fumed at the "intrigue, corruption, and sale of public office" that "humiliat[ed] the American character . . . and the constitutional rights of the people."[38] Jackson and his supporters insisted that the selection of Adams "lacked democratic legitimacy."[39]

Jackson's outrage motivated him to abandon his earlier inclination to be "President of the nation and not of a party" and, after the 1824 campaign, he joined forces with Martin Van Buren to build a national party organization to mobilize voters and bypass the system that rewarded insiders.[40]

Elections Are Democracy
Jackson and his campaign developed a two-pronged strategy. The first was to narrow democracy to mobilizing voters for the short-term objective of winning elections.

Adjusting to the emerging political environment, Jackson's campaign prioritized the instrumental value of targeting the discrete, isolated episodes of elections instead of organizing as a broad, continuous process. Jackson singled out elections as "the panacea for all the ills of government." "The right of suffrage," he insisted, is the "great constitutional corrective in the hands of the people against usurpation of power, or corruption by their agents."[41] Democracy became both potentially more adept in directing government power and narrowed to the window of campaigning for office. The earlier investment during the 1780s in developing the skills and networks of citizens and their communities was now assessed as less rational.

Building Political Parties as National Organizations

Second, the competition to become president and Jackson's ambition to succeed propelled his campaign to build substantially on Jefferson's start to erect an efficacious national party organization. This commitment to party development followed the splintering of the Democratic-Republican Party after the 1824 election. One faction supported Adams in 1824 and later nominated Henry Clay in 1832 before becoming the National Republican Party and then the Whig Party. Jackson's supporters retained the Democratic-Republican Party label until the 1832 Democratic National Convention officially renamed it the Democratic Party.

The splintering of the Democratic-Republican Party fueled opposition to the work of Jackson's allies to construct a comparatively effective, national party organization. President James Monroe (who departed after the 1824 election) derided political parties as the "curse of the country" because of their damage to the public good; John Quincy Adams, who replaced Monroe, vowed to "break up the [last] remnant of party distinction."[42] Jackson himself echoed this antiparty sentiment in the run-up to the 1824 election; his ambition and controversial defeat to Adams converted him to party building.

Van Buren, whom Jackson recruited to steer him to victory in 1828, forcefully advocated for political parties as an antidote to the hoarding of government privileges by Washington insiders and the House selecting winners in closely contested presidential elections. He argued that political conflict—and specifically partisan competition—was unavoidable and, indeed, indispensable to sustaining the form of representative democracy that the Constitution's framers intended.[43] Efforts to mute party competition by Jackson's predecessors advantaged insiders over the mass of citizens who were left divided, unfocused on their interests, and bereft of the organization necessary to mobilize opposition.[44] Jackson came to defend the political party as a vehicle of "the people," and Van Buren insisted it would "keep these masses together."[45] Political parties were the organization for mass democracy because they could widen citizen participation and create the Electoral College majorities for a single candidate that was necessary to avoid shady dealings in the House.

Van Buren was a precocious modernizer. Drawing on his earlier experiences in New York,[46] he ushered in a new generation of professional politicians to replace the stubborn reliance on social connections and ad hoc campaigning. Van Buren brought a "passion for organization" that was guided by specified routines and procedures, hired individuals with expertise, and judged performance by voter turnout and other quantifiable metrics.[47] In contrast to previous campaigns, Jackson's 1828 and 1832 organizations developed the capacities to mobilize distinct segments of white voters across region, ethnicity, and class.

Focused on the potential for a large electorate, Van Buren's campaign fully cast off the dated eighteenth-century presumption that voters would defer to "their betters" in favor of aggressive targeted techniques of voter appeal during Jackson's presidential races. The Jackson campaign—with its headquarters in Nashville, Tennessee— orchestrated frequent spectacles of rallies and parades to excite and turn out supporters. The Jackson organization's boisterous and aggressive public campaigning was a departure from the earlier practice of smaller, less frequent, and often uncoordinated events but was critical in the nineteenth century when candidates were expected to refrain from directly pleading for votes.[48] Although Jackson largely abided by the norms of his age by relying on party organization instead of extensive personal appeals, he did disturb some contemporary observers by personally promoting his campaign in meetings with delegations and using newspapers to distribute his letters and views expressed in interviews.[49]

In addition, Van Buren organized an early effort to establish mass communications by creating a dense network of newspapers that crisscrossed every state. Building coalitions in urban and rural areas in the North and South was a campaign priority. Van Buren reached out to disparate factions and sculpted the campaign organization to build and maintain these valuable alliances.[50] His elaborate operation of voter appeals, newspapers, coalition building, and more cost money, which triggered an organizational process for fundraising.[51]

Van Buren's embrace of organizational capacity as necessary to mobilize voters within a country saddled with uneven communications and difficult travel meshed with more general moves toward erecting political institutions. His efforts followed more than two decades of building the government's central authority and capabilities and raising money to pay for it.[52]

Jackson's Populism

Jackson's crusade for "the people" and against corruption accelerated the emergence of nineteenth-century populism, which would later flourish in the protests of farmers after the Civil War.[53] He articulated a broader and more searing populism than Jefferson along three dimensions—each of which fits the pattern of self-serving elite manipulation.

The first prong of Jackson's populist appeal was his attack on corruption in America, especially its seat of national government power—Washington, DC. His experiences running a Tennessee farm and serving in the military instilled a deep-seated suspicion of a distant government that favored those with connections. Jackson scorned the national government interventions that Adams and Clay promoted as "executive patronage" and "legislat[ing] on behalf of the favored few at the expense of the many."[54] "When I view the splendor and magnificence of the government [in Washington, DC]," Jackson confessed, "I shudder for the consequence"—creating a "money aristocracy" and "robbing the people" by saddling them with debt and unreliable paper money.[55] For Jackson and many voters, the economic collapse in 1819 resulted from government activism and the reliance on debt and paper money. Limited government that starved the corrupt was the antidote.

Jackson's populist attack on corruption targeted the Second Bank of the US (BUS) and the presidential nomination system run by the Congressional Caucus. A quick word about America's tortured history with national banks: Hamilton created the much-criticized First Bank but was unable to rally support to continue it past 1811; the Second Bank replaced it with President Madison's approval in 1816. It handled the government's money—income, payments, and debt—and seeded branches in multiple states. In a new country struggling to conduct the basic functions of government, the bank's job was to sustain the good standing of the country's credit to borrow money and facilitate commerce. Unlike the contemporary Federal Reserve Bank, however, the Second Bank's role was meager: it was inconceivable that it would set monetary policy (the raising and lowering of its interest rates to manage economic growth), regulate private banks, or step in as a lender of last resort in emergencies when banks collapsed, which occurred about every decade in the nineteenth century.[56]

For Jackson, the Second Bank was a ready-made target to mobilize masses of Americans behind his populist outrage against elites and catapult himself into the White House. He and his supporters blamed banks and political insiders for capturing government power to enrich themselves and for putting a chokehold on credit that hit everyday people and fueled foreclosures. The bank's finances certainly reeked of privilege: only a few hundred wealthy (white) men controlled most of its stocks and it became the world's largest monied corporation.[57] Jackson thrashed the Bank for equipping "a few Monied Capitalists" to get rich and to use their wealth to bribe government officials. Jackson's populist rage crystallized in his veto of the congressional reauthorization of the Second Bank in 1832 and his charge that the "rich and powerful . . . bend the acts of government to their selfish purposes." Evoking his reputation as a war hero, Jackson brandished his veto pen to "take a stand against . . . any prostitution of our Government to the advancement of the few at the expense of the many."[58] Instead of serving the people, the Bank swelled its power and opulence and made "the rich richer and the potent more powerful." The vehemence of Jackson's attacks was fed by his own searing experience with banking.[59]

In an ironic twist of history, the son of Alexander Hamilton (the first promoter of a national bank) prepared an analysis for Jackson that the BUS was unconstitutional because Congress created it by asserting powers it lacked and threatening popular sovereignty. The bank, Hamilton's son reported, concentrated in "the hands of a few men, a power over the money of the country."

While Jackson slammed the BUS for privileging the rich, he castigated the Congressional Caucus for fixing the nomination of presidential candidates and trying to block his path to the presidency. With the Democratic-Republican Party dominating presidential elections by winning six consecutive races as of 1824, the "King Caucus" wielded the power of deciding who would be the party's nominee and therefore president.

The King Caucus's supremacy was unchallenged for nearly two decades after George Washington stepped down. But Jackson unleashed withering attacks on it for protecting a "corrupt aristocracy" that was "attempt[ing] to cheat the people out of their constitutional rights" and "force public opinion to take up a particular candidate."[60] If the caucus system remained, he warned, the people would be stripped of their power and a dictatorship would emerge: a small number amounting to less than a quarter of Congress would select the Republican Party candidate and the eventual president by "coerc[ing] the people to follow them."[61] After 1824, the King Caucus was silenced.

The second prong of Jackson's populist appeal to lift his presidential ambitions was to summon "the people" to rise up and drive out the corruption. He anchored himself in the tradition of "old Jeffersonian Democratic republican principles."[62] Jackson fashioned his public identity as a champion of the "common man" and defender of "the people" and "humble members of society" against the parasitic privileged insiders who promoted the Bank of the US, the King Caucus, and Washington's giveaway projects.[63] His campaign framed a stark choice: "Shall the [Adams] government or the people rule?"

Jackson championed the "constitutional right of suffrage" as anchoring America's egalitarian commitment. Political power, he insisted, resided with the "independent exercise of their free suffrage" and the "majority . . . govern[ing]." "There is no other corrective of [the federal government's] abuses," he insisted, "but the suffrages of the people" and "a fair expression of the will of the majority."[64] By extension, his power would depend on "elect[ion] to fill the presidential chair . . . by the people" in order to "legislat[e] the people's will."[65] Jackson's crusade for "the people" accelerated the collapse of the social hierarchy and the traditions of deference and aristocratic pretensions that had hung on since the Colonial Era.[66]

The third prong of Jackson's populism was his campaign's cultivation of personal charisma. Beginning in earnest in 1828, his campaign intentionally accented Jackson's heroism, virtue, and humble origins as a representative of the people unsullied by the intrigue and corruption of Washington, DC. The strategic purpose was to invite a personal and even emotional bond with Jackson, who was portrayed as locked in a titanic battle for the people and the egalitarian Spirit of 1776. The pattern of self-serving elite manipulation of populism took a turn to personal promotion that Jefferson avoided.

Organization and Populism Matters

Jackson's allies and staff were exceptionally effective in tethering his 1828 and 1832 campaign organization and populism to mobilizing "popular self-assertion" and votes.[67] His overwhelming nationwide victories broke free of the pattern of close or deadlocked elections since 1796. Jackson's winning margins were not outdone during the nineteenth century.

In 1828, the combination of Jackson's populism and Van Buren's campaign organization was remarkably successful in turning out voters. About 1.15 million votes were cast in 1828 compared to 365,928 four years earlier—more than a threefold increase.

Jackson won 55.9 percent of the vote (642,809 votes) and 68 percent of the Electoral College vote (178 votes) compared to John Quincy Adams's 43.68 percent (500,967 votes) and 83 Electoral College voters. These results, Jackson pronounced, were a "triumph of the great principle of self-government over the intrigues of aristocracy."[68]

Jackson won reelection in 1832 against Henry Clay by more impressive margins: securing 76 percent (219) of the Electoral College voters along with a larger winning margin in the popular vote: 54.74 percent and 702,735 votes compared to Clay's 36.93 percent and 474,107 votes.[69] The campaign's work to build an organization and populist message that would appeal to voters and broaden coalitions was rewarded by wins in Republican states in New England (Maine and New Hampshire) and much of the South. Jackson's strident veto of the rechartering of the Bank of the US was,

in Van Buren's account, "popular beyond my most sanguine expectations" and contributed to widening the campaign's broad appeal
throughout the nation.[70]

Neither Jefferson's nor Jackson's turn to party organization registered with their opponents as necessary to winning elections.
Ironically, the Federalists both pioneered the development of the
government's administrative capacity and failed in the case of John
Adams's 1800 campaign to appreciate the significance of harnessing
elections to organizational innovation. In 1828 and 1832, Jackson's
presidential elections demonstrated the strategic advantages of
marrying populist appeals with a mass-mobilizing party organization, but his opponents did not immediately learn the lesson. Critics
continued to pine for the older, more sedate style of campaigning
and belittled Jackson's populism and Van Buren's voter outreach
as "mere effervescence."[71] Defeat would prove a bitter teacher; the
effectiveness of Jackson's campaign would exert enduring influence on how American elections are conducted. Van Buren was
rewarded by Jackson for loyalty and effectiveness: he was elected
vice president in place of the troublesome John C. Calhoun in 1832
and then received the party's nomination to succeed Jackson.

Channeling the Mobilized

Historians understandably single out the expansion of white male
suffrage as a salient feature of Jefferson's and Jackson's legacies—
along with the racial and gender exclusions.[72] Their significance
extends, however, beyond quantitative measures of voting to the
particular institutional form of American democracy that they
initiated. They pioneered political party organizations devoted to
voter mobilization and a national party convention to select presidential candidates. Jefferson, and especially Jackson, advanced
these institutional forms in response to two tangible challenges—
one jeopardized their political aspirations, and the other imperiled

the political system's stability. Their linkage of democracy with political party and its candidate selection mechanisms would initiate an institutional pattern that would endure for two centuries, come to dominate candidate nominations, and threaten representative government.

The Political Project: Harvesting Votes

The new era of growing voter turnout raised a practical political challenge for election campaigns—how to harvest voters for a preferred candidate. This was particularly true for Jackson's campaign; it recruited voters who were casting a ballot for the first time in an era when identification with a political party was still forming. The campaign faced the unpleasant possibility of turning out voters who cast ballots for another candidate due to a late conversion or confusion in races with multiple candidates—sometimes from the same party. For Jackson and Van Buren, the strategic challenge was to anchor voters and reliably harvest ballots.

To solidify votes behind their preferred candidate, Jackson and Van Buren developed what was then the novel mechanism of a national party convention of state delegates to exercise the power of nominating the candidates for president and vice president.[73] The idea of a national party convention started to receive "serious and sustained attention" before the 1824 election.[74] The *Albany Argus*—the newspaper associated with Van Buren and his allies in New York State—asked whether "a National Convention . . . may not be the best mode to concentrate the public opinion in the nomination of President and Vice-President of the U.S.?"[75]

Van Buren seized on the then obscure idea of a national party convention in 1827 as "the best and probably the only practicable mode of concentrating the entire vote of the opposition [against President John Quincy Adams]."[76] He continued to tout the strategic value of the national party convention as a mechanism to "concentrate" and "unify" voters during Jackson's campaigns (especially in 1832) and his own run for president in 1836.[77] "[The] national convention," according to the president of the Democratic convention that selected Van Buren, was "the best means of concentrating the popular will and giving it effect in the approaching election."[78] By equipping the "mass of the community" to select the nominee, it would then be "incumbent upon all party members to support the general will."[79] Van Buren's campaign succeeded in mobilizing voters and solidifying their support behind him; he secured a popular majority and 170 Electoral College votes (surpassing the 148 threshold to win) in a crowded field with five candidates.

The national party convention to select presidential and vice presidential candidates addressed a tangible political problem—solidifying and harvesting votes. It was also a political tool to register Jackson's populism and attacks on the corrupt congressional caucus. The national convention also stimulated the growth of state party organizations by relying on them to select the delegates to attend the national convention—a practice that would endure for 140 years.

The party convention, Jackson promised, would equip "the people . . . [to] assume their rights of choosing a President themselves" by "send[ing] delegates, fresh from the people, to a general convention, for the purpose of selecting candidates for the presidency."[80] In Jackson's titanic battle for democracy, he singled out the national convention as equipping the people to "retain in their hands, the election of President and Vice President."[81] His linkage of democracy with party candidate selection would set the parameters for future reform.

Political Control in a System of Elite Competition

As the founding generation aged, many strained to reconcile the egalitarian values of the Revolution with the reality of universal white male suffrage and the arrival of the "common man" in government during the first third of the nineteenth century. The "old revolutionaries," Gordon Wood explains, "found it difficult to accept . . . that their fate now rested on the opinions and votes of . . . unreflective ordinary people."[82] The country's leading legal mind expressed alarm at America's "democracy of numbers and radicalism."[83] The trepidations were amplified by a prominent European commentator's observation that "the advance of the people has been like a torrent, sweeping and levelling all before it" until "wealth and intelligence are compelled to bend to poverty and ignorance."[84]

Although Jefferson's mobilization of voters had stirred questions about the country's governance, Jackson's coarse language, origins outside the founding tradition, and direct appeals to the masses "shocked and dismayed" economic and political elites who worried that his "audacious tactics would [incite] . . . the thoughtless multitude."[85] Jackson's cabinet, which lacked men of high social standing and worldly reputations, was mocked as constituting a "millennium of the minnows."[86] The elite's disdain for Jackson was showcased by John Quincy Adams's public protest of Harvard University's "disgrace[ful]" decision to grant an honorary degree to a "barbarian."[87]

Underlying the disquiet was the renewed worry that the "common man" would use their vote to "share the plunder of the rich," as New York conservatives predicted, and revive the Robinhood spirit.[88] The country's second president—John Adams—identified rising popular participation in the nineteenth century as a threat to the government's "great object [of] . . . render[ing] property secure."[89] The *Richmond Whig* newspaper chastised Jackson and his Democratic Party for "classif[ying] the rich and intelligent and denounc[ing] them as aristocrats." It disparaged Jackson for "degenerat[ing] [the Constitution's Republic] into a Democracy" after having "caressed, soothed, and flattered the heavy class of the poor and ignorant because they held the power which they wanted."[90] The aging Noah Webster castigated Jackson for creating a "democratic devil" by insisting on the egalitarian principles that men are created equal.[91] Reviewing the disquiet among America's privileged, a British traveler reported that Jackson had been "raised... to the office of President by the mob ... [he] led."[92]

The focus of Jackson's critics on the disruptive impact of his populist appeals neglects, however, the other dimension of his legacy: reconstituting political stability in a system of mass political participation. Jackson—and Jefferson—accepted existing laws about the eligibility of voters, even though it hurt their prospects; deferred to the Electoral College vote, even though it potentially threatened their superior popular vote margins; and acquiesced to a shady process in the House of Representatives that they believed "stole" their election. Alternatives existed. Jackson—and Jefferson—could have launched protracted challenges—especially to the House outcomes—and possibly found traction given the fragile legitimacy of a young Republic recently removed from a contentious ratification battle over the Constitution and the deep elite divide over government activism.

Jefferson and, more notably, Jackson rejected the path of subverting the Constitution and, instead, pursued a different alternative—designing new institutions that invited citizens to participate in elections while also sustaining government authority and deflecting disorder that would threaten private property.

By the 1830s, Jackson and Van Buren pinpointed the most significant threat to social order: elite divisions that pit regions against each other. Flipping the script of contemporary democracy doubters, they identified the villains not as active citizens but rather as ambitious politicians and, especially, the highly visible competitors for the White House.

Although Van Buren politically benefited from the collapse of the Federalist Party, he nonetheless appreciated that its rivalry with the Democratic-Republican Party had constrained elite disputes. In the face of dueling partisan loyalties, he credited the

Democratic-Republican Party with creating welcome cross-region affiliation: "attacks upon Southern Republicans were regarded by those of the North as assaults upon their political brethren and resented accordingly." In the absence of the Federalist Party and the growing prevalence of antiparty sentiment, he predicted a "Pandora's box of evils"; it descended on America half a century later in the gruesome Civil War. In Van Buren's prophetic scenario more than three decades before the Civil War, he warned that "geographical divisions founded on local interests or . . . prejudices between free and slaveholding states will inevitably take their place."[93] Van Buren argued that elites and presidential candidates—not voters—would ignite searing regional divisions and split America.

Van Buren turned to political parties as a remedy. He argued that the competition of political parties could be leveraged to focus disputes among politicians toward safe topics and away from the explosive topic of slavery. "Substituting party principles for personal preferences," he argued in 1827, would "create . . . party feelings to keep [the] masses together" and counteract sectional animus.[94] The common bond among party allies from the North and South, he suggested, would moderate regional differences, avoid party disputes over first principles, and "restore a better state of things."[95] "Debates over the scope of federal power," James Ceaser explained, would make it possible for rival parties to "exist together without each feeling the need to destroy a seditious rival."[96]

Van Buren's plan anticipated the argument by political scientist E. E. Schattschneider that political parties could be an effective means for inviting salient disputes over "safe" issues that favored the advantaged while obscuring topics from public debate that threatened the political order.[97] While Van Buren's use of party competition would fail to prevent the Civil War, political parties were competitive in all parts of the country by the 1836 election and, for a period, contributed to holding off America's violent regional schism over slavery.

Egalitarianism and America's White Supremacist Order

Jefferson's and Jackson's strategies to leverage the egalitarian rights of white men to advance their own political rise accepted—indeed, contributed to—the enslaving, murdering, and oppressing of African Americans, Native Americans, and women. The egalitarian values and rights that became anchored in American political institutions during the early nineteenth century reproduced the "white supremacist order."[98]

The Early-Nineteenth-Century's White Democracy

Jefferson and Jackson preached the gospel of empowering "the people" but practiced the sins of slavery and misogyny. Historians have challenged Jefferson's once towering reputation by spotlighting his ownership and fathering of slaves and contempt for women.[99] For his part, Jackson was an unremorseful slaveholder who first gained national notoriety for the bloodthirsty murder of Native Americans—bragging at one point that "we shot them like Dogs." Jackson played a role in forcefully removing indigenous peoples from their ancestral homelands in the Southeast and brutally marching them until they were west of the Mississippi River.

During the first third of the nineteenth century, white male democracy strengthened as slavery became more entrenched in the South and remained in parts of the North. While northern states eventually turned against slavery, Connecticut, New Jersey, New York, and other states in the region reduced the voting rights of blacks in the decade or so after 1816. Fear of the rising electoral power of blacks in New York prompted its 1821 convention to disenfranchise the great majority even as it expanded citizen rights for white citizens by lowering property qualifications among other reforms.[100]

The South's exclusionary system that enslaved blacks also set back the rights of whites and fueled conflict. When white men in South Carolina and other southern states pressed for voting rights, slave owners resisted because of fear that widening egalitarian rights for whites might inspire slaves. It might also undercut land-owner domination by empowering poor white men to support a "Robinhood Society" that taxed them.[101]

Party organizations and nominating conventions reproduced and reinforced the exclusion of most adults during the nine-teenth century due to race and gender. While Jefferson and Jackson mobilized white men in order to win the presidency, both candidates accepted the political, civil, and economic coalitions that barred blacks, Native Americans, and women from voting. Indeed, racial and gender exclusions continued or expanded. The ideology and practices of white supremacy recognized white men as exceptional and deserving of citizenship rights while marking women and people of color as inferior and undeserving.

America's Antagonistic Racial Orders

Even as two racial orders took root in the early Republic (one based on egalitarianism and the other white supremacy), the double ac-tion of widening and narrowing democracy produced differences, resistance, and inconsistencies across states and at the national level during the nineteenth century.[102] Egalitarian values stirred the conscience in some. Jefferson accepted and relied on slavery but he also voiced support for ending slavery "in any practical way" and backed the termination of the transatlantic slave trade over the South's objection.[103]

Meanwhile, labor markets in the North relied on free labor and increasingly coalesced with religious and political groups to op-pose slavery. Northern states eventually came together to outlaw slavery in their region and oppose its expansion westward to new territories and states. Most also granted the right to vote to black men regardless of property. Women joined with abolitionists and, after the 1848 Seneca Falls Convention, launched their own fight for equal rights and the power of the vote.

Slavery was morally unstable, colliding in time with the egalitarian promise of the Declaration of Independence. Abraham Lincoln distilled the irreconcilable contradiction: "This government cannot endure, permanent half slave and half free."

The Legacies of Jefferson and Jackson

The grand principles of the Declaration of Independence and the calculating design of the Constitution were debated in the late eighteenth century but tested in the fires of the early nineteenth century. The dual legacies of Jefferson and Jackson were, first, to elicit the mass democracy that the Constitution's framers feared. They orchestrated the "long swing" in widening the right to vote from the Constitution's ratification into the mid-nineteenth century, distinguishing the United States as the first country to extend the franchise with few or no explicit economic barriers.[104] The second legacy attempted to tame the first by designing what would become enduring forms of representative politics: political party organizations and the national nominating convention.

The conjunction of three factors during the early nineteenth century shaped the institutional patterning that would structure future directions of American democracy. First, intense elite competition—and the looming prospects of violent regional divisions—opened cracks in what had been the unity of purpose among the Constitution's framers. Second, the ambition of Jefferson and Jackson to prevail in a presidential election process biased toward deadlock and favoritism propelled them to put into practice the rights of citizens in order to mobilize mass voter turnouts that lifted them to momentous presidential election victories. Third, they eased elite trepidations about the potential disorder of activating mass political participation by renewing the search for order in the institutions and authority of representative democracy. Their institutional innovations—channeling voters through political parties and their nomination process—cast a shadow over coming generations of ambitious politicians and reformers as they weighed their options, opportunities, and constraints.

The political dynamics of Jefferson's and Jackson's handiwork would exert enduring effects, but not without tumult and revision. In 1836, Andrew Jackson bequeathed the White House to his loyal ally Martin Van Buren. He draped his passing of the baton of power in populism by holding a national party convention. True to the pretense of populism, Van Buren's nomination was presented as "fresh from the people" but was announced by convention delegates that Jackson had carefully hand-picked—as if they were "the breath of his nostrils."[105]

The clash of pretense and manipulation would fuel, over the coming decades, powerful movements to return power to "the people" and restore democracy. The origins of those counterattacks lay in enduring contradictions: promising to return power to citizens while putting the new political forms in the hands of unresponsive political parties, and heralding "the people" while supporting enslavement and the decimation of Native Americans.

PART II

DISRUPTING DEMOCRATIC INSTITUTIONS

The early-nineteenth-century attention to building durable (though incomplete) democracy was abandoned during the twentieth century. Ambitious politicians recklessly introduced the direct primary during the Progressive Era and embraced it following the stormy 1968 Democratic Convention. Leading reformers of their day opposed the shift to primary elections, presciently anticipating their routine fracturing of American politics into warring factions.

4

Progressive Frustrations: Institutional Limits and Reform Prophesies, 1880s–1920s

Harsh words among members of Congress are familiar today but not gunfire and knife fights. Nearly a century ago, though, "Fighting" Bob La Follette was targeted on the floor of the US Senate. His offense: he used a Senate filibuster to block legislation requested by President Woodrow Wilson in 1917 to arm merchant ships in response to the outbreak of World War I in Europe. Wilson and his allies in Washington insisted the Armed Ship Bill was essential to protect America and repudiated La Follette's opposition as an "evil endeavor, in which no loyal American would have engaged," according to the *New York Times*.[1] La Follette retorted in this and other exchanges over US intervention into World War I that "cruel greed" and "profit" were "the real motive[s]." War was "the social reformer's doom," he charged; it would bring "awful suffering . . . [to] the masses."[2]

The venomous exchanges unleashed bedlam on the floor of the Senate on March 3, 1917, when a crucial vote loomed. The Wisconsin senator sent his son to retrieve the bag that contained his gun. Meanwhile, two senators ominously moved toward him—one with a gun to shoot La Follette and the other with a "rat-tail file" to disarm the would-be assassin by "put[ting] the file down [his] collarbone and into his heart."[3]

Violence was averted in the Senate, and La Follette's opposition was trampled by a stampede to enter the First World War in April

1917. The Wisconsin senator's ringing dissent showcased, though, his fiery style of uncompromising populism that he deployed to forge a new—and, in his view, truer—form of democracy: direct primaries that equipped citizens to use their vote to choose the delegates to party conventions, which selected party candidates.[4]

The design of the direct primary and the timing of its initial adoption resulted from the conjuncture of three distinct but intersecting trajectories. The first is the intensifying competition among political and economic elites over the country's direction. Second, ambitious entrepreneurs like La Follette turned to fiery promises to deliver power to "the people" to mobilize support and overtake barriers to their political careers. Third, La Follette's innovation of a direct primary extended an institutional pattern of candidate selection that started a century earlier with Jefferson's embrace of mass-mobilizing political parties and Jackson's embrace of party conventions to empower "the people" in candidate selection. The past equipped Progressive reformers with a tangible focus on convention delegates but it also narrowed their options for feasible change.

Even as La Follette and other prominent progressives routinely appealed to mobilize the public and strengthen its power, they rejected the explicit assaults of antiregime populists against the authority and legitimacy of representative government itself. While the direct primary's advocates abhorred sedition, they also showed little concern with the enduring consequences of institutional reform for the durability of democratic procedures and rules—a preoccupation of James Madison and early-nineteenth-century state builders.

Progressive reforms pose other puzzles. Direct primary advocates appealed to the commitments of Jefferson and others to political equality and "consent of the governed," but their handiwork contributed to the exclusionary structures of race and gender in the nineteenth and twentieth centuries. In particular, southern states seized on primary elections to sustain racial hierarchies. Claims about the democratic intent of Progressives often omit race and the contested and contradictory character of the new candidate selection mechanism.[5]

Contemporary observers often mistakenly blame the prevalence of presidential primaries today with their launching by Progressives a century ago.[6] The reality, however, is that the reform was opposed and stopped in the early twentieth century. Established party organizations effectively resisted primaries to preserve their institutional position and political power. The opposition, though, was broader and more compelling. Progressive state and local reformers and prominent intellectuals like Herbert Croly and Walter Lippmann were alarmed by the threat of direct primaries to the authority, legitimacy, and functioning of representative democracy. Their resistance forced a debate over the form of American democracy and surfaced an alternative direction: fewer elections of greater importance within the framework of representative institutions. For nearly half a century after the adoption of presidential primaries peaked in the 1920s, their expansion was watered down, blocked, or repealed. By the 1968 Democratic nominating convention, it was still possible for Hubert Humphrey to be selected as the party's presidential candidate without running in a single primary. Although today the presidential primary is commonly equated with democracy, a critical mass of Progressives a century ago argued the opposite: that it would weaken representative government.

This chapter examines the origins of the presidential primary, its adoption, and its stalling out by the 1920s. The origins and development of America's elaborate candidate selection process was shaped by sustained conflict, defeat, and decades later, an unexpected revival. We begin by situating the push for direct primaries within the broader Progressive agenda to mitigate monopolies and trusts.

Elite Competition and Institutional Change

In 1832, Andrew Jackson heralded party conventions as the mechanism to put power over candidate selection in the hands of "the people." Jackson's soaring democratic rhetoric quickly gave way to a process in which dueling factions vied for control over candidate nominations in state and presidential contests.

The scrum of party conventions chafed against the democratic ideals associated with political parties, candidate selection, and American elections that Jefferson and Jackson instilled. The result was a series of flashpoints. In 1884, Republican reformers—known as Mugwumps—bolted from their party to the Democratic Party in protest of the sway of money, and in the process aided the election of Democratic presidential candidate Grover Cleveland.[7] Into the 1890s and the early twentieth century, the agrarian and labor populists organized millions of Americans into a grassroots movement against self-serving political parties, which were in cahoots with the economic interests that suppressed unions and deflated farm prices, manipulated financial markets, imposed high interest rates, foreclosed on properties, and in the case of railroad monopolies, charged exorbitant transportation fees. Some of their proposals are familiar today, like federal income taxes; others failed to gain legislative traction, especially those that directly assaulted capitalism and private property with calls for public ownership of banks.[8]

By the late nineteenth and early twentieth centuries, the Progressive Era emerged with a robust reform agenda to restore economic fairness and opportunity by "go[ing] back to the first principles of democracy," as La Follette pronounced in a speech at the University of Chicago in 1897.[9] Progressives introduced the Australian ballot to equip citizens to vote in secret, while other steps aimed to overhaul voter registration and election procedures more generally. Reforms of the federal civil service starting with the Pendleton Act (1883) targeted the link of government jobs to political favors. They also set out to revive Alexander Hamilton's early promotion in the Federalist Papers and the Washington administration of national administrative capacity to direct America's economic growth.

Progressives defined the solution to corruption and democratic decline as requiring a frontal challenge to the political parties that had solidified geographic strongholds: The Democratic Party ruled in the South and parts of the West, and the Republican Party dominated the North. Within each party's regions, they directed political communications and policy debates, organized voters, and used jobs and other favors to discipline government officials. The two parties created formidable political machines that benefited—and served—state and local interests and fended off threats close to home or from national assertions of power and policy.

For ambitious Progressive politicians, reform was personal. The rules of the political game at the turn of the previous century obstructed their entry and advancement. Rejection by the rigged political system motivated Progressive entrepreneurs to agitate for reform of a system that offered little opportunity to compete for government power. Political conflicts and divisions unsettled the old order and created crevices for political entrepreneurs to fight for a foothold in local, state, and eventually national government office.

La Follette Discovers the Personal Rewards of Reform

Robert La Follette's career illustrates the significance of closed party organizations to spurring ambitious reformers to strut across the political stage as "a man on horseback . . . seeking to popularize a particular . . . reform," in Croly's memorable description.[10] The Wisconsinite's drive was incubated in early tragedy and aggravated by the political machine's obstruction of his political career. His father (Josiah La Follette) died when he was an infant, and his mother instilled in her son a deep sense of loss that would later provoke him to exhume Josiah's remains and devote much of a day to handling his bones. The haunting grief was compounded by his mother's decision to remarry an older—and brutal—man (John Saxton) on the false pretense of receiving financial security. Saxton's whippings fed the future politician's abiding resentment that culminated in his stepson's revenge—emotional banishment: the adult La Follette never spoke of his stepfather and omitted any mention of him from his autobiography.[11]

The financial pinch that La Follette experienced as a child would revisit his early political campaigns and intensified his incentive to win. Political success brought economic sustenance. "We poor fellows," he confided, "have to earn a living [and] can only occasionally take a hand in politics." Electoral loss bruised not only his ego; it imperiled his family's finances.[12]

La Follette started his political career as a naïve and dogged twenty-five-year-old who stumbled into a fight with the local political boss by pursuing the Republican Party nomination for a county office. Despite warnings from the local political machine, he tirelessly campaigned for his party's nomination as district attorney of Dane County, Wisconsin, in 1880. Addressing the party boss in this and later races, "I know of no reason why I should consult you. I've been out in the country consulting the people, and I'm going to consult a good many more."[13] He appealed directly to voters by unleashing a blizzard of speeches and publications over the heads of the party machine. He was rewarded with nomination and election as district attorney and four years later as a member of Congress.[14]

While the local party machine was vulnerable to La Follette's public blitzes, the state political machine held tight control over Republican Party nominations for state office and used it to defeat his first two gubernatorial campaigns in the closing years of the nineteenth century (1896 and 1898). "The bosses," La Follette revealed, "did not regard the selection of a candidate for governor as a matter in which the voters of Wisconsin were entitled to have any voice."[15] When the state party faced delegates who declared their support for La Follette, it reverted to bribery and intimidation. In a (failed) effort to bully the financially strapped La Follette, a member of the Wisconsin political machine told him that they shelled out a small fortune—$263,000 in today's terms—to secure the necessary delegates.[16]

After the Wisconsin political machine squashed La Follette's campaigns for governor, he recrafted his campaign and its message to break through the obstruction and broaden his appeal across parties. In his autobiography, he recounted his efforts "to try the experiment of campaigning for reform in an off year" by delivering speeches around the state and disseminating them in a newspaper he purchased.[17] He responded to the growing size and interest of his audiences by transforming his campaign strategy to craft an image of a hard-charging reformer battling for democracy. La Follette attached his personal quest for office with the appeals of Jefferson and Jackson for democratic revival.

His growing recognition produced an invitation to speak about his reform agenda at the University of Chicago in 1897 and the University of Michigan in 1898. In 1900, reform was the motor for his first successful campaign for governor. He delivered rousing speeches for eight hours a day in small towns and county fairs and blanketed Wisconsin voters with printed materials. Political machines offered voters crass favors; in contrast, La Follette offered stirring appeals, information, and concrete promises to improve their lives.[18] La Follette's ferocious public campaigning eventually defeated the machine's obstruction and propelled him to a string of high offices in his home state and Washington, DC: US House of Representatives (1885–1891), governor (1901–1906), and US senator (1906–1925).

The Disruption of Reformers

The challenge of reformers to the established political parties ruptured the Republican Party in 1912. Following Teddy Roosevelt's decision to step down in 1909, he came out of retirement to run for president in 1912 as a Progressive alternative to his anointed successor, Robert Taft. Where TR pressed business to strike a "Square Deal" with labor, he panned Taft for failing to adequately respond to the damaging effects of monopolies: "I am sure he means well, but he means well feebly.... He is utterly unfit for leadership and this is a time when we need leadership."[19] The former president chastised Taft as aiding "the forces of reaction and of political crookedness." Taft retaliated by denigrating TR as "the greatest menace to our institutions that we have had in a long time."[20] Taft handily defeated TR for the Republican Party's nomination on the first ballot by drawing on loyalties purchased with federal patronage, the self-interested support of the Republican Party machine, and conservative forces opposed to TR's Progressive agenda.

The ambition of Progressives split the Republican Party and rattled its established power centers. The division also intensified party competition by advantaging the Democratic Party in 1912. After losing four consecutive elections, the Democratic Party's nominee, Woodrow Wilson, prevailed with a plurality (41.8 percent) over TR (27.4 percent), Taft (23.2 percent), and Socialist Eugene Debs (6 percent). The institutional position of political parties and the path to political power were scrambled.

Ambition rather than reformist zeal alone drove the new political entrepreneurs and triggered disruption. La Follette's determination produced a string of initially improbable electoral wins in the early twentieth century but also damaging misjudgments that dulled his political prospects. After overcoming his initial gubernatorial defeats, La Follette entered office in 1901 with a sweeping reform agenda that set a model for other states; but he also fueled confusion, opposition, and distrust among lawmakers, which contributed to a string of legislative defeats. Even allies in the state capitol pushed back on his hard-driving political style as "messianic" and "browbeating." Some of his proposals passed years after he left office, but La Follette lost battles to enact a host of legislative proposals, including his plan to rewrite the state's taxes by establishing a state income tax, reinstating the inheritance taxes, and increasing corporate taxes.[21]

La Follette's single-minded ambition may have contributed to derailing the most promising opening for Progressives to establish a toehold in national politics: TR's 1912 campaign. The Wisconsinite refused to support TR in the "stop-Taft" alliance against the conservatives within the Republican Party.[22] After losing the Republican nomination to Taft, TR bolted to the Progressive Party, which startled La Follette, who had encouraged its development as his own vehicle to run for president.[23] A clash ensued that split Progressives who were loyal to La Follette from those who hoped TR would provide the exceptional national visibility and alliances to catapult their movement into the White House. La Follette's explicit reason to oppose TR's nomination was the former president's uncertain commitment to the Progressive agenda, though most assumed that the Wisconsinite's own aspirations provided the driving reason, along with personal animosity.[24] A number of Progressives resented La Follette's unrelenting hostility to TR as a contributing factor in his loss. By the 1916 elections, the momentum for reform receded, and the Progressive Party faded—as did La Follette's reputation.

Progressive Reformers: Fighting "Iron-Hearted Power"

Frank Norris's 1901 novel, *The Octopus*, described a train traveling across California. "It whistled for road crossings, for sharp curves, for trestles; ominous notes, hoarse, bellowing, ringing with the accents of menace and defiance."[25] Norris extends this sensory description of a racing train into a searing metaphor for the brutal seizure of farmland by a railroad monopoly in the San Joaquin Valley. The train becomes a "galloping monster, the terror of steel and steam, with its single eye, cyclopean, red, shooting from horizon to horizon." In case we missed the real-world connection, Norris delivers the literary equivalent of a body slam. The train, he reveals, is "the symbol of vast power, . . . leaving blood and destruction in its path; the leviathan, with tentacles of steel clutching into the soil, the soulless Force, the iron-hearted Power, the monster, the Colossus, the Octopus."

Norris crystallizes the tumult of the late nineteenth and early twentieth centuries as old economic and social networks collided with sweeping change. The new titanic monopolies and business trusts in railroads, oil, steel, and banking propelled rapid industrialization and triggered labor organizing, employer repression, and electoral fights over worker rights and economic support. Divides over class, religion, ethnicity, race, and gender took on greater public prominence and spilled into workplaces, streets, and elections. America's emerging middle class was swept up in the tumult, and new pressures for "association and social solidarity" unsettled its values of individualism.[26]

Progressives responded to the excesses of business conglomerates by seeking to renew American democracy and build the administrative capacity to reduce corruption, inequality, and the sense of vulnerability that Americans harbored. They defined monopolies and trusts as a clear, tangible enemy and targeted them with economic and regulatory restrictions. Teddy Roosevelt condemned corporate "trusts" and the "malefactors of great wealth." La Follette singled out Standard Oil for having "driven people all over this country out of business [and] crushed competition." Railroads put a chokehold on America: "To permit the railroads to control the commerce of the country," La Follette charged, "permit[s] the railroads to control the country." Economic salvation lay, he declared, in the "emancipation of the people of this country from monopoly control" by breaking up trusts and allowing small, independent farmers and businesses to thrive.[27]

La Follette connected the attack on economic "hard times" and corporate power to the need to restore America's founding principles of political equality and popular sovereignty. "[My] own party leaders . . . work for corporations and railroad control [and] . . . do not represent the people."[28] "The supreme issue" that links debates over railroads and other trusts, he proclaimed, is "*the encroachment of the powerful few upon the rights of the many,*" separating "the people and their government."[29] "The influence of financial interests" and "hostile forces [associated with political machines]," he warned, were "thwart[ing] the will of the people and menac[ing] the perpetuity of representative government" through "bribing, bossing, and thieving."[30] They—and not citizens—were "running their caucuses, naming their delegates, conducting their conventions, nominating party candidates . . . [and] controlling legislatures." Under the watchful eye of the political machine, government officials "fee[l] responsibility to his master alone, and his master is the political machine of his party." The result, he charged, is that "the people ceased to be sovereign [, and] gone [is] the government of equal rights and equal responsibilities, [which had been] . . . the jewel of constitutional liberty."[31]

Teddy Roosevelt, Woodrow Wilson, and a stable of astute writers agreed. They too recoiled at the ability of political machines and big business to dominate the political process through the use of bribes and state and local power centers. Instead of checking private interests, elected officials often represented or worked directly for the railroads or other large monopolies.

The Democratic Battering Ram

Progressives at the dawn of the twentieth century flipped the Constitution's original framework. Instead of limiting government to maximize the liberty of property owners and individuals, they saw monopolies and trusts as the primary menace and welcomed government intervention to offset them. Herbert Croly, one of the Progressives' leading intellectuals and a cofounder of the *New Republic* magazine, singled out the "monarchy of the [C]onstitution" and its conservative shackles as a barrier to progress.[32] The alternative, Woodrow Wilson explained in 1913, was to deploy government as a check on the unbridled power of monopolies and an agent to restore political and civic rights: "Freedom today is something more than being let alone." "The program of a government of freedom," Wilson insisted, "must be positive, not only negative" in order to create "fair play between individuals and . . . such powerful institutions as the trusts."[33] To convert government into a force for creating freedom, Progressives expanded government's responsibilities and national administrative capacity to intervene in economic and social affairs.[34]

Progressives wielded Jefferson's and Jackson's political strategy (activating citizens) for Hamilton's ends (expanding national power). Progressives countered the superior resources and organization of party machines and big business by weaponizing political equality and democratic responsiveness to rally broad and sustained citizen support.

Routinely mobilizing citizens required, they appreciated, changes to the interpretation of the Constitution. The Constitution's framers designed it, as we discussed in Chapter 2, to discourage frequent appeals by politicians and avoid a return to the intense public engagement and "Robinhood Society" environment that blossomed during the dozen years following the Declaration of Independence in 1776. Progressives reinterpreted the Constitution to normalize frequent and direct public appeals as acceptable and, indeed, necessary.

Presidents were a particular focal point of Progressive efforts to reinterpret the Constitution to welcome public appeals to increase the reach and impact of government. TR popularized the idea of presidents using their office as a "bully pulpit." Chief executives possessed untapped reservoirs of power by capitalizing on their unique visibility and access to "the people" and returning to the early-nineteenth-century tradition of visiting Congress to deliver the State of the Union address.[35] Woodrow Wilson, as scholar and president, helped pioneer this Constitutional reinvention: He calculated that the president could overcome the resistance of Congress and private interests if he became the "spokesman for the real sentiment and purpose of the country [and] g[ave] direction to [public] opinion."[36] If presidents seized on their opportunities for public promotions, Wilson insisted, they would marshal the political resources to supply national administrative and programmatic direction despite the defiance of monopolies and state and local party organizations.

As Progressive politicians fought for a new Constitutional interpretation, they seized the opening to routinely make public appeals to promote policy agendas and candidacies against formidable, entrenched interests. They singled out "the people" as the source of their authority and legitimacy. "The people [had] ceased to be sovereign," La Follette thundered in an 1897 speech in Wisconsin and vowed to "secure [a government that was] a more direct expression of the will of the people."[37]

Pragmatic Populism

The appeals of Progressives for public support stirred long-standing fears of demagogues who exploit newfound power to undermine democratic procedures and rules—fears that continue to resonate in our own time.[38] "Populist disfigurement of democracy" is blamed for fascism and authoritarianism in Europe and Latin America, where charismatic leaders have used emotional appeals to replace the procedures and checks of constitutional government with promises to become the direct expression of the "will of the people."[39] "The danger to democracy today," Jan-Werner Muller cautions, is "populism. . . . [It] promises to make good on democracy's highest ideal ("Let the people rule!") . . . [and] speak[s] the language of democratic values [but produces an end result that is] antidemocratic."[40] In the United States, some historians charged that nineteenth-century populism was a movement of white farmers who responded to their decline by scapegoating immigrants, Jews, and others.[41]

US populism, however, has also been a powerful political tool to incite "secular redemption" and democratic renewal.[42] The nineteenth-century agrarian and labor populists argued for returning to the guarantees of the Declaration of Independence and Constitution for political equality and representation. By contrast, European and Latin American populists toppled the rule of law and democratic practice to concentrate power in the hands of a national charismatic leader.[43]

Progressives like La Follette were avowedly *pragmatic populists* who mobilized millions while abiding by the Constitution, rule of law, and civil liberties. The Wisconsinite repeatedly anchored his populist appeals in "the foundation of the representative system."[44] For La Follette, his respect for the Constitutional framework endured over the decades even as he suffered legislative and electoral defeats and was hung in effigy in retaliation for his opposition to arming the merchant marines prior to America's entry into World War I.[45]

Pragmatic populism trumpeted core democratic values: political equality and popular sovereignty. La Follette heralded America's founding values of "equal voice, equal rights, and equal responsibilities" and the "fundamental principle . . . that each citizen shall have equal voice in government."[46] Restoring political equality animated his political agenda. He consistently lambasted the political machine for replacing "government of equal rights" with "manipulation, scheming, trickery, fraud, and corruption."[47]

The direct primary, the Wisconsinite repeatedly promised, was the constitutional means to strengthen the scheme of representation by equipping voters to hold the "trustee . . . to account directly . . . in the discharge of his trust."[48] It would ensure, he vowed, that "every citizen will share equally in the nomination of the candidates of his party"—"every member of a party [would possess] equal voice in making . . . nominations [of candidates]." He embraced institutional change to rebuild "the spirit [and] the very life of representative government."[49]

La Follette and Progressive political reformers made missteps, as we discuss. Unleashing an antidemocratic insurrection against the Constitution is not one.

Designing the Direct Primary

The agitation by political entrepreneurs clamoring for a new opportunity structure and their pragmatic populism generated the impetus for reforming the rules of the game at the turn of the last century. The particular content and form of institutional change were not dictated, however, by the propulsive force of populism. Rather, the direct primary's design flowed from a separate trajectory—the institutional pattern that equated democracy with a mass-mobilizing political party and the selection of candidates by delegates at party conventions who were "fresh from the people," as Andrew Jackson put it.

"The Most Fundamental of All Reforms"

Why did reformers latch onto the inner mechanism of political party nominations as imperative for American democracy? Other democratic countries built new political parties, constructed enduring coalitions with a broad range of interests—farmers, labor, or business—and generally changed the structure of politics. Some have come to use primary elections, but none use them as extensively nor attach as much importance to them as the United States.[50]

La Follette's thwarted personal ambition and populist inclinations created a template for a trial-and-error search for a novel signature reform that would energize his campaigns and rally support to "attack and, if possible, overthrow the whole system." His hunt focused on existing political institutions—"all the laws relative to caucuses and convention." Confining himself to working within these established parameters, La Follette discovered that in the 1800s a small number of counties in Pennsylvania, New York, California, and elsewhere were quietly using a direct primary as part of the process for selecting candidates and party officials.[51] These efforts were largely unknown through the country, and few appreciated their broader potential as a practical threat to the domination of candidate nominations by party machines and as a winning political issue. La Follette's innovation was to propose the wide adoption of direct primaries, require their widespread use in selecting candidates for office, and direct them toward toppling the political machine.[52]

La Follette trumpeted the direct primary in his 1900 gubernatorial campaign as "the most fundamental of all reforms." The political machines, he charged, "stand between the voter and the official [and] thwart the will of the voter, and rule official conduct."[53] He offered a path forward: equipping citizens to nominate candidates through their own votes and compelling "[government] officers [to] respond to public opinion."[54] "Whoever seeks to thwart or defeat [the direct primary]," he declared, "is an enemy of representative government" and will face a "fight" that "will continue to victory [with] . . . no halt and no compromise."[55]

Under La Follette's pressure, Wisconsin pioneered the use of direct primaries to select delegates among individuals competing to attend the party convention. (The "delegate primary" was later replaced with candidate primaries in which the name of the candidate and not the delegate appeared on the ballot.) Wisconsin's Republican Party embraced delegate primaries in its 1898 convention platform. Within a few years, the Wisconsin legislature approved a referendum for direct primaries to select candidates for all state-level offices. It passed with 62 percent support in 1904. The primary for state offices was expanded to presidential races in 1911.

The Constraint of Reform

While La Follette and his allies prided themselves in designing a novel political reform, the changes they proposed were constrained and enabled by two features of America's institutional pattern of politics. First, they were tethered to a path of political development pioneered by Jefferson and Jackson that equated democracy with political parties and their internal operations to nominate candidates.

Second, institutional patterning constrained La Follette but also created advantages for drawing support. He was positioned to present the direct primary in the early twentieth century as an incremental change: states could adopt it and, if they disliked its effects, reverse their decision. The reform did not threaten sweeping structural change.

In addition, building on an existing and familiar system of party nominations retained procedures and rules that were known by the political class and many citizens. Familiarity with the party and convention processes for nomination helped woo politicians and their allies who may have immediately recoiled at the prospect of learning an entirely new process.

For instance, TR channeled his challenge to Taft for the Republican Party's 1912 nomination into presidential primary elections—the first of its kind. He calculated that the primary offered the most feasible route to overcome the party machine. When TR's gambit prompted the Taft campaign to refuse to face primary voters, he seized on it as a campaign issue that was readily understandable to politicians and engaged citizens. "Are the American people fit to govern themselves, to rule themselves, to control themselves?" he asked in a much-touted March 1912 speech in New York's Carnegie Hall. "I believe they are. My opponents do not."

Woodrow Wilson publicly came out in favor of the direct primary in his first message to Congress as president in 1913. In his precedent-breaking decision to present his State of the Union address in person, he called for the "prompt enactment of legislation [to] . . . provide for primary elections throughout the country." For Wilson, his support of the primary boosted his reform credentials without deeply disturbing supporters in the Democratic Party establishment; it was seen as a manageable or perhaps unavoidable change.

What Should Be the Form of American Democracy?

La Follette and like-minded reformers capitalized on the convergence of three trajectories: elite division that dissipated opposition to reform; political advocacy by motivated entrepreneurs; and an institutional trajectory rooted in reforming political parties and their selection of candidates. They propelled twenty-four states to adopt presidential primaries by the early 1920s.

The trajectory of direct primaries stops, however, at about this point. The primary's interrupted development defies mechanical models of institutional change that assume a near-automatic extension and knee-jerk correlations of its initial launch with its routine use today.[56] Missing is the sustained, widespread, and intense pushback that halted its development and, in certain respects, reversed it. Also lost is a significant feature of this resistance: sustained debate over the form of American democracy and proposals to move in the opposite direction of direct primaries—fewer elections of greater importance.

The Limits of Reform

The introduction of the direct primary in the early twentieth century was predictably opposed by entrenched interests that benefited from existing local and state party machines.[57] The power of entrenched parties was augmented, however, by a surprising source: Progressives who shared La Follette's commitment to confronting monopolies and trusts but opposed his candidate selection reform. The broad assault on the direct primary, and specifically the presidential primary, had by mid-century upended La Follette's plan and prevented it from controlling nominations. After the 1916 elections, the presidential primary was adopted and used by only one additional state. Of the twenty-four states that did adopt presidential primaries, three states used it only once. The backlash against it was so strong that nine states repealed it. Iowa and Minnesota, for instance, held presidential primaries in 1916 and repealed them the next year.

When not rolling back presidential primaries, many states that retained them weakened them or narrowed participation in them to party members through "closed" primaries and tighter restrictions on membership. New York and Illinois bolstered the power of state conventions in the 1920s to select delegates, and New Jersey barred voters who contributed to one party from participating in another party's primary.[58] Southern states used the poll tax, literacy tests, and other measures to exclude African Americans, as we discuss later.

Louise Overacker, a leading scholar of primaries in the 1920s and later decades, reported that "the presidential primaries in the states . . . [are] at a standstill" and "cannot possibly control the choice of the [presidential] convention" because they failed to matter for the majority of delegates.[59] Even by the 1960s, presidential primaries existed but were unable to dictate nominations, as they do today.[60]

Why did the presidential primary stall? The challenges not only display the nature of political power at the turn of the century but also reveal compelling critiques of the direct primary that anticipated later flaws as well as posing alternative directions that were conceivable a century ago. Three sources of resistance to direct primaries stand out.

State and Local Political Parties Fought Back

Despite the assault of Progressives on the political machine, networks of state and local parties remained formidable due to their influence over government contracts and jobs and they were eager to defeat or neutralize direct primaries. The first significant use of the presidential primary—Taft and Teddy Roosevelt's competition for the 1912 Republican nomination—illustrated the continued power of the old order. The contest confirmed TR's lasting popularity, but the nomination was nonetheless dictated by the Republican Party's national committee controlled by party officials and Taft.

President Warren Harding, who was beholden to the "Ohio Gang" of political bosses and business titans, openly "craved" the return of the old-style party conventions. "I had rather have men appeal for support on the pronouncement of party conventions," he proclaimed in 1922, "than to have the appeal of the individual for his particular locality."[61] A city attorney for Chicago testified to a reform conference in New York City in favor of the existing party organization as a "powerful, well controlled engine."[62] From New York State, a Senate Majority Leader coarsely derided the direct primary as "an abomination [that] . . . ought to be skinned alive." He too recommended a return to the state convention system and won bipartisan support.[63]

The early-twentieth-century research of Indiana University political scientist James Albert Woodburn dispelled the hopeful promises made on behalf of direct primaries. They "promote rather than check electoral corruption . . . [by encouraging] a large and corrupt use of money." Far from cleaning up elections, candidates who have "money . . . ha[ve] as good a chance for the nomination in a primary as in a convention."[64] The Chicago city attorney agreed: the "illiterate and degenerate voters, who control . . . the direct vote system . . . can be purchased for a 'drink.' "[65] Media reports and studies of state and local elections in New York and elsewhere confirmed the continued use of money and inside dealing to steer nominations.[66]

Political figures who assailed direct primaries were, of course, defending their own interests and were not shy about acknowledging that. Indeed, they used this candor as a weapon against La Follette: he was taken to task for chastising party machines for doling out patronage while he did it himself. The Wisconsinite routinely gave out state jobs for game wardens, inspectors, and more to retain the loyalty of supporters and build his own political organization.[67] Critics, according to one historian, assailed him for "being a selfish hypocrite and political trickster who professed to champion the rights of the people only to obtain political power." Independent analysts and defenders of the political establishment underscored La Follette's false claims of moral superiority and truthfulness.[68]

Statecraft

Political figures and Progressive intellectuals challenged the direct primary for neglecting what Herbert Croly considered "prudent statecraft."[69] Early institutional designers placed a priority on aligning the choice of citizens and the national interest with the incentives and structures that dictate the pursuit of power by candidates.[70] Their aim was to sort out presidential candidates who were authoritarians, demagogues, and threats to the authority and legitimacy of the Constitution and representative democracy.

For La Follette and supporters of the direct primary, statecraft and institutional design to balance citizen voice and quality leadership took a back seat. Their priority was to anchor government decision making and elite behavior in the amorphous concept of "the people."

Critics mocked the populist adulation of "the people" and were incredulous at the proposition that this monolith could police elected representatives. The result, they warned, *would* degrade the quality of candidates and imperil democratic government.

Henry J. Ford—Princeton University professor and president of the American Political Science Association from 1918 to 1919—warned that reformers mouth the "sentimental cant" of "giving power to the people," but in practice dissipated power and thwarted the "select[ion] of the wisest and best for public office."[71] Primary contests shifted the incentives toward freewheeling candidates who built their own organizations and loyal followings. The new candidate selection process creates, the Chicago attorney testified, a vacuum with "no responsible head" to either select a strong candidate or "prevent bad and unwise nominations."[72] An officer of the Municipal Association of Cleveland echoed this conclusion at a conference on Progressive reform: the primary tends to select candidates who are "[not] acceptable . . . from the point of view of a party well-wisher [or] . . . a citizen desiring to see competent and faithful persons selected to administer public affairs."[73]

The result, detractors warned, would be "pestiferous demagogues" and "brazen-faced men of a lower type of character." Among voters who are distracted and poorly informed, the candidates most likely to win excel at the "repulsive and disgraceful undertaking" of "begging for an office" by making outlandish promises and practicing the deceptions of a demagogue.[74] A series of studies during the initial launch of the direct primary reported that it "tends to weaken and destroy the party" and diminish America's capacity to govern in the public interest.[75]

The Political Rationality of Factions

Supporters of good government and Progressive reform pilloried the direct primary for imperiling representative government by shifting power to factions. Croly slammed La Follette and his allies for their "absurd multiplication of elections." They swelled the number of elections in the name of engaging citizens but had the opposite effect: "public interest . . . flag[ged]."[76] Multiplying elections would outstrip the interest and knowledge of citizens who could not be "magically transform[ed] . . . into selfless patriots."[77]

With everyday citizens drained, control over nomination fell to "embittered and unscrupulous factions" committed to their narrow agendas instead of the national interest or broad coalitions. The Chicago city attorney testified at the New York conference on political reform that primaries rewarded candidates with intense pockets of support: they win crowded races by "receiv[ing] a plurality [and are] nominated by a small minority." Professor Ford agreed that the primary "impairs [the] responsibility [to govern] by making power the football of faction" and "scrambl[ing] power among faction chiefs and their bands."[78] The Cleveland official similarly blamed the introduction of primaries for "leav[ing] the party weak and unorganized" and fostering "severe and bitter [divisions]."[79] The effect is to splinter the class and ethnic interests that the party had previously stitched together.[80] For ambitious politicians searching for success, the most rational path for advancement in an environment with direct primaries is to appeal to organized factions.

FDR's 1938 Purge and the Defeat of the Primary

Franklin Delano Roosevelt's losing battles with conservative Democrats to pass his New Deal agenda underscore the continuing control of state and local party establishments over candidate nominations decades after La Follette's campaign for primaries. Following FDR's inauguration in March 1933, he unleashed a barrage of legislation to tackle the Great Depression that was opposed by conservative—and often southern—members of Congress in his own Democratic Party. After conservative opposition continued to block his priorities in his second term—such as the Fair Labor Standards Act and an executive reorganization bill—FDR struck back by supporting liberal Democratic candidates who ran against the "traitors" in the 1938 midterm primary elections.

In his June 24, 1938, "fireside chat," the president heralded his determination to increase Democratic votes for his popular legislation by using the "direct primary . . . to make the nominating process a more democratic one." Primary elections equipped him, he reasoned, to mobilize public support in a "clear-cut [choice] between candidates for a Democratic nomination" who would be loyal liberals instead of anti–New Deal "traitors." FDR's gambit to build a loyal New Deal coalition in Congress pitted the institutional power of two candidate selection systems—the primary against the traditional state and local party organization.

FDR's effort to "purge" obstructionist Democrats in congressional primaries largely failed.[81] After the 1938 elections, he abandoned his efforts to chase out his party's conservatives and create a Democratic Party unified in backing the New Deal. He followed the advice of Jim Farley, Democratic Party chair, that he accept conservatives and "promote harmony [and] teamwork."[82] Following FDR's defeats, "damage control" became a priority, and he mended fences with conservatives he had targeted.

The source of FDR's defeat was his exaggerated expectations of primary elections and underestimation of the party establishment. It proved too strong even when pitted against a popular president during a national emergency.

Alternatives to the Direct Primary

The clash between the advocates and critics of direct primaries framed an enduring question: what should be the form of American democracy? Two of the Progressive Era's intellectual leaders—Walter Lippmann and Herbert Croly—criticized the party machine and agreed that it was imperative to modernize the national government to manage industrialization and America's place in an increasingly global world.[83] Croly shared the concern of many Progressives with the country's "dangerous inequality in the distribution of power." The "concentration of wealth and financial power," he cautioned, was "inimical to democracy because it tends to erect political abuses and social inequalities into a system."[84]

Lippman and Croly were also stinging critics of the direct primary and favored rolling it back. They parted ways, however, on how to achieve responsible governance. Lippmann's criticism of the direct primary reflected a fundamental conviction that the role of citizens is excessive and needs to be substantially diminished. "No amount of . . . direct primaries," Lippmann derisively asserted, "will make a democracy out of an illiterate people." "The voter," he continued, "cannot grasp the details of the problems of the day because he has not the time, the interest or the knowledge." Instead of achieving "a better public opinion because [the voter] is asked to express his opinion more often . . . [, h]e will simply be more bewildered, more bored and more ready to follow along."[85] Lippmann's views were not isolated; Professor Woodburn referred to "ignorant and irresponsible voters," and the Cleveland municipal officer observed that the "ordinary individual has little fitness to judge of the ability of a candidate for office."[86]

Croly shared Lippmann's criticism that La Follette's blizzard of elections prevented all but a small number of citizens from thoughtfully participating in them. He complained that the direct primary's efforts to "keep power in the hands of the "plain people" . . . [had] precisely the opposite [effect] . . . [by] afford[ing] the political specialist a wonderful opportunity [to devote] . . . their time [to] nominating and electing candidates to these numerous offices."[87]

Rather than demoting citizens (as Lippmann suggested), however, Croly aimed to "simplify the machinery" of representative democracy to align it with the reality of busy citizens, possessing uneven knowledge and expertise. He recommended that "only decisive decisions and choices [should be] submitted to the voter." Rejecting the approach of La Follette and his supporters, Croly reasoned that the "way to make votes important and effective is not to increase but to diminish their number." The authority and legitimacy of representative democracy would be protected and strengthened by submitting *"only decisive decisions and choices... to the voter."*[88] Citizens would be better prepared, more engaged, and more likely to turn out in greater numbers for a small number of decisive battles between the parties.

Croly identified three steps to recommit governance to "republican institutions" by retaining the founding principle of popular sovereignty (as Jefferson and La Follette insisted) and incorporating government authority bolstered by improved administrative capacity (as Hamilton argued).[89] Croly's first step was to anchor the accountability of governing elites and political parties in voting. The dependence of elected officials on winning or retaining sufficient votes is "necessary [for] . . . decisive action." He linked this electoral imperative with lawmaking and the national party's "organized control over the legislative proposals."[90] "Party organization performs a great service," Ford insisted, "because it . . . locates power somewhere . . . [and assumes] real responsibility for the behavior of government."[91]

Second, Croly argued that national political parties connected the "method of representation" to "expert administration in a progressive democratic community": it inserted a "centralized responsible organization" into governing and producing "efficient and responsible . . . social policy."[92] The "cost of government in time, ability, training and energy should fall . . . upon the leaders" of the organized political party and its members holding the reins of government rather than citizens with inadequate time and resources. Countering Jefferson and La Follette, Croly proposed that "efficient representation" based on using administrative agencies and officials was feasible under the watchful eye of national political parties alert to the verdict of voters in the next election.[93] Professor

Ford similarly argued that reinvigorated political parties were decisive to "promote good government."[94]

Third, political parties were the proving ground to train and "encourage leadership that would lead toward the national interest."[95] "A democracy," Croly reasoned, "should encourage the political leadership of experienced, educated, and well-trained men but only on the express condition [that their actions face the accountability of] . . . severe penalties [for wrongdoing]."[96] Croly looked to national political parties to generate leaders who connected electoral success with governing that advanced the broader public interest.

Promoting Equality and Practicing Racism

Alexander Keyssar's meticulous historical account of voting rights traces the rolling back of the franchise to the period from the mid-nineteenth century through the Progressive Era. Men and women across racial lines were deprived of the vote in response to the rising antagonism of the middle and upper classes toward wide access to the franchise. The backlash hit African Americans far harder; their disenfranchisement was achieved with brutal violence and was far more severe.[97]

Progressives spoke glowingly in public about universal values. In practice, their reforms—perhaps unwittingly in some instances—benefited whites, villainized immigrants, and aided the South's embrace of a Jim Crow system of segregation and violence toward people of color.[98] La Follette's crusade for the primary occurred in this context of disenfranchisement and racial antagonism and, in certain respects, was subsumed by it.

Political Equality for Whites and Blacks

La Follette's commitment to the Declaration of Independence's promise—and the Constitution's guarantee—of popular consent and political equality animated his advocacy of direct primaries; it also propelled his support for civil rights. Growing up during the Civil War, he admired Lincoln for saving the Union and for freeing the slaves. The Wisconsinite campaigned with "righteous indignation against the South," regularly insisting that the "past of 1865 is no more to be forgotten than the past of 1776."[99] The South's oppression of blacks, he argued, also set back the rights of whites by restricting their ability to challenge the Democratic political machine's ties to affluent whites.[100]

La Follette's support for civil rights was evident in his voting record. He supported legislation to create opportunity for black people, such as federal aid to southern farmers. He also publicly lambasted lynching as an "everlasting shame"—the murder, he said, of "innocent, God fearing, law abiding, colored citizens."[101] The NAACP and leading African American leaders like W. E. B. Du Bois recognized La Follette's principled stand for civil rights and supported him.[102]

Many Progressives, however, did not share La Follette's civil rights commitments. Some were outright racists and in positions of enormous power. Woodrow Wilson outwardly embraced white supremacy. He publicly extolled the film *Birth of a Nation*, which exalted the KKK and promoted negative stereotypes of African Americans. Wilson also supported the segregation of federal employees.

Many Progressives were not explicit white supremacists but acquiesced to it as the price for achieving what they considered more worthwhile priorities. Teddy Roosevelt's 1912 Progressive Party campaign distilled the division between Progressive southerners who insisted on a "lily-white party" as the price of their support and northern reformers, including Jane Addams, who promoted social policy and women's suffrage but failed to rank black rights as their highest priority.[103] TR's campaign fit a pattern among northern Progressives: they did not share the racial animus of southerners but they "seldom contested the increasing division of Americans into separate enclaves."[104] In 1912 and 1924, the Progressive Party platforms loudly advocated for expanding American democracy through adoption of the direct primary and other reforms and yet were silent about the rights of African Americans.[105]

The Direct Primary and White Supremacy

The rules of politics are not neutral. For decades, white supremacists seized on the arrival of the direct primary as a helpful instrument to dull the impact of voters color and dodge effective constitutional challenges.

The "white primary" produced outright exclusion from the 1920s to the 1950s. In southern states after the Civil War, the Democratic Party dominated, and its primary decided who would hold office due to the political weakness of Republican candidates. Following the ratification of the Fifteenth Amendment in 1870, African American men enjoyed the constitutional right to vote and were poised to influence elections. When the white vote split among a number of white candidates, black voters could become kingmakers or conceivably elect a black candidate. By excluding blacks from voting in the direct primary, white supremacists used it, according to a North Carolina newspaper editor, to "keep white men united" behind one white candidate.[106] It also secured the Democratic Party's domination against challenges from candidates that rallied struggling whites.[107]

Southern white supremacists were also attracted to the direct primary as a strategy to effectively undermine the Fifteenth Amendment. For many years, they argued successfully in Courts that political parties were private associations that could discriminate by excluding African Americans. In short, the direct primary performed a double whammy: it disenfranchised blacks and, for several decades, dodged a pitched constitutional battle over the Fifteenth Amendment.

Legal skirmishes over the direct primary pockmarked the 1920s and 1930s and invariably favored southern white supremacists. That started to change, however, with the Supreme Court's 1944 decision in *Smith v. Allwright*. This ruling eventually struck a mortal blow by barring political parties from using the direct primary to deny the constitutional rights of African Americans to vote. After this decision, South Carolina, Alabama, and Arkansas maneuvered to dodge the Court's decision and continued to disenfranchise blacks. But a process started that weakened the control of white supremacists and altered the balance of power among racial groups—a process that would continue through the Voting Rights Act of 1964.[108]

As the white supremacist use of the direct primary was blunted and eventually stopped, La Follette's reform evolved into a mechanism for reproducing racial hierarchies within the US constitutional framework and democratic procedures. It was more subtle but still effective.

The Voting Rights Act and other legal and political changes opened the door to greater black representation. The direct primary enabled candidates of color to unseat entrenched white legislators and increase the numbers of black representatives in America's national and state capitols.

Even with this expansion of representation, however, racial disparities in the recruitment and election of presidential and legislative candidates remained. The proportionately lower representation of legislators of color compared to white officials is a product, in part, of the primary process that splits the black vote and favors candidates with more organizational and financial resources, as critics of the primary warned in the early twentieth century. We explore these developments in later chapters.

The Progressive Era: Limits and Constraints

Progressives have faced a century of withering and often conflicting criticism: timid conservatives, overpromising schemers, or reckless redirectors of American political development. The legacy of Progressive political reform defies one verdict, but a common theme weaves through the political reforms and, in particular, La Follette's direct primary campaign: the limits and constraints owing to misjudgments, resistance, and the shackles of the past.

Radical Agendas and Legislation

Progressives are criticized for not seeking to transform gender and race relations. Instead of pursuing a radical agenda of government seizure of property and assets to achieve structural economic change, they responded to middle-class values and anxieties.[109] They accepted the concepts of capitalism even as they worked to tame its excesses and intentionally left its edifice intact.[110]

For this group of critics, the Progressives are flawed for what they never tried. Prominent Progressives from La Follette to Teddy Roosevelt were practicing politicians committed to winning votes to secure office and pass legislation. They accepted—as do successful Western politicians and effective reformers from most eras—the underlying social and economic structures. La Follette was clear about the starting point for himself and his colleagues: "I am not for a class party—or a party composed of organized labor and organized farmers and organized socialists." He practiced the arts of populism but swore off "organized strife for class or group control."[111]

The reform records of Progressives and nineteenth-century populists present dueling roles and records. The Populists, the People's Party, and their allies designed a radical agenda to form cooperative alternatives in agrarian communities, remove "money power" from the political system, and greatly expand the scope of government intervention in the economy and workplace.[112] They were, though, locked out of the legislative process and unable themselves to enact these proposals into law or build enduring and widely used programs.[113] By comparison, the Progressives battled to win elections and wield influence in state and national legislatures against the well-funded opposition of political machines and corporate trusts. They accepted as a matter of necessity the imperative of searching for allies, building coalitions, and appealing to citizens with differing values and priorities. By contrast, Populists generated an agenda whose legislative success depended on Progressives and, later, New Dealers to rescue farmers, stabilize the financial system, and tackle other priorities.

The Curse of Overpromising

A second group of critics take Progressives to task for overpromising and failing to achieve their own objectives. They set out to remove the excesses of monopolies and political machines. But their efforts to break up monopolies and concentrated wealth stumbled, leaving the agenda to the New Deal to tackle effectively. On another front, reformers rallied behind the Hamiltonian vision of creating coherent, national administration of economic and regulatory policy but left a legacy of "incoherence and fragmentation"—a "hapless giant" that was tangled by multiple and competing lines of authority that crisscross the executive and legislative branches.[114]

The shortfalls of the Progressive Era are undeniable. Reformers like La Follette and others overpromised and underdelivered, yet this pattern is familiar to reform episodes. Reformers at the turn of the twentieth century might arguably be faulted for erring more frequently or with greater consequence, but their counterparts during the New Deal and Great Society as well as the presidencies of Ronald Reagan, and Barack Obama, which also required modifications, accommodations, and reversals.

Falling short is not simply a verdict on reformers; it also speaks to their circumstances. Progressives confronted dense and widespread networks entrenched in local communities and states. Incomplete and partial initial outcomes were inevitable.

The contemporary and historical commentary about the direct primary often neglects the intense, widespread, and effective opposition it provoked. Political entrepreneurs—like La Follette— pushed for a new opportunity structure but collided with amply equipped state and local party networks. They also clashed with other Progressives, who recoiled at the deleterious impacts of direct primaries on the authority and legitimacy of representative government and national institutions.

While the direct primary is pervasive now, that outcome was not obvious by mid-century. It might well have remained marginalized in the battle for power and position if not for the undercover operation in 1969–1970 that revived the primary without adequately considering the reasons it was stymied.

The Long Shadow of Progressives

A third group of critics blames the Progressive Era for contemporary ills. The policies and changes introduced by the Progressives, an array of detractors charge, occurred at "the pivot point in the development of modern American government." The results are declared catastrophic: they "pushed the nation down the wrong path" and "se[t] the government on an unsustainable course."[115] Instead of criticizing the Progressives for what they did not seek to accomplish or failed to accomplish, the third line of criticism blasts them for the changes they did make and the disastrous consequences for our own time.

Today's doubters of democracy skewer Progressives for introducing a "more-elections approach." Progressives are guilty, critics maintain, of establishing primaries to radically redirect control over presidential nominations "from elected officials and party officials and toward the electorate and activist base."[116]

Democracy's doubters illustrate the tendency to single out the Progressive Era as the cause of contemporary ills based on tenuous, elongated chains of effects. Blaming the direct primary on Progressives ignores their opponents within their ranks that stymied it, as well as the institutional inheritances that limited their options and distorted their plans to reformulate American politics.

Progressive Warning to Later Reformers

Advocates of the direct primary during the past half century have persistently ignored the perceptive doubts voiced by critics about its democratic pretentions from its start. The ready excuse of "unanticipated consequences" is not available to this group of reformers. The dreadful consequences of primaries over the past half century were, in important respects, anticipated if reformers cared to listen. Early-twentieth-century critics of primaries singled out two features that would later metastasize in American governance and politics.

The Political Rationality of the Direct Primary

The effect of the direct primary, Croly and others cautioned in the early twentieth century, is to splinter voters into factions, proliferate their formation, and motivate candidates to cater to them. Where the party machine consults "conflicting interests [until] a ticket satisfactory to the majority is agreed upon," the primary encourages schisms and the pleaders of specific interests and causes by making it possible for them to nominate candidates who cater to their positions as opposed to the wishes and wants of most Americans.[117] For candidates, their drive to secure nomination was expected to motivate them to adopt policy positions and build a personal organization devoted to mobilizing these narrow factions instead of pursuing the broad, civic, republican values heralded in the late eighteenth and early nineteenth centuries.

In addition, Croly and others warned (as outlined earlier) that structuring political participation toward incessant primary elections focused on the inner workings of political parties, which narrowed the interest and engagement of most citizens. Members of factions devoted the greatest attention to the internal party nomination process, while voters without intense preferences or loyalty to an organized group were less motivated to participate in a primary.

They also cautioned that the primary reversed the effort by generations to design the rules of elite competition and voter behavior to steer candidates toward shared national interests as they calculated the question "What is rational to win?" The primary's design put a premium on the short-term objective of winning the nomination instead of the longer-term process of organizing and engaging voters and broad coalitions around shared interests.

The warnings of Croly and others failed to deter La Follette and his allies. The puzzle is that primary advocates both decried the pursuit of narrow, selfish ends by corrupt parties while redesigning party nominations to channel politics into a labyrinth of rules and administrative processes. Why did their misgivings about parties fail to temper their enthusiasm for a reformed version of them?

The answer lies in the Progressives' faith in administration.[118] The promoters of primaries trusted that the corruption of party machines would be checked by rigorous rules and procedures guiding the internal operations of political parties.

La Follette and his allies championed the values of political equality and yet designed a process that fostered disparities in political voice and representation. They claimed to create a bulwark against the ad hoc trading of favors by party bosses, but channeled citizens into a political process that controlled the terms of political participation and favored factions that wielded the substantial resources needed to track candidates, issues, and varying rules of eligibility.

The Authority and Legitimacy of Representative Government

La Follette and other advocates fueled a spiral of attacks on the authority and legitimacy of representative government. They elevated unrealistic expectations of citizen control, which in turn triggered chronic disappointment with reforms that failed to deliver idealized democratic institutions and impassioned searches for elusive reform to achieve popular sovereignty. The effect was to hone political conflict on betrayals of untrustworthy democratic institutions rather than on the fights over policy between parties, as Van Buren, Croly, and others counseled.

Why the direct primary was rehabilitated in the 1970s and reached its current heights is the topic of the next chapter.

5

Political Elites and the Failure
to Protect Democratic Institutions,
1960s–1972

"Nobody goes hungry." That was the ethic of William and Christine Mikulski's grocery store in the Highlandtown neighborhood of East Baltimore. It was an ethic that steered their daughter—Barbara Mikulski—to embrace a commitment to "Heal the Sick and Love thy Neighbor."[1] Mikulski credits her parents and Catholic education to her early social work career in Baltimore during the 1960s and later pioneering career in the US House and US Senate where she became the longest-serving woman in congressional history (1977–2017).

Mikulski's early career illustrates an era-defining disconnect between formal and practical politics in the 1960s—one that would shatter the mid-century Democratic Party and clear a path for the direct primary that Progressive critics warned against. Mikulski "wasn't political" nor a "party person thinking about party politics" during the 1960s, yet she excelled at the basic skill of politics: organizing. She trained the poor and disadvantaged in the war on poverty's disruptive tools of "maximum feasible participation" to confront inequality.

Although initially distant from electoral politics, Mikulski eventually challenged the unresponsiveness of the formal political establishment with the tools of grassroots politics and protest that she had honed as a social worker. Her impetus: a plan by the ossified Democratic Party in Baltimore City Hall to jam a sixteen-lane

highway through her neighborhood on the East Side and dis-
place thousands of blacks and "ethnics"—working-class Polish,
Greek, Lithuanian, and Ukrainian Americans. When Baltimore
started to destroy rowhouses in 1968, Mikulski organized a coalition that brought it to a halt. After beating City Hall's highway
scheme, she then beat it again at election time by knocking on
fifteen thousand doors in her "outsider" campaign for a city
council seat.

Mikulski's infusion of grassroots organizing and resistance into
electoral politics was not isolated but part of a national pattern of
popular protests in the 1960s. It successfully activated previously
excluded youth, women, and people of color against entrenched
political parties and unpopular policies—notably, the Vietnam War
and racial injustice. Mikulski's mantra of "Show up, Stand up, Speak
up" echoed the mindset of political organizers around the country
who disrupted the established political system as a means to pursue
social change.

Grassroots political organizing was one of three discrete
developments that intersected to catapult the direct primary from
the sidelines of American politics to center stage, even though it
was not a priority of grassroots reformers in the 1960s and 1970
and was vehemently opposed by Progressive Era commentators
half a century earlier.

The second element was the intensifying competition and division among political elites. Eugene McCarthy, Robert Kennedy, and
George McGovern bristled at the barriers to their advancement to
president. The selection of Hubert Humphrey by the Democratic
Party's insiders crystallized their frustration and that of a new generation of political activists who reviled "normal politics" and the
establishment's unresponsiveness on Vietnam, race relations, and
other major issues.

Seeking to placate the opposition to Humphrey's nomination
at the riotous Chicago Democratic National Convention in 1968,
the party approved a seemingly innocuous commission, which

insurgent leaders would later seize. Under the direction of party chair Fred Harris and its first leader (McGovern), the commission advanced a concealed scheme to replace the party's candidate nomination process with direct primaries and dislodge Democratic power brokers in favor of "new voices"—youth, women, and people of color. Where protest disrupted the political establishment and created pressure for change, the division among elites opened space for alternative leaders to promote structural change and seize the opportunity for themselves.

The third element concerns the content and direction of reform and the unexpected and ill-advised return to direct primaries to dictate party nominations in the 1970s. The advocates for the direct primary heralded it—as did La Follette—as expanding democracy and correcting the "abuse" of "democratic assumptions" by state and city Democratic Party operations that McGovern's commission identified.[2]

This chapter traces the revival of the presidential primary in response to the convergence of elite divisions and rivalry with institutional patterning. We begin by locating this unexpected turn in the conflict and elite rivalry of the 1960s that created an opening for sweeping change.

America's "Sizzling Cauldron"

Bob Dylan was born and raised in northern Minnesota and at twenty-three years old put the comfortable in America on notice: "The Times They Are a-Changin.'" For politicians steeped in the status quo, he presciently warned in 1964, "The battle outside ragin' / Will soon shake your windows and rattle your walls."

The "unraveling of America" is how historian Allen Matusow described the flip from the social cohesion and insularity of an affluent, white middle class in the early 1960s to the assault on the political establishment and onset of economic malaise.[3] Disruption of the status quo in the 1960s contributed to the fracturing of governing elites and fiery divisions within America.

Social and Political Fracturing

John Kennedy was inaugurated into an America on the upswing after the Second World War. Social historians portray a country with high hopes for the future and confidence in solving problems, including poverty and racial disparities, and reviving the world order in America's romanticized image. "Americans," John Blum reports, exuded "confidence in the superiority of their economy, their technology, and their weaponry."[4]

Rising standards of living and shared affluence among professional and blue-collar workers in the 1950s and 1960s propelled the growth of a white middle class with discretionary income. Princeton economist and New York Times columnist Paul Krugman describes this period as a "fairly equal society" in which economic disparities among whites were subdued, though Black Americans remained disproportionately impoverished and lacking economic opportunities. "The vast income and wealth inequalities of the Gilded Age had disappeared [and] the poverty of the underclass [was] viewed as a social rather than an economic problem."[5]

As the well-being of Americans broadened and government revenues grew, a new generation of politicians and policy experts designed modest remedial programs and optimistically projected the prospects for social betterment.[6] Poverty, racial disparities, education, juvenile delinquency, and other social ills became targets. John Kennedy's 1961 inaugural address famously gave voice to the idealism and hopefulness: "Ask not what your country can do for you—ask what you can do for your country." The normally aloof novelist Norman Mailer gushed that the new president was a "superman" instilling an "unwilling charge" to Americans.[7]

Then came the shots.

The shock of Kennedy's 1963 assassination produced a startling turnaround for Lyndon Johnson, a southern conservative who was on the cusp of possible indictment and replacement on Kennedy's 1964 ticket.[8] Despite initial reservations from liberals, Lyndon Johnson's programs ignited their "euphoria." A broad coalition of voters produced a landslide for Johnson in the 1964 election and swelled the Democratic majority in the US House majority by thirty-eight seats. The legislative tide for liberalism rose in 1965 with the passage of the Voting Rights Act, the Medicare program for seniors, a historic education bill, and more. Even with the surge of liberal legislation, American politics retained a substantial degree of pragmatism across party lines, with Republicans joining Democrats on much of this agenda. On particular issues, politics remained "largely consensual."[9] That abruptly changed.

Barbara Mikulski's revolt against the Baltimore political establishment was not an isolated incident; protest and social disorder erupted for nearly a decade after the mid-1960s. Her searing speech at Catholic University in 1970 catapulted her to national prominence as an advocate of the forty million bluecolor "ethnic Americans" who are "victim[s] of class prejudice." These hardworking citizens, she charged, are caught in a "sizzling cauldron" in which they "pa[y] the bill for every major government program and ge[t] nothing or little in the way of return." Meanwhile, earlier criticisms of American poverty, discrimination, and the nation's presence in Vietnam that had percolated on college campuses and among intellectuals—like Michael Harrington's sobering 1962 portrait of poverty—were seized on by people of color, youth, and women. It was a time of "takin' it to the streets," as the rock-and-roll hit put it.

The steaming outrage of protesters against America's policies extended to what they saw as its shriveled democracy. The New Left charged in the 1962 Port Huron Statement that elections and traditional politics failed to penetrate institutions that were cordoned off from citizens. The alternative was outside the arena of elections. *"Participatory democracy,"* campus organizer Tom Hayden proclaimed, was the path to justice and to inspiring students and allies off campus.[10]

Lyndon Johnson became the target of the liberals, hippies, and New Left rebelling against the political establishment. For his part, the president was bewildered by the "reject[ion] . . . of his strenuous efforts to liberate the poor and the black."[11] Johnson deluded himself into believing that the backlash could be tamed by crafting misleading messages targeted by White House public opinion polling. After securing landmark breakthroughs in social policy and civil rights, Johnson was unable to accept the poisonous effects of his Vietnam debacle, his deceptions to sustain it, and the cumulative effects on the political system's eroding legitimacy.[12]

The mobilization of the left spread off campuses into the country as the economy struggled and discord grew over US policies. America's affluent middle class was staggered after 1966 by the "Great Inflation," pushing the "high cost of living" to the top of Gallup polling on the country's most important problems. Even Johnson's legislative victories underscored limits rather than accomplishments in the eyes of liberals and social justice advocates. Passing the Voting Rights Act and other civil rights legislation were historic achievements; they also became targets for what they failed to do: end deep-seated racial barriers. Black communities revolted against the continuation of rampant discrimination, political underrepresentation, and clashes with police. The 1965 summer riots in Los Angeles's Watts neighborhood spread to cities across America in 1966, 1967, and 1968, displaying the fury of demeaned blacks and the long indifference of government. Johnson was cornered between these protests and majorities of whites concluding that his administration was moving too fast on civil rights.[13] The years of dodging demands for civil rights to sustain southern white support for the Democratic Party—as President Kennedy had done—produced damaging political costs.[14]

The 1964 Democratic Convention in Atlantic City showcased the searing political conflict between the righteous demands of the Mississippi Freedom Democratic Party (MFDP) for seats in the state's delegation and the state's racist Democratic Party establishment that excluded blacks and favored segregation. Johnson accepted a deal that refused to seat MFDP delegates in order to hold the South in the 1964 election but committed to banning segregated delegations in 1968. Johnson—again—ended up with a no-win outcome: MFDP protests garnered damaging headlines and the Mississippi white delegates that he did seat walked out in opposition to the party's civil rights planks.[15] (The Democratic National Committee adopted rules in January 1968 to ban racial discrimination, which were expanded in 1972.)

Vietnam accelerated America's unraveling as Johnson widened the draft, television icon Walter Cronkite grimly announced the daily US casualties, and US soldiers bombed and massacred innocent Vietnamese people. The eroding support for Johnson's war started with liberal intellectuals (including MIT professor Noam Chomsky), disaffected students, and the New Left; it spread to growing numbers of Democrats and eventually the general public.

Before 1967, Gallup polls show that stable majorities believed that sending troops to Vietnam was not a mistake, including 60 percent in August 1965 and 59 percent in March 1966. But opposition grew rapidly as the costs started to register. The economic costs of the war set up a damning choice: guns for Vietnam or funding for Johnson's Great Society programs. The deepening US involvement provoked growing numbers of Americans to take to the streets and stirred escalating congressional opposition. For the first time, Gallup's July 1967 poll reported that 41 percent now thought that sending troops was a mistake, 52 percent disapproved of Johnson's handling of the war, and 56 percent concluded that the United States was losing the war or was stuck in an impasse. The eroding confidence in Johnson's optimistic reports on the war's progress accelerated after the Vietnamese Tet New Year in January 1968, when the forces battling America—the Vietcong—surprisingly launched its largest military operation in over one hundred towns and cities.

Democrats Turn on Each Other

As America's economy and confidence crumbled and festering policy debates and rising distrust escalated into full-scale resistance, the Democratic Party split into unruly factions. The star *Washington Post* reporter David Broder bemoaned the open "antipathies" that developed within the Democratic Party; the "party's leading figures are convinced that their enemies (always defined as Democrats of another faction) are about to succeed in cutting the party's throat."[16]

Hubert Humphrey's Dilemma

Before 1968, Lyndon Johnson firmly led the Democratic establishment. As Johnson's policies provoked rising opposition in the country, the factions within the Democratic Party prepared a ferocious and debasing assault against his reelection campaign in 1968. Nearly three weeks after a surprisingly close primary win, Johnson abruptly ended his campaign during a nationally televised address on March 31, 1968. With no warning, Vice President Hubert Humphrey was thrust into the presidential campaign.

Party rules and the tumult of 1968 trapped Humphrey in a paradox that was both seductive and toxic. Humphrey's nomination was advantaged by the establishment's continuing control over the nomination process after La Follette's ineffectual effort at change. But as Humphrey reached for his prize for assiduously following the party's longstanding rules, he enraged the discontented.

Following Johnson's withdrawal, Humphrey stepped in to secure the "political base" that he had courted as senator and then as vice president by meeting the requests of party leaders around the country and aiding mayors and governors in need of the administration's help. Humphrey's ties to organized labor produced commitments from nearly all delegates from Michigan, Ohio, and the heavily unionized states in the Northeast.

Humphrey expected, as had presidential candidates for decades, to reap the reward of securing support from the national, state, and local party organizations. They continued to control the selection of delegates to national conventions; by 1968, only 38 percent of delegates were selected by primaries, with fewer even bound to specific candidates.[17] The result: The party establishment chose nearly a third of the delegates before the 1968 primary elections even began, and Humphrey jumped to a healthy lead in the delegate count.[18]

Like prior presidential candidates backed by the party establishment, Humphrey skipped the primaries as unnecessary and risky. Wendell Willkie, the Republican Party's 1940 presidential candidate, entered the 1944 Wisconsin primary to overcome opposition among party leaders irked by his cross-party wartime assistance to FDR. His large defeat in the Badger State ended his political career.

Up next: Democratic senator Estes Kefauver of Tennessee. Senator Kefauver leveraged his national fame from conducting organized crime hearings to win twelve of fifteen primaries and over three million votes. Nonetheless, party leaders opposed Kefauver and selected his chief opponent, Adlai Stevenson, who received a mere seventy-eight thousand primary votes.[19]

Humphrey's losing primary battle with John Kennedy in 1960 left a searing reminder of the risks.[20] "Any man who goes into a primary," Humphrey concluded, "isn't fit to be president. You have to be crazy to go into a primary."

Even as the backing of party leaders convinced Humphrey in 1968 not to enter the primaries, several Humphrey advisers flagged the risks in a time of upheavals. US senator Walter Mondale—co-chair of Humphrey's 1968 campaign, Minnesota protégé, and future vice president and Democratic presidential nominee—pleaded with him that "he should run in the primary . . . to be connected with the public and become their candidate." Although Humphrey sided with advisers who warned of the risk of running and losing or falling short of expectations, Mondale insisted that entering the primary was a "risk worth taking and that it was a mistake to skip them." After the election, Humphrey would regret his decision to stay out.[21]

Humphrey's following of party rules that had been in place for decades secured his nomination, but in exchange he absorbed withering criticism not only for abiding by the process but also for serving with the increasingly unpopular Lyndon Johnson. If Humphrey criticized the president or flagged in defending him, he risked losing the support of key party leaders—especially Johnson's loyalists from the South. Humphrey was cornered, and his campaign reeked of his predicament: campaign journalist Theodore White reported that Humphrey's "words, phrases, speeches sounded old [and] tired," and he delivered them with "layer upon layer of reservations" about policies he opposed that he felt bound to defend.[22]

For the first time, the once powerful position of being chosen by party leaders was a political curse, and Humphrey's allies ached for him. The vice president became a bullseye for critics of Johnson and long-accepted rules for party nominations. Forgotten was Humphrey's considerable record of championing redistributive social policies and civil rights, including his clarion call to delegates at the 1948 Democratic National Convention to "get out of the *shadow* of states' rights and *walk* forthrightly into the bright sunshine of human rights." Mondale was galled by the "lecturing" to Humphrey about liberal causes even though critics like Kennedy were "late arrivals" and less than reliable supporters of them.[23] Historians later discovered in White House archives that Humphrey resisted Johnson's conduct of Vietnam, earning him the president's cold shoulder and venom.[24]

Prior to 1968, the likely presidential nominee approached the national convention with stature and confidence owing to party leader support. Not Hubert Humphrey. He arrived at the Democratic Convention "scarred and embittered by four years of demeaning servitude to Lyndon Johnson and by the desertion and denunciation of his old liberal friends."[25]

McCarthy and Kennedy Fight Back

The mix of elite division, personal ambition, and popular unrest congealed in 1968 into a frontal assault on the Democratic Party's nomination process. Eugene McCarthy and Robert Kennedy reflected and contributed to the split in the Democratic Party, leading contending factions that opposed the Johnson administration and the party's nomination process.

Eugene McCarthy initially targeted Johnson before moving on to challenge his fellow Minnesotan senator Hubert Humphrey after Johnson's withdrawal, and then assailed the Party's nomination process. McCarthy brought an iconoclastic persona to the political stage: he combined hard-charging barnstorming and cut-throat competitiveness with a fascination for poetry and mysticism that baffled colleagues and reporters. At various junctures, he himself worried that his campaign speeches more resembled poetry than decisive campaign statements.[26]

McCarthy's unorthodox style leveraged 1968's countercultural moment to wage a punishing challenge to his Senate colleague.[27] McCarthy became a rallying point for liberals and large university audiences of disaffected youth opposed to the Johnson administration, especially its Vietnam policy. Upon launching his campaign in November 1967, McCarthy decried America's "deepening moral crisis" and the administration's handling of Vietnam, charging that it was "afraid to negotiate" with America's adversaries in North Vietnam.[28]

McCarthy shocked the political world in the March 12, 1968 New Hampshire primary—the first in the country—by winning the "moral victory" of 42 percent against the sitting president (Johnson received 49.6 percent). McCarthy's startling result was aided by the low expectations prior to the election; polls registered his support as only 10 percent to 20 percent.[29]

McCarthy's success revealed Johnson's political vulnerability and the political path for a challenger. After New Hampshire and Johnson's withdrawal, McCarthy won the next primaries in Wisconsin (56 percent) and Pennsylvania (71 percent) and a plurality in Massachusetts.

McCarthy's success stirred Robert Kennedy's private deliberations over "skip[ping] the primaries . . . or challenging [Humphrey and] McCarthy." Kennedy opted for the against-the-odds path of entering primaries—as did his brother—to win over party leaders and "brea[k] through at the Convention." Beating Humphrey and McCarthy would convince "the old-fashioned delegate-brokers," White reported, that "Kennedy was, beyond doubt, the man who would win [the presidential race and] . . . do more for [their] local ticket in November."[30]

Convinced that McCarthy and Humphrey were vulnerable, Kennedy entered the primary battle for the Democratic nomination on March 16. He remade his public persona to fit the moment. He jettisoned his privileged upbringing and place at the apex of political power as a US senator, attorney general for his brother John Kennedy, and ruthless calculator who resisted his brother's outreach to Martin Luther King during the 1960 election. Kennedy's new identity channeled those who lacked power and political voice—students, blacks, and the poor. Instead of disdaining street disruptions, he befriended radical student leader Tom Hayden.[31]

Kennedy's star rose as the primaries progressed. While McCarthy prevailed in Kennedy's home state of Massachusetts on April 30 (49 percent to 28 percent), Kennedy won a string of five primaries from May 7 to June 4 when he secured a potentially decisive plurality victory in California's winner-take-all contest. The next day he met with his ecstatic supporters in a large hotel ballroom and, with growing confidence, promised to "go on . . . and win" the nomination at the Chicago Democratic convention. Moments afterward, Sirhan Sirhan assassinated him.

Tragedy mixed with upheaval and protest in 1968. As the country buried Kennedy only a few months after Dr. Martin Luther King's death, Humphrey and McCarthy withdrew from campaigning for several weeks.

The Rules Marched On

As America mourned Kennedy's assassination, the longstanding rules for assigning delegates for the Democratic nomination proceeded unabated, with Humphrey gaining many of Kennedy's delegates. Oregon's Republican senator Mark Hatfield concluded in June that McCarthy had "no chance" of stopping Humphrey's nomination in two months.[32] As predicted, Humphrey won the Democratic Party's presidential nomination on the first ballot.

While political insiders accepted Humphrey's steady march to the nomination as following long-established rules, supporters of McCarthy and Kennedy vibrated with an outrage supercharged both by grief and opposition to the Johnson administration. McCarthy won a plurality of primary votes (2.9 million votes or 39 percent), yet he lost the nomination to Humphrey—who received about 150,000 votes but 67 percent of delegates (McCarthy's delegate count amounted to 23 percent).[33] The president of the leftist organization Students for a Democratic Society was enraged that the assassinations of King and Kennedy was followed by the embrace of "Humphrey, with his incredible debt to Lyndon Johnson and everything that was corrupt and sick about the Democratic Party."[34]

The frenzied politics of 1968 crystallized in an extraordinary challenge to the Democratic Party's nomination process. A commission chaired by Iowa governor Harold Hughes and inspired by McCarthy's supporters documented what it described as the "undemocratic" conduct of state Democratic Party leaders in allocating candidates. In addition to unilaterally selecting delegates before the primaries started, state party leaders disproportionately steered the distribution of delegates toward Humphrey at McCarthy's expense. For instance, the New York Democratic state committee selected fifty of the sixty-five delegates to reward allies. Its chair matter-of-factly explained that he would face a "revolution" if he "ignored the people who helped me with the organization work and appointed strangers just because they're for McCarthy." The Connecticut and Kentucky parties heavily tilted delegates toward their favorite candidate—Humphrey—and provoked the McCarthy delegates to the state conventions to walk out in protest.[35] A year later, the DNC's McGovern-Fraser Commission would confirm this pattern in seventeen hearings around the country. In Missouri, the governor selected the national convention delegation on his own; Iowa's Democratic Party granted McCarthy 8 percent of its delegates even though he received 40 percent of the support in the state's caucuses. Although 880,000 blacks lived in Florida, its Democratic Party entirely excluded them from its Executive Committee for a century and only a few were selected as delegates.[36]

The Hughes Commission converted these long-standing practices into a political harpoon directed at the Democratic Party. The practice of party officials running their party—a concept widely accepted in other representative systems—was labeled undemocratic and a threat to social disorder by a commission supported by a losing candidate's campaign.[37] "State systems for selecting delegates to the National Convention display," it charged, "considerably less fidelity to basic democratic principles than a nation which claims to govern itself can safely tolerate." What started as the grievances of a losing candidate took on broader and more ominous meanings at the Democratic National Convention.

The People, the Thugs, and the Democratic Party

The breakdown of the "old politics" of interest balancing and reconciliation exploded on national television at the Democratic

National Convention in Chicago in August 1968. In the lead-up to the gathering, the Students for a Democratic Society (SDS) and protest organizers castigated government policies as "unrepresentative of the interests of vast numbers of people" and ridiculed Humphrey's nomination as "unrepresentative government." Their bitter disdain was displayed by Yippie leader Jerry Rubin's nomination of a large pig named "Pigasus" as the Democratic candidate.[38] The remedy, they declared, was filling the streets with protesters and practicing democracy in action. They chanted, "The party belongs to the people," and "The streets belong to the people."[39]

The "Police Riot"

The Democratic Party's internecine battles and protests may have faded in significance without the fuel of Chicago's "police riot," as an official investigation about the events described it. With Mayor Richard Daley's city government denying permits for peaceful gatherings of what they described as meddling "outsiders," demonstrators amassed and mayhem ensued. Police responded by firing volleys of tear gas with weapons supplied by the US Army. When protesters fled, the police gave chase with batons raised high over their heads to "crac[k] against skin and bone" while some chanted, "Kill, kill, kill," (according to a *Chicago Daily* reporter). With the "police completely out of control," "everyone became a target, demonstrators, [clergy] . . . journalists, and innocent bystanders." Police supervision broke down, and some cops removed their nameplates and badges to avoid later discipline.[40]

Playing out during an unusually hot August, the police assaults and fleeing crowds produced a "satanic smell" of "rotting cloying meat" and unwashed clothes and bodies.[41] The violence and odors permeated Chicago. Humphrey's hotel shower filled with tear gas, and McCarthy's hotel rooms were converted into a makeshift medical unit filled with bleeding demonstrators.

The Chicago police and their master, Mayor Daley, supplied a face for the New Left's depiction of America's authoritarianism. Ruling as the all-controlling political boss that La Follette reviled, Daley directed the police "not to go easy on protesters" and to "shoot to kill arsonists and maim looters."[42] To impose his will, Daley assembled forty thousand officers drawn from city police, state National Guard, five thousand US Army troops equipped with flamethrowers and bazookas, as well as one thousand federal agents. The mayor transformed the Democratic convention into "Fort Daley" and encased it in barbed wire.[43]

"Billy clubs, tear gas and Mace" was *Time* magazine's contribution to the news media coverage. Walter Cronkite reported to the nation that the police who assaulted his colleague Dan Rather were "thugs," and Theodore White described the convention as a "contagion of madness . . . [and] a sickening loss of control."[44] Novelist Norman Mailer likened the police assaults to "a scythe through grass . . . cutting a channel," while fellow fiction writer William Styron relayed the scene of police knocking down "a young man . . . and beat[ing] [him] senseless."[45]

Humphrey "Nominated in a Sea of Blood"

The chaos and bloodshed in the streets—and the media's visceral coverage of it—had political reverberations. The protesters seized on the spectacle of police brutality, chanting, "The whole world is watching."[46] Daley became a target of stinging rebukes, and the police retaliated against journalists for covering them. "The word is out to get newsmen," several cops acknowledged. At least twenty reporters were hospitalized.[47] Reformers in the country—like Barbara Mikulski struggling seven hundred miles east to open up politically ossified Baltimore—were appalled and recommitted to changing the Democratic Party.

Police riots on the streets of Chicago ignited the "warring factions" inside the convention hall. At Daley's instructions, security forces patrolled the convention floor to muffle critics of the Vietnam War by seating them far from the stage and physically abusing them, including the "jack booting" of fourteen New York delegates off the floor. The heavy-handed tactics enraged delegates and attracted the attention of reporters beaming the proceedings to the country. Carrying a copy of the "hated *New York Times*" was enough to stop a New York delegate from gaining entry to the convention.[48]

The pandemonium on the streets fired up a second front: the political scrum over the nomination. Supporters of McCarthy and Kennedy fought to seize control of the convention from party regulars and block Humphrey's nomination. McGovern, who stepped into the nomination battle as a successor of Kennedy, hammered the Democratic Party for the street carnage. Even after the convention adjourned, McGovern pressed for an investigation into "American youth being savagely beaten by police simply because they were protesting policies about which they have had very little say."[49]

As Humphrey fought off a challenge to his nomination by his rivals, he faced a third front: Lyndon Johnson. Humphrey feared that the president might repudiate him at the convention; Johnson harshly criticized Humphrey to party officials and sabotaged his Vietnam "peace plank" on the party platform to bring Democrats together. The cruel irony is that McCarthy's supporters were incensed by the president's attacks on him and mistakenly assumed that Humphrey was responsible as an extension of a nonexistent "Johnson-Humphrey plot."[50]

Humphrey Prepares for Nixon and Makes Concession to Protesters

Presidential conventions are designed to unify the party and slingshot candidates into the fall campaign. Not so for Hubert

Humphrey. Humphrey's closest advisers surveyed the damage in Chicago and concluded it was a "mean Convention" that "humiliated" the Minnesotan and left him "a wreck." Theodore White gloomily summed up Humphrey's decline from a vigorous liberal champion to a "puppet of the old machines . . . nominated in a sea of blood."[51] Thinking ahead from the August convention to the November elections, Humphrey and his advisers worried that Chicago might be their "wake" or "funeral" that protesters prophesied. Years later, Walter Mondale agreed, blaming the convention for Humphrey's loss to Nixon. Pouring salt on the wounds of the "staggered" Humphrey was the refusal of McCarthy, his fellow Minnesotan, to follow tradition by rallying behind his party's nominee and supplying fulsome support following the convention's decision. Humphrey's stalwarts blamed McCarthy for their razor-close popular loss to Richard Nixon: half a million votes out of nearly 73 million ballots or 0.7 percent. While Nixon ultimately scored a large Electoral College margin—301 to 191—the outcome hinged on California, Ohio, and Illinois, which the Republican won by three percentage points or less.

In August 1968, Humphrey and his team were far from conceding; they maneuvered to revive his prospects against Nixon. One strategy was to bring together the party's warring factions by proposing new initiatives on race and Vietnam. With little to show for their efforts, though, Humphrey's team reached for a spur-of-the-moment compromise with Governor Hughes and his supporters.

Before the convention, Hughes and his colleagues converted their criticisms of the 1968 primaries into a scathing report, "The Democratic Choice," that revived America's tradition of equating democratic decline with political parties.[52] Harkening back to La Follette and Progressive reforms, the report declared a "crisis of the Democratic Party" and linked it to a broader "crisis for democracy in America and especially for the two-party system." Hughes and his allies pressed for "open public participation" in selecting convention delegates and ending the control of state and local parties.

At the convention, Humphrey supporters on the influential Rules Committee initially blocked the Hughes report because it was the work of an "unofficial, largely self-appointed group . . . of McCarthy supporters . . . [proposing] radical changes in the convention rules," in the words of Texas congressman James Wright Jr. Wright and other delegates did leave open, however, the possibility of "careful and sympathetic consideration" for a future party commission. Faced with the prospect of no progress, Hughes and his supporters rallied behind a proposal to create a commission to study reforms to increase popular participation in the selection of delegates to presidential conventions and submit a report at the 1972 gathering.

On the 1968 convention's last day, it approved a commission to study the party's nomination process to identify steps to "welcome" members and ensure that "delegates to choose a Presidential nominee must reflect the up-to-date views of the members." The motion from Governor Hughes indicated that the commission would "undertake to assure that all Democrats of the state will have meaningful and timely opportunities to participate fully in the election or selection of delegates and alternatives."

Most convention delegates approved the commission as a seemingly harmless gesture to "throw liberals a bone" and respond to the mayhem on the streets. Democratic powerhouse Anne Wexler underscored another reason for the convention's approval of a commission that would later trigger a monumental move to direct primaries: the presumed innocence of the proposal and distractions outside the convention hall meant that "there was no organized attempt to stop it [by Humphrey or the Party leadership]."[53]

As the fall campaign commenced and Humphrey searched for ways to energize his campaign, he trumpeted his support for a reform commission. He urged the party's chair to proceed quickly with starting its work to "develo[p] recommendations . . . [to]

maximize democracy in the nomination process." Revealing his motivation, the Democratic nominee stressed the importance of recruiting members who were particularly concerned about the criticisms leveled by McCarthy's backers and the Hughes report.[54]

Humphrey's strategy of using party reform to soothe the the ire of McCarthy supporters, Kennedy mourners, and street protesters repeatedly failed. The convention adoption of a commission was hardly noticed or was assumed to befall the well-known curse of studying a well-known problem.[55] Indeed, the prospects for the commission rested on a series of long-shot twists: the Democratic Party appoints the commission; it recruits open-minded members instead of known reform opponents; the commission and party adopt recommendations that genuinely respond to the scorching criticisms in the Hughes report; and independent state parties transform their selection of delegates. Under normal circumstances, each one of these should have derailed the 1968 convention's closing decision. The unexpected happened, however. Humphrey never got a bounce from his conversion to party reformer, but his sop to reformers created an opening that would transform the form of American democracy.

Subterranean Reform

Following the Chicago convention and Humphrey's close loss to Nixon, an undercover reformer—Fred Harris (one of Oklahoma's US senators, a rising young star in the Democratic Party, and co-chair of Humphrey's campaign)—launched a surreptitious plan. His scheme would transform participation in the presidential nomination process and shunt aside the national and state party establishment and its allies. Harris's quiet coup poses two puzzles. The first is Harris's success in imposing concentrated costs on the people and organizations with the power to stop reform while promoting the purported interests of a diffuse and largely unorganized group of citizens and dissidents with little institutional influence. Second, the Democratic Party returned to the internal mechanism—direct primaries—that Progressive reformers savaged as a threat to democracy half a century earlier.

While Harris's plan may have failed at another time, he pushed for change during a powerful convergence: popular discontent created a rhetorical arsenal for Harris to exploit; elite divisions weakened the resistance of the Democratic Party to an organizational threat; and political ambition motivated presidential hopefuls to invest their reputations in promoting reform with uncertain consequences. George Wallace's populist appeal to racial resentment in the 1968 presidential campaign won 13.53 percent of the popular vote and reinforced Harris's inclination toward reform that would create a path for incorporating (and presumably defeating) these discordant factions.[56]

The Quiet Coup

A miscalculation by Humphrey gave Harris's covert operation an opening. Under pressure from Harris, Humphrey rewarded him for his leadership of his presidential campaign with a position as chair of the Democratic National Committee (DNC) over the strong objections of his advisers. Power brokers like Max Kempelman warned Humphrey that Harris was a "mistake and [would] hurt the party" because he was driven by his "own personal goals and couldn't be trusted on the important issues of the party."[57] Mondale agreed. He also warned that Harris's interest in reforming the DNC was to "position himself as a great reformer to pave his way to the presidency by offering new leadership with a different flavor following the 1968 convention."[58]

Under normal circumstances, Harris's rush at the party organization to promote himself as the "chairman of reform" would have been repelled by well-positioned state and national Democratic leaders determined to protect their bases of support. His ambitious inside job, however, exploited the power vacuum following Nixon's victory and Humphrey's withdrawal. He stalled resistance by concealing his intentions and welcoming the misconception that only modest adjustments would be made to improve fairness.[59]

"[N]obody understood [Harris's plans]," his DNC executive assistant marveled, "until he said it out loud [following his appointment]." Even then, his goals were vague and made it difficult, as Mondale observed, to "find out the commission's position other than they wanted reform." Harris's ruse misled not only Humphrey but also groups that bore the brunt of Harris's deception—national and state party leaders and labor.[60]

Once appointed in January 1969, Harris made two decisive organizational moves. First, Harris carefully selected commission members who would support reform of the party's structures and not provoke a damaging backlash that would put a harsh spotlight on his radical intentions. He excluded party leaders and marginalized a critical Democrat ally—organized labor—by limiting its representation.[61] Mondale, who was sizing up his own presidential prospects, was alarmed that "the names of the commission were fast walked through" and "left out" labor leaders like Bill Dodd from the autoworkers, whom Mondale considered indispensable to the Democratic Party. Mondale worried from the commission's outset that Harris was aiming to "change rules without regard to the party establishment."[62]

Even as Harris started to outline his objectives in general terms, few Democratic power brokers stood up to his still vague vision of reform. With little pushback, he exhorted commission members to "create the most open and representative party ever," and Vice Chair Hughes recommended shifting power from the "small group of men" who run the Democratic Party to "all of [the party's] members, from the precinct to the national convention."[63]

Second, Harris surrounded himself with a carefully selected and close-knit cabal of staffers who were "party insurgents" and shared his radical agenda to widen substantially public participation and disrupt the established party organization. He recruited key staff from the Hughes investigations who had catalogued the flaws of the Democratic Party's nomination process during their scrutiny of its treatment of McCarthy, wielded a nearly unrivaled familiarity with reform proposals, and shared a firm commitment to structural change.[64] Mondale's initial worries deepened as he came to appreciate that Harris and his staff disdained regular party politics and traditional party constituencies like organized labor.

Political ambition propelled not only Harris but also George McGovern. The sitting US senator and eventual 1972 Democratic presidential nominee similarly latched his presidential hopes to establishing credentials as a bold reformer and weakening the party establishment that opposed him. His push to substantially expand public participation opened the doors to his intense and devoted backers and well-organized grassroots campaign to secure the party's nomination in 1972. While McGovern may not have anticipated the rapid adoption of presidential primaries, his disruption of long-standing Democratic Party nomination rules neutralized party opponents and advantaged his grassroots campaign strategy.

The Staff Takeover

The commission's staff enjoyed a lopsided advantage in motivation and expertise. Members of the commission devoted little time or attention to its work. They were tied down by full-time jobs and met only intermittently before the report's public release in April 1970.[65] "I must admit," a staff adviser professed, "I was amazed at the way [the commission] let us run things [without] . . . lobbying in advance [or] any calling back and forth between members. There was only us."[66]

Even if commission members engaged and tried to steer its work, the staff was equipped with a coherent agenda, expertise, and the latitude to frame the group's questions and pose alternatives to advance structural reform.[67] Theodore White's description of "runaway staff" is fair but incomplete; their plans followed Harris's map and were overseen by the commission's chairmen—George McGovern and, after he announced his presidential campaign in January 1971, Minnesota congressman Don Fraser.[68]

The staff capitalized on the disconnect of commission members to fundamentally redesign the party's presidential nomination process. The result, according to Byron Shafer, is that "the over-whelming share of the document going out to publication was effectively identical to the draft document [prepared by staff for the Commission's August 1969 meeting]." In total, the commission made minor adjustments to the staff's work, added a guideline to the report's initial seventeen core guidelines, and deleted none of its recommendations.[69]

The commission members' disinterest had repercussions. It preempted public attention and debate that their disagreement would have triggered among the general public and state and local party leaders across the country. It was a sequestered and hidden process. The commission's detachment unleashed the staff with the extraordinary latitude to overturn the party's process for presidential nominations and, in time, reshuffle the political system. Commissioners did not approve of these drastic changes but failed, as a group, to challenge or even understand the impact.[70]

The trio of DNC players (Harris, McGovern, and the staff) sidestepped a familiar hurdle to transformation: effective resistance by organizational interests facing diminished power and resources. They disrupted the long-standing presidential nomination process by capitalizing on divisions among party elites and allies and welcoming aspiring presidential candidates to promote it to serve their own political interests.

The Return of the Direct Primary

The commission's adoption of the presidential primary proceeded in three phrases.

Step 1: The commission blitzed national and state party establishments with calls for democratic renewal that summoned Jefferson's and Jackson's indignation and the pointed complaints of La Follette. "The problems encountered in Mayor Daley's city were indicative," the commission charged, of the "sickness" that infected state party operations around the country and routinely produced "delegates [that] are not chosen in a democratic manner."[71]

The path forward, according to the commission report, *Mandate for Reform*, was to return to democratizing internal party operations. The aim, it vowed, was to "strengthen our Party and American democracy" and "regenerat[e] the Democratic Party as a more responsive and dynamic servant of the American people."[72]

The report claimed to channel the New Left's call for "participatory democracy" and the ethos of citizen mobilization embraced by Barbara Mikulski. The commission steered the party's administration of nominations toward embracing the "maximum participation among interested Democrats in the [selection of] National Convention delegates" and creating "popular participation . . . [and] popular control of the Democratic Party." The purpose of this deeper engagement, according to McGovern, was to "assur[e] that the people rather than the bosses select the presidential nominee."[73]

The reform cabal directing the DNC seized on the "tumult of Chicago" to undercut recalcitrant national and state party officials. Failure to "open the door to . . . [participating in] the choice of [the Democratic Party's] presidential nominee," it cautioned, would threaten the party's "survival." Worse still, inaction risked the country's stability by steering "people committed to orderly change" toward the "anti-politics of the street"—that is, the bedlam at the 1968 Democratic convention.[74]

The commission strong-armed state party organizations to comply with its dictates. *Mandate for Reform*, which was approved in November 1969 and implemented in 1970, commanded the "adoption of these Guidelines by all states" and defined its recommendations as "the minimum action [they] *must* take to meet the requirements [to attend] . . . the 1972 Convention" (emphasis added). As part of its process of implementation, the Commission's staff issued 465 "violations" by states along with a checklist of failings and the necessary changes to comply. (Every state was called out for at least six shortcomings, many received far more.) The effect "entirely repudiated over half of all state plans [for delegate selection]."[75]

State Democratic Parties treated the DNC's eighteen guidelines as posing a dire choice: reform or face rejection by the next national convention's Credentials Committee. The intended effect was to preempt state resistance, public scrutiny, and debate that might have stalled reform.[76]

Despite the state acquiescence, the DNC's guidelines were not "binding": McGovern and his staff bypassed the normal authoritative roles of the national party and the next convention. States were herded by the commission's exaggerated claims of sweeping authority to "require" compliance and mete out punishment.

Step 2: Deploying artful deception, the commission's leadership and staff pressed states to change but without insisting on the adoption of specific new mechanisms that might spark a backlash. On the one hand, *Mandate for Reform* took aim at common practices by state parties. It called for the elimination of party caucuses and the "delegate primary" while requiring that the names of presidential candidates be on the ballot. (The delegate primary featured contests among individuals seeking to become a delegate to the national convention; today's primary elections feature the names of the candidates for office, with those winning a certain number of votes securing delegates committed to them.) A longtime state power center—state committees—were limited to controlling only a tenth of the delegations to the national conventions to select presidential nominees.[77]

On the other hand, the commission counted on state and local parties to behave as strategic actors. The state chairs had "more important fish to fry at the state level than they saw for themselves in the squabbles over presidential nominations." Accepting presidential primaries to skirt a potentially costly battle with the DNC was a reasonable trade: the selection of presidential candidates was already nationalized and slipping out of the hands of state party organizations.[78] Without a specific directive, states accepted national presidential primaries to preserve their power over what mattered most to them: control over district and state caucuses and conventions.

The finesse by McGovern and the staff held off resistance from commissioners. Most of its members favored reforms of conventions and caucuses that would expand participation. By not specifically recommending presidential primaries, the artfully crafted commission guidelines traded on the detachment of commissioners and averted opposition.

While the commissioners were oblivious of their own report's recommendations, the staff anticipated that states were likely to choose the presidential primary. Through their work for Hughes during the 1968 nomination contests, the staff was well acquainted with candidate selection mechanisms. Once the commission eliminated the methods that states most widely used to choose delegates, the staff projected that primaries had a strong potential to emerge dominant.[79] What else could the states use that was familiar and available?

Step 3: The adoption of presidential primaries by Democratic state parties rapidly spread across the country, with the Republican Party generally following along after 1972. The GOP was not driven by the elite divisions and ambition that propelled Democrats. Indeed, renegades like the party's 1964 presidential candidate Barry Goldwater found openings. The impetus for the GOP was state laws passed by mostly Democratic legislatures and the lure of media coverage, which favored Democratic candidates battling in the 1972 primary races.[80]

With both parties conducting presidential primaries, the number rose rapidly from fifteen in 1968 to twenty-seven in 1976 and thirty-seven in 1980, where it has hovered a bit higher or lower depending on the competitiveness of presidential nominations. Because of the adoption of primaries to replace party control, the proportion of delegates chosen by primary elections to both party conventions more than doubled—from about 40 percent in 1968 to 94 percent by 2020.[81]

The primary produced a fundamental shift in political power and America's incentive system. The adoption of primaries flipped control over the selection of national convention delegates. Nearly three-quarters were chosen through the state mechanisms of caucuses and conventions in 1968; primaries selected almost three-quarters by 1980. Within a decade of the McGovern-Fraser Commission, the winner of primaries became the presidential nominee. Politicians looking for a successful career in politics took note.

Primaries and Race

The Democratic Party's reforms occurred in the context of expanding rights to vote since World War I and pitched reactions against it. Women won the right to vote with the passage of the Nineteenth Amendment in 1920, nearly doubling the size of the electorate. The determined movement for the rights of African Americans precipitated civil rights legislation and judicial decisions, which created national democratic rules that removed nearly all the formal restrictions on the franchise. As the McGovern-Fraser Commission was issuing its recommendations, the "United States, formally at least, had something very close to universal suffrage."[82]

The clash over recognizing the democratic rights of African Americans was etched into the Democratic Party and became a rare flashpoint on the DNC commission. At the 1968 Chicago convention, southern delegates fought the party's steps to make good on the commitments in 1964 to integrate future delegations, as promised to Fannie Lou Hamer and the Mississippi Freedom Democrats. Georgia's state party chair recoiled at the seating of civil rights leader Julian Bond and an integrated delegation, concluding that the "white conservative vote in the South is not wanted by the present leaders of the Democratic Party." Speaking for a previously segregated white party, James Gray pronounced that "we all feel . . . sore and battled" and have a "score to settle." True to his word, five of the state's most powerful Democratic politicians followed through by leaving the party after the 1968 convention.[83]

Meeting just a year later, the DNC commission became another site of America's dueling racial orders. The guidelines issued by *Mandate for Reform* directed states to send delegations to the national convention that included "minority groups, young people and women in reasonable relationship to their presence in the population of the state."[84]

The commission's commitment to explicit demographic targets and increasing the participation of groups that had been underrepresented precipitated ongoing strife. On the commission, the policies to reverse the Democratic Party's history as a white organization stirred one of the few pointed disputes among commissioners over what would be described as "quotas."[85] This dispute burst into the public eye, with the demographic targets slammed for imposing "reverse discrimination." At the 1972 Democratic National Convention, Chicago mayor Daley exploded at the replacement of fifty-nine Cook County delegates with an alternative slate to meet the new requirements for diversity.[86]

The fracas over race coincided with Barbara Mikulski's jump from neighborhood organizer and Baltimore political newcomer to national politics. Mikulski's 1970 speech in favor of shaking up the Democratic Party brought her national attention and an invitation to serve on, and eventually chair, a new Democratic Party commission in 1973. Its mission: Retreat from the "imposition of mandatory quotas" and fixed quantitative ratios by granting states the flexibility to design plans to "encourage full participation by all Democrats, with particular concern for minority groups . . .women and youth, in delegate selection and in all party affairs." Participation by blacks and women would decline in the next convention, though still stand above prior levels.[87]

The Democratic Party's halting, fractious, and prolonged acceptance of civil rights coincided with a search for an "alternative Democratic coalition." Starting in the early 1970s and continuing for decades, the Party aspired—with uneven results—to build a new political force from the previously marginalized—women, youth, and people of color. The coalition included liberal political organizations—such as Americans for Democratic Action and the National Women's Political Caucus—as well as establishment reformers from inside government.[88]

Political History and Blundering Political Elites

Fred Harris, George McGovern, and their staff succeeded where La Follette failed a half century earlier: establishing presidential primaries nationwide. Keen observers of "protest-induced reformism" credit the reforms to the populism and civil disorder of the 1960s and Chicago's riotous convention.[89] The protests did persuade delegates to the 1968 convention to approve a commission on the nomination process on its last day and supplied a rhetorical arsenal for McGovern. Beyond these influences, though, the tangible impact was limited. The protest account emphasizes the significance of citizen agency, and yet the consequences of the reform to establish primaries curtailed citizen influence by favoring factions and undercutting the participatory democracy that the New Left proposed, as I suggest in the next chapter.[90] Moreover, the 1968 Chicago protests and the later DNC reforms are correlated without a causal connection: neither the records of the commission's decision making nor interviews with commissioners and senior party officials present persuasive evidence that the civil disorder exerted a discernible influence on the tangible decisions.[91]

Elite-level dynamics account for the adoption of primaries. Divisions among Democratic Party elites, fatigue from the taxing presidential nomination battle, and the close loss to Nixon created an opening for reform. Humphrey's withdrawal after the demoralizingly close loss to Nixon and his ill-considered decision to appoint Harris DNC chair ceded power to upend the party organization. Inattentiveness by national and state party officials and organized labor (aided by Harris's strategic ambiguity) removed a potential check that would have previously blocked the transformation. Indeed, Humphrey's stewardship and the veto by the party establishment were anticipated by many delegates at the 1968 convention who nonchalantly approved a commission on nominations.

In the vacuum after the 1968 elections, ambition filled the void created by elite disarray. Harris and McGovern calculated that advocating reform and winning the backing of party liberals would translate into an advantage in a competitive and divided field of presidential candidates in 1972. McGovern did successfully capitalize on the open structure he created to win the 1972 Democratic nomination before losing in a landslide to Richard Nixon. By contrast, Harris's ambition to "build a political career" came to naught; within a short period, "new people replaced him and he was old news in a couple years."[92]

The DNC reformers engineered structural change against the odds, but why did they choose the particular design of a direct primary? Prior accounts of primaries assume that it was a foregone conclusion because of the effectiveness of Progressive reformers in establishing them.[93]

The reality, however, is that La Follette's agenda to establish primaries throughout the country was defeated by Progressive Era opposition. From the perspective of mid-century, the McGovern-Fraser Commission's reform was not a foregone conclusion. If reform occurred, there were options that did not entail eviscerating the Democratic Party organization.[94] For Mondale, parts of the Democratic Party were autocratic, but Harris and McGovern were wrong that "everyone in the Democratic Party were corrupt, backward, and bankrupt." The party organization contained "some of the [country's] best people" who achieved civil rights and other progressive breakthroughs. Sensible reform of the Democratic Party, he suggested, should have focused on strengthening these elements rather than weakening the party's organization.[95]

While the adoption of primaries was not foreordained, the maneuvering by Harris and McGovern for thoroughgoing changes left them searching for feasible options. The institutional patterning since the early nineteenth century set the parameters for reformers when it coincided with crippling elite divisions and soaring political ambition.

Harris and McGovern's makeover of the Democratic Party's nomination process failed to consider the tradition since the Republic's birth of designing institutions to protect democratic representation and restrain elites. Harris and McGovern sought to reinvigorate American democracy without corralling, as Madison and Croly did, elite ambition to serve broader interests. The consequences undermined rather than advanced political equality and popular sovereignty, as we discuss in the next chapter.

PART III

REVIVING AMERICAN DEMOCRACY

The proliferation of primary elections since the 1970s precipitated – in conjunction with other developments – a sharp turn toward instability and hateful polarization. The first priorities to restore democratic resilience are to check irresponsible ambitious politicians and bolster community participation within a system of political representation.

6

The Ills of Primary Elections and Democratic Deformation

How did a country that produced the foundations of mass democracy become its fire pit? Donald Trump is a shrill warning of the fragility of American democracy, but he alone is not the problem. The vulnerability is broader and deeper.

Trump's supporters stormed the Capitol on January 6, 2021, after the president implored them from near the White House to "walk down to the Capitol" with a challenge—"You will never take back our country with weakness." Trump's agitation of the crowd of more than ten thousand added to the provocations of previous speakers: the call for "trial by combat" by his personal lawyer Rudy Giuliani and the threat to disloyal Republican members of Congress that "we're coming for you" from his son Donald Trump Jr.

Centuries of eloquent proclamations about the elevated virtue and responsibility of the governing class were mocked by Trump's defiance of the Constitution and, just as telling, the acquiescence of Republicans in Congress. Even after Trump's supporters invaded the Capitol, 147 Republican senators and representatives followed Trump's instructions and voted not to affirm Biden's Electoral College victory despite the dictates of the Constitution and law.[1]

The repudiation of the law was compounded by the kind of demagoguery that would have alarmed James Madison and other authors of the US Constitution. Trump and congressional Republicans roused their party's loyalists by spewing falsehoods about voter fraud in the 2020 election that were disproven by voter recounts, signature verifications, and the rulings of more than sixty courts (including the US Supreme Court with three Justices nominated by Trump). Seventy percent of Republicans accepted their groundless charges, and Trump's mischief solidified his standing as "far and away [the] top choice" for the GOP's presidential candidate in 2024, years before the election arrives.[2] Following the throng they helped manufacture, Republicans in Congress and in legislative districts turned on GOP lawmakers who voted to affirm Biden's win and called out Trump's conduct. Representative Liz Cheney was targeted with the most public initial retribution: House Republicans stripped her of her leadership post in May 2021. Her response cut through the swirl of misinformation: Trump is intent to "unravel the democracy to come back into power."

The threat to American democracy is not primarily from aberrant individuals, as initially compelling as Trump's and Wallace's messianic personalities may appear. The faulty structures of politics are the root cause.

In the most immediate sense, the robust adoption of primaries in the 1970s is responsible for the rise of Trump despite clear indications—before his nomination—of repudiating American democratic rules, procedures, and norms. The primary equipped Trump to speak to voters on a uniquely visible public platform, clear the barriers to ballot access by having his name placed on state tickets across the country, and secure a major party's label with its legions of loyalists. With the nomination in the hands of primary voters, the Republican Party and its leaders lacked the institutional tools to stop Trump in 2016 or another Trump candidacy if he decides to run for a second term.

Trump was not the first renegade candidate to use primary elections. In 1972, Alabama's racist governor George Wallace was a front-runner for the Democratic Party presidential primary before a would-be assassin sidelined him.[3] He followed a script similar to Trump's. In a crowded field with establishment figures (including Humphrey and Maine senator Edmund Muskie) and candidates favored by party activists (including Shirley Chisholm and McGovern), Wallace's messages stood out for "often teeter[ing] along the razor's edge of violence." Like Trump, he appealed to the grievances of financially vulnerable and politically disaffected white voters. Siding with the "average man," he targeted the media, "pointy-headed intellectuals," and the political establishment, ominously warning the national Democratic Party to "watch out because . . . average citizens are going to run you over" to take "our party back because it belongs to us."[4] Wallace—like Trump—received extensive (free) media coverage for sensational statements and actions. Both were also intensely opposed by nearly all the party leaders; but they were powerless in the primary system to stop them.

Wallace's strident antiestablishment populism won 37 percent of the delegates in eight states; the eventual nominee, George McGovern, won only 19 percent of the delegates in these states. Although the shooting of Wallace pushed him out of the campaign, he stunned the Democratic Party by winning more than 40 percent in five states (Florida and Michigan included), 30 percent in two more, and over 20 percent in two additional states.[5]

Because of its deformed political institutions, America now faces the recurring threat of antiregime presidential candidates. Like wolves in the forest searching for weak prey, ambitious politicians are gearing up to present themselves as "Trump 2.0," and "racial nationalists" are recruiting renegades to reprise the strategy of Trump and Wallace.[6]

Primaries present a dire threat but they are also an expression of more deep-seated and momentous perils. The authority and legitimacy of democracy have eroded to critical levels. Political inequality based on organization and race is now embedded in political structures. Political campaigns aimed at agitating racial resentment are increasingly common and prominent in defining political divisions. Primary elections either gave rise to each of these or augmented already existing impulses. Now, efforts to alter America's calamitous direction face towering obstacles, including a deformed understanding of democracy itself. Heroic narratives of American history, politics, and its "great leaders" collide with a record of actions and developments that endanger American democracy.

This chapter begins by revisiting the previous chapters to identify the barriers to changing the current course of American politics. It then catalogues the damaging consequences of primaries for political polarization, political inequality, entrenched racial disparities, and erosion of democratic authority and legitimacy.

Barriers to Change

American democracy is at risk, yet change is obstructed by three sturdy barriers. The urgency of reform will not, on its own, produce needed reform.

The Construction of an Idea of Democracy

The words of the Declaration of Independence are familiar today but were startling to many in 1776. Its brazen pronouncement that everyday people had rights—including the right to govern themselves—astonished Europeans, where most lived under monarchs and in societies topped by aristocrats. A dozen years later, the French Revolution's Declaration of the Rights of Man and the Citizen modeled itself on the Declaration of Independence and its recognition of equal rights and popular sovereignty.

While leaders of revolutions embraced democratic rights, the ratification of the Constitution commenced the work of integrating values into institutions. Few were as influential as Thomas Jefferson and James Madison in shaping the founding of the republic and expressing unease with the potential of political parties to foment dangerous factions. Yet Jefferson's defeat at the hands of John

Adams in 1796 motivated the pair to reverse course and embrace political parties as their weapon to instigate a "revolution" in mass voting. Expediency eclipsed earlier principle, and Jefferson was rewarded with the White House in 1800.

Andrew Jackson later swaddled himself in Jefferson's legacy by strengthening the mass mobilizing capacity of the political party and extending the influence of "the people" to the selection of presidential candidates. Jefferson's turn to parties and Jackson's move to open up the party nomination process set the parameters for reforms by subsequent ambitious politicians. La Follette and the later duo of Fred Harris and George McGovern, who instigated the wide adoption of presidential primaries starting in 1972, similarly linked democracy with political parties and the responsiveness of its nomination process.

The democracy-nomination formulation continues. Bernie Sanders revived the populist appeal for a "political revolution" that would "protec[t] an American democracy of one person, one vote" and reach the "millions of Americans [who] have become disillusioned with our political process." He aimed his populist fire in 2016 on state Democratic Parties. He ripped the Nevada party that "used its power to prevent a fair and transparent process from taking place." He described New York's closed primary that barred independents and Arizona's long lines as "absurd and undemocratic process[es]" and "an embarrassment to American democracy."[7]

In 2016, Donald Trump used Sanders to amplify his complaints. "I watched Bernie winning [primaries]," he told a Rochester, New York, audience in April 2016. "Then I see, he's got no chance . . . because the system is corrupt and it's worse on the Republican side." The GOP unfairly distributed delegates to Ted Cruz, he complained: "I'm up millions of votes on Cruz [and am only] up by . . . [about two hundred] delegates." He tied these charges of a "fixed" and "corrupt system" to his populist pitch to give "voice" to "the forgotten men and women of America." "We live in a democracy," he charged, but "the system is rigged against our citizens" by "the bosses."[8]

The complaints by Sanders and Trump are the normative by-products of an understanding of democracy that has been constructed over time. The recipe is familiar: Ambitious politicians tie their political prospects to castigating internal party mechanisms as failing to satisfy a peculiar American idea of democracy.

The reality, however, is that primary elections repudiate the seminal democratic standard of political equality. Because participation is limited to the better educated, established, and organized, primary elections obstruct "equal political activity among citizens" and discourage lawmakers from providing "equal consideration of the preferences and interests of all citizens."[9]

The false notion of democracy is a daunting barrier to altering primaries. Reforms to equalize political voice by altering the nomination process perversely face charges of subverting democracy.

Institutional Design and Political Rationality

Over the past half century, Washington political analyst Norm Ornstein pioneered reforms of campaign finance laws and more with both Democrats and Republicans. Yet the January 6 insurrection and prior months of Trump's baseless charges of voter fraud provoked an outburst against reformers in the GOP he had relied upon as responsible problem solvers.[10] Trump, Ornstein pointed out, "benefited greatly as major figures within his party failed to offer a different vision or act to counter his destructive behavior." Instead, responsible Republicans and former collaborators— Senators Bob Corker, Jeff Flake, and Rob Portman—"pull[ed] the plug [on running for re-election] rather than facing a potentially bruising primary . . . to help the GOP revert to a right-of-center, problem-solving party [and stop] . . . a xenophobic cult of personality." Ornstein was particularly disappointed in Portman, who surrendered a career in the executive and legislative branches as a serious statesman on pension reform, global trade, and budget deficits. After not voting for Trump in 2016, Ornstein called him out for "acquiesce[ing] to the president's style and program."[11]

Ornstein's Republican disappointments are products of the primary system and illustrate *three* mutually reinforcing dynamics that cow even those who know better.

The New Brokers of Power

Officeholders follow the policy goals of the new brokers of nomination under threat of punishment. With the weakening of party as a filter to nomination after the 1971 reforms, the political vacuum was quickly filled by a new network of party activists, organized groups, and donors who intensely embraced liberal and, especially, conservative policy demands.[12] New political groupings also developed; the opportunity to exert influence in a receptive political arena along with courting by ambitious candidates enticed advocates—from born-again evangelicals to environmentalists—to become active.[13] "Primary electorates," Gary Jacobson explains, "are much more partisan and prone to ideological extremity."[14]

Candidates, in turn, adjusted to the new rules by embracing the policy demands of the new networks that controlled nominations even though they constitute small minorities within their party and the country. Candidates who were not initially hard-edged partisans or ideological were replaced by more amenable politicians (especially immediately following the DNC reforms) or converted to the policy goals of party activists.[15] Jeff Sessions felt the primary sting. He was a prominent Republican senator who was among the early Trump supporters in 2016 and was rewarded with the position of attorney general, but Trump turned on him when he followed Department of Justice policy by recusing himself from Robert Mueller's investigation of the Trump campaign's possible collusion with Russia. Trump exacted revenge by endorsing Sessions's challenger in the 2020 US Senate primary—political neophyte and football coach Tommy Tuberville—who won by over twenty points before cruising to a similarly large general election victory.

Within this system of incentives, it was rational for formerly principled Republicans to capitulate to Trump's perilous conduct and his loyal following.

In contrast to Trump, Biden ran as a favorite of the party organization and not as a threat. Party factions played a role, however, in both of their nominations.[16] The Democratic nomination featured a sharply drawn conflict between cliques devoted to electability and defeating Trump and those committed to progressive ideological principles. The first three state nomination contests in January and February 2020 were won by the moderate Pete Buttigieg and, most impressively, the Progressive favorite—Bernie Sanders, who thrashed Biden 46.8 percent to 20.2 percent in Nevada on February 22. After Nevada, political observers were harshly critical of Biden's campaign and were preparing to declare his candidacy doomed.

Biden prevailed, however, because of his earlier successes in the "invisible primary" when he built a formidable coalition of activists, former leaders, and influentials in the Democratic Party; large donors from party allies; and a plurality of African American voters. Sanders's support among Progressives and small donors was notable but not enough.[17]

Biden's advantage among party factions registered in the fourth primary on February 29 when he scored a twenty-nine-point win in South Carolina. With this demonstration of his core strength, his competitors among moderates withdrew and the Delawarean settled into a straightforward and winnable contest with Sanders .

The effectiveness of a policy-demanding network has produced a Republican Party that is nearly saturated with conservatives. Voters and officeholders in the Democratic Party have become decidedly more liberal, though differences in its memberships, aims, and institutions are more pronounced than among Republicans.[18] After party activists and their allies used primaries to enforce fealty to their policy demands, successful primary challenges based explicitly on ideology have generally become less common than they were after 1972, though the Tea Party and, more recently, Progressives spurred upticks. The potency of punishment by primary remains because of anticipation of retribution; politicians rarely defy fealty to party activists and their allies.[19]

Defending the Turf

Power brokers of candidate nominations fiercely defend their institutional positions against reform. Party activists denounce any weakening of influence as akin to an unconscionable selling out of party values while interest groups and donors fight to defend their inside track to advancing their policy agendas and securing favorable government regulations and funding. Faced with threats to the survival of their influence in politics, they respond with an intensity that is difficult for reformers to match.

Deploying Democracy to Defend Political Inequality

Elected officials and organized interests defend the primary system as democratic to deflect criticisms or proposed reforms. Righteousness linked to self-interest is a powerful barrier that rallies allies and misleads the casual observer.

In short, the primary system is highly resistant to change. The normative claims about primaries are married to the mutually beneficial interests of the party activists and their allies as well as politicians elected in the current system. While McGovern and Harris wanted to open up Democratic nominations, the effect of the primaries has been to entrench a narrow set of factions and their political loyalists.

The Dangers of Misguided Political Elites

Edmund Burke famously made the case for citizens deferring to elected officials. Talking to his constituents in Bristol, England, in

1774, Burke painted an alluring picture of officeholders who were guided by the "duty" to exercise "mature judgment [and] . . . enlightened conscience . . . [without] sacrific[ing them] to you, to any man, or to any set of men."[20]

Burke's sympathizers trace the failures of American politics to democracy and its violation of his Bristol guidance. Primaries are attributed to the " 'more democracy' illusion" and demands that there is a "democratic imperative to expand opportunities for citizen participation and control."[21]

The reality is quite different, however. Primaries and the ensuing vulnerability of democratic institutions result from the competition and ambition of political elites. Jefferson, Jackson, La Follette, and McGovern each collided with the political establishment and turned to reforming political parties to secure a path to greater power. Their self-serving calculations initiated and reinforced a pattern of reform that loaded the dice for the faction-favoring primaries. They hid their tracks by seizing on populism as a pretext to unsettle the political establishment and mobilize support for them as the vehicle for reform.

Elites ignored or bypassed warnings. Herbert Croly's prescient cautions during the Progressive Era that primaries would proliferate divisive factions and undermine the authority and legitimacy of representative institutions faded with time. McGovern, Harris, and their staff deceived members of their commission and the broader Democratic Party about their intentions to demolish important organizational capacities in order to implement their plans.

Lost was the preoccupation since Madison with designing electoral institutions to reward candidates with "good character" and erect "filters" for candidates hostile to the Constitution and rule of law. Progressive Era critics warned precisely that primaries invited "pestiferous demagogues" and "brazen-faced men of a lower type of character" who relied on false and divisive public appeals.[22] The skill set to win presidential nomination via a primary—strident public appeals and a knack for cutting deals with factions—replaced the older pattern of showcasing good character and building support in state and national networks.

As predicted, the primary opened the door to antiregime candidates. Wallace was the first. Trump was the most effective, exploiting the communicative power of the presidency to project the most disruptive messages of any predecessor. Trump's approach bares a haunting resemblance to European right-wing authoritarian populists like Hungarian prime minister Viktor Orban, who took advantage of economic insecurity, demographic change, and immigration to rally supporters against democratic institutions.[23]

The survival of American democracy may depend on urgent reforms, and yet the primary system creates daunting obstacles. Worse, the consequences of primaries have made these barriers still higher.

The Consequences of Primaries

The Democratic Party's commission to examine party nominations produced the "reconstitution of the total matrix of institutions for presidential nomination in the national Democratic party."[24] The "revolution" of political party nominations contributed to five extraordinary consequences. The presidential primaries that McGovern launched were rarely the single and direct "cause" of these complex and multifaceted components of contemporary America. But they opened a path for their development by both weakening the filter of party organization that previously dampened them and motivating politicians and groups to exploit new opportunities.

Enabling Partisan Polarization

Today's extraordinary partisan polarization is a by-product of the direct primary along with the emergence in the 1960s and 1970s of salient civil rights issues. Of course, the polarization of American politics is not a simple story with one explanation.[25]

Primaries Inserted Civil Rights into Nomination Contests

The widespread adoption of primaries starting in 1972 coincided with the arrival of new issues, disagreements, and cleavages. Congressional Republicans were decisive supporters of civil rights legislation in the 1960s, but the leadership of Presidents Kennedy and Johnson and subsequent partisan division on implementing the new laws imprinted the Democratic Party as the primary champion of racial justice and prompted voters (especially in the South) to reconsider their mainly inherited partisan devotions.[26]

Primaries created a new forum where political activists, organized groups, and donors were able to insert the new issues and divisions at the center of candidate competition for nomination to a degree that was not typically possible when political bosses controlled the nominations.[27] The issues of race along with social and religious concerns became increasingly aligned with visible left-right thinking and partisan divisions among politicians and, in time, the electorate. Over a period of time, the interplay of primaries, advocates of liberal or conservative policies, and ambitious candidates for the presidency and Congress had a momentous impact: consistent ideological polarization across economic, social, and racial policies replaced shifting differences on a few issues as was the case in the past.[28] Public opinion surveys show that individuals with conservative attitudes toward social welfare policy (think: Obamacare), race, and cultural issues such as abortion now reliably affiliate with the Republican Party. Americans with liberal views on these issues have become the core of the Democratic Party.[29]

The sorting of political parties based on ideology changed voting patterns. Most states in the South and near South elected conservative Democrats into the 1960s; now they are Republican strongholds, though the 2021 Democratic Senate wins in Georgia may suggest change. States in the North that elected moderate and liberal Republicans in the past are increasingly Democratic.[30] Exit polls on Election Day routinely reveal that nine out of ten Democrats and Republicans vote for the party with which they identify.

Two profound shifts have occurred during the past half century. Each political party became more internally unified. The liberal Republicans of the 1960s—like New York's Jacob Javits—are gone, and conservative Democrats have mostly faded as well. As this ideological cleansing occurred, both major political parties diverged from the other, becoming more polarized than at any point in the past.[31]

Empirical Research Confirms the Impact of Primaries

My research with Penny Thomas and Ling Zhu examined the empirical impact of presidential primaries on the ideological polarization of presidents.[32] Studying the period 1952 to 2000, we found that the increasing numbers of primaries produced immediate and continuing effects on presidential polarization in the years following the McGovern-Fraser recommendations in 1971.[33]

The pattern of presidential candidates moving further apart on policy after the robust adoption of primary elections in 1972 did not exist before the McGovern-Fraser Commission's recommendations.[34] In the period 1952 to 1968, presidential primaries had no statistically significant impact on polarization.

Our findings suggest, then, that primary voters are pulling candidates to the left and, especially, the right. Frequently studied additional influences on polarization failed to consistently matter.[35]

Two Puzzles

Two riddles are posed by the primary-fostered polarization of elected officials.

Riddle #1. Why aren't voters tossing out officeholders who are more liberal and conservative and rejecting the choices presented by party activists? Most Americans hold comparatively moderate attitudes toward policy issues and governing. For instance, everyday Americans (including Democrats and Republicans) favor what activists detest: compromise. This was evident during the first few years of the Trump presidency: Republicans used their majorities in the US House to pass bills that repealed Obamacare and aimed to restrict funding for Planned Parenthood, while most Americans favored more moderate positions.[36] Fifty-eight percent of Americans preferred politicians who compromised rather than rigidly held to their ideological positions.[37]

Riddle #2. Americans favor moderate attitudes toward government policies like health reform, but they are hostile and distrustful of individuals in rival political parties. Why are Americans agreeable on policy issues and furious at rival partisans? And, no, Donald Trump is not the original cause; rancor preceded him, though he fanned it.

The bonding of voters to political parties is the key to answering these riddles.

Let's start with Riddle #1. Voters are not removing extremists from office because they have sorted into loyal partisan teams. Instead of the older hodgepodge of liberal and conservative ideologies and split-ticket voting, liberals more consistently reside within the Democratic Party and conservatives in the GOP than half a century ago.[38]

Primaries facilitate the odd pairing of partisan polarization and public moderation. Party activists and their allies (especially in the GOP) use their control over nominations to put polarized choices in front of voters during the fall campaign even though the mass of voters is moderate and in agreement on broad policy goals.

Unpacking Riddle #2 brings us to a series of fundamental questions: Who are we, what do we believe, and who is in our group?

The center-stage gladiator match between political parties cements their dominance as a political identity.[39] Saying, "I am a Republican," tells you what policies I likely favor as well as how I define myself and the world in which I live. As our parties polarized and Americans are fed a steady diet of Joe Biden squaring off against Republican leaders or Donald Trump pitted against Democrats, our political identities have increasingly diverged at a deep level—it now defines our psychological makeups and generates feelings of intense dislike.[40] Racial resentment by GOP loyalists—fed by Trump's "white protectionism"—intensified these shifts and racialized the partisan polarization.[41]

Primaries are the psychological equivalent of Friday-night booster events for the home team. Presentations by primary candidates articulate variations on common themes and activate emotional connections to their party, despite disconnects on policy. The in-group experience that contributes to the social polarization of political identity is rewiring our judgments, behavior, and emotions. The result: Psychological and emotional loyalty to party resembles the devotion and, at times, fanaticism of sports fans for their team and against opposing teams.

Reinforcing Political Inequality

For generations, America embraced the principles of political equality and popular consent even as it denied these rights to slaves as well as Americans of color and women. Congress and the courts since the 1960s have nearly swept away formal restrictions on citizenship rights, but primary elections sustains racial and economic disparities.

Inviting the Practice and Mindset of Factions

The institutional form of primaries is hostile to the practice and understanding of political equality and popular consent. It instills among elected officials and citizens the "narrow or group-interest" mindset of faction instead of the embrace of the common good that John Rawls envisions.[42] The language and maneuvering integral to primaries are constrictive rather than expansive. The result: Politicians, observers, and the media conceive of the American electorate as sliced into narrow "lanes" in order to win the support of competing segments of party activists, groups, and donors. As government officials adopt this standpoint, Rawls warns, they openly skew their attention to the factions that control their renomination.

Talk of shared interests, values, and principles are uncommon, and action based on them rarer. Everyday citizens and the unorganized struggle to find themselves in a conglomeration of squabbling factions.

In addition to cultivating a factional mindset, primary elections enable, reinforce, and heighten the "organization of bias" that has long favored the organized and well-resourced.[43] Turnout is low, typically a half or less of general election participation. As a result, party activists and the most loyal partisans are overrepresented in primary elections. The impact of factions in primaries is further amplified by organized groups and donors who devote money and resources to capitalize on the opportunity to steer Democratic and Republican nominations.

What has the practice and mentality associated with primary elections meant for the government's attention to citizens? In the decades after the Second World War, the Democratic and Republican Parties competed to respond to the policy preferences of the majority. Ambitious politicians appreciated that advancing their careers depended on pleasing the "median voter" at the midpoint of public opinion and party leaders who focused on winning elections.[44] The result was that both parties gravitated toward agreement on salient policies from expanding New Deal programs like Social Security, protecting the environment (hat tip to Richard Nixon for historic steps on both), and bolstering national security (hat tip to the Carter/Mondale administration for pioneering stealth technology and cruise missiles).

As primaries disciplined ambitious politicians, their policies often responded to party activists and their allies rather than median voters. This has contributed to persistent gaps between government policy and the preferences of citizens.[45] Everyday citizens exert little or no impact on the decisions of presidents and members of Congress. Not surprisingly, fifty-six percent of Americans in a 2021 Pew Recent Center study reported that elected officials do not care what ordinary people think compared to 32 percent in Germany.[46]

Donald Trump simultaneously fanned public distrust and favored insiders. He hyped Washington as an unresponsive "swamp" and the American system of representation as "not democracy" but "a rigged . . . [and] very unfair system."[47] As if to prove his point, he closed deals among Republican and conservative factions to cut taxes to benefit corporations and the best off and attempted to repeal health coverage from the uninsured and inadequately insured and strip protections for Americans with severe health conditions. Lopsided majorities of Americans opposed these and other policies. Only 30 percent or so expressed support for the tax cuts, and two-thirds or so opposed the Trump administration's attempt to strip protections against preexisting conditions.

Deceiving Swing Voters

A relatively small number of independent-minded voters may tip control of Congress or the presidency. Skillful politicos turn to several tactics to simultaneously abide by the agendas of party activists, groups, and donors while still appealing to the decisive set of swing voters. Presidents and members of Congress work hard to disguise decisions that are at odds with what most Americans prefer by relying on the complexity and obscurity of the legislative process and government policy.[48] Congressional leaders are magicians in engineering votes that leave no fingerprints to trace to unpopular decisions. President Trump, for instance, struck at one of the most popular features of Obamacare—prohibiting insurers from denying coverage due to preexisting medical conditions—through a relatively obscure Justice Department legal filing.

Another tactic of deception: Politicos under the direction of cold-blooded and highly paid political consultants use polls and other methods to identify words, arguments, and symbols that simulate the (false) appearance of responsiveness.[49] In the run-up to the 2020 elections, Trump increased his support among voters of color compared to 2016 after modulating his attacks on Latinos and accenting Biden's authoring of the 1994 crime bill that added to the mass incarceration of African Americans.[50] Presidential use of public opinion surveys started long before Trump. Richard Nixon conducted "image studies" to analyze voter perceptions of him and tested—along with Reagan—the popularity of competing presentations of administration policy. White House message testing led, for instance, to Reagan's description of his expansion of US nuclear weapons as "peacekeeper missiles." Barack Obama promoted the passage of health reform with a promise that polled well but was not feasible: "If you like your health care plan, you can keep it."[51]

Bottom line: The empowering of narrow factions with enormous power has motivated politicians to turn to deception as a routine matter. Primaries are not solely driving American politics but they created a new institutional environment that favored the growth of new interests, political activists, and issues supported by insiders, stakeholders, and narrow factions.

Diverting Democracy

The passionate denunciations of elite corruption from Jackson and La Follette to McGovern were twinned with promises to tame political parties by lashing party nominations to a labyrinth of rules and legal mandates. This administrative impulse is not unique. It fits a familiar American pattern in the responses of reformers to the concentrations of economic power during the Progressive Era, market breakdowns during the Great Depression, and the Great

Society's attention to inadequate education, illness, inaccessible medical care, and more.[52]

The Democratic and Republican Parties now routinely issue decrees that spawn—along with court rulings—elaborate, often arcane strictures that route disputes over candidacies and policies into debates over internal practices. The corralling of political participation into highly structured and elaborate processes has three effects. First, the "smart" political strategy calibrates the investment of money and candidate time and messages to serve the short-term objective of winning a fast-approaching election. The outcome is familiar: campaigns are laser-focused on a discrete pool of frequent voters, groups, and donors who already share viewpoints and interests and have the highest probability of lending support. Online communications have accelerated selective short-term mobilization.

As primary elections concentrated political engagement among a relatively small number of activists and voters, Democratic and Republican candidates calculated that it was a rational allocation of limited resources to underinvest in politically disaffected or intermittently engaged citizens who sit out elections. The flip side is the calculations of elected officeholders. Catering to the activists and voters who frequently participate is worthwhile. Attending to the interests and preferences of infrequent voters receives attention but is considered an "unwise" target for large investments.[53]

Second, US primaries focus political energy, as no other democratic country does, on year-long intraparty contests that magnify comparatively minor intraparty differences in contrast to the momentous divide between parties. By comparison, intraparty disputes are important in European political parties but take a back seat to the competition over broad themes between distinct parties. With a focus on interparty disputes, organizations of mass-oriented political parties and trade unions mobilize everyday citizens, including people who might otherwise be inactive.[54] Rather than the selective mobilizing that takes place in America, European parties encompass a broader range of interests.

Third, the eighteen-month process of quietly recruiting staff, donors, and party activists followed by the grueling six-month primary season consumes massive organizational and financial resources that might otherwise be available for organizing citizens and encompassing associations. Bernie Sanders ran in the 2016 and 2020 Democratic primaries as a proponent of revolution to inspire activism among long-marginalized groups. But his campaigns and the $228 million he raised in 2016 and $211 million in 2020 were siloed toward the inner workings of the Democratic Party.[55] Building a broad, encompassing organization of citizens—including many who were disaffected—was not a priority because Sanders's fight for power was channeled within the narrow confines of primary battles rather than sustained community organizing.

Primaries channel political participation into the inner administrative processes of political parties. Primaries divert resources and political focus from organizing citizens, including the disaffected, which we flag in the next chapter as valuable to restoring American democracy.

The Direct Primary and Reconstituting Racial Orders

America's celebration of Jefferson and Jackson for creating democratic revolutions is tainted by their complicity with the subordination of women as well as the enslaving, murdering, and oppression of African Americans and Native Americans. This contradiction is rooted in the contending racial orders of white supremacy and egalitarianism.[56]

The battle of Jeffersonian ideals against white supremacy continued with the introduction of primary elections. Bruce Cain attributes the advent of the primary with "expand[ing] citizen democratic opportunities."[57] While that was La Follette's stated aim, the "white primaries" diminished the democratic rights of southern blacks by protecting Jim Crow segregation until the mid-twentieth century. The persistence of explicit racism in the Democratic Party's nomination process produced the exclusion of Freedom Democrats in 1964 from the Democratic convention in Atlantic City in favor of Mississippi's all-white delegation.

Yet as the formal apparatus of white supremacy was pulled down by Supreme Court rulings and civil rights legislation, primary elections created a unique platform to transmit messages of white antagonism to tens of millions.[58] George Wallace used the primary to spew his racialized populism, and Trump employed it to stoke racial resentment by denigrating Mexicans as "drug dealers, criminals, rapists" as well as demeaning other people of color.[59] The primary gave Trump and Wallace the singular opportunity to reach tens of millions of voters with their messages and gain access to the ballot with the incomparable political payoff associated with a major party's label.

"Descriptive representation" has increased, but the election of black candidates remains partial. Because of racially polarized voting, the preponderance of African American legislators were elected from majority-minority districts.[60] In the South, majority-minority districts accounted in 2015 for 95 percent of all southern statehouse seats held by African Americans, 96 percent of state senator positions, and all of the seats in the US House of Representatives. An only slightly less stark pattern is evident outside the South. The representation of Latinos from majority-minority districts largely mirrors that of African Americans.

The elections of candidates of color have increased with partisan polarization in which whites disproportionately vote for Republicans and people of color for Democrats. Since 2010, racially polarized voting has contributed to the increased election of minority candidates in districts where 40 percent to 50 percent of the electorate are voters of color.[61] Outside majority-minority districts, candidates of color have only limited success winning white-majority districts.[62]

The depressed representation of African Americans is not due to a lack of interest. African Americans are more likely to consider themselves qualified for office and consider a run for office than whites.[63]

The convoluted primary process contributes to the underrepresentation of voters of color. It puts a premium on recruitment, fundraising, and the power to clear out rivals. These practical limitations on candidates who are black, indigenous, and people of color favor white politicians and depresseddiverse political representation. Only 7 percent of US House primary elections included an African American candidate between 1994 and 2004.[64]

The proliferation of factions is a factor in the underrepresentation of people of color.[65] Even in majority-minority districts, African American candidates lose when the primary splits voters of color and white candidates are advantaged with superior organizational and financial resources.[66] Without the organizational and financial resources to build effective political institutions, communities of color struggle to narrow the number of black candidates and prevent dilution of the black vote for African American candidates.

Primaries not only invite voters of color to split their vote, but they also help whites avoid the same predicament. In some southern states, primaries use runoff elections when no candidate receives the majority of votes. While lacking the white primary's explicit racist intent, the runoff election has the effect of allowing white voters to coalesce behind a white candidate when a candidate of color has done well in the primary.[67]

The tendency of primaries to proliferate factions has the effect of politically isolating black candidates and voters. The process segments candidates of color based on race, obscures their nonracial status as citizen, and interferes with evaluations of skills, experiences, and accomplishments that white voters consider when choosing among white candidates.

Barbara Mikulski's iconic 1970 speech that spotlighted the plight of white ethnic Americans also called for "an alliance of white and black." This soaring promise proved difficult as the electorate was factionalized and white candidates were advantaged by their racial identity as well as financial and organizational resources.

Depleted Democratic Institutions

James Madison engineered the Constitutional Convention in 1787 to establish the authority and legitimacy of government— including representative institutions. Madison's double-sided strategy—control the direct expression of political equality that erupted in the 1780s and lay a foundation for representative rules and procedures—was extended by Jackson's political strategist Martin Van Buren, who anchored representative institutions in the political party nomination process in the 1830s.

The authority and legitimacy of representative institutions that Madison and others nurtured is now threatened by the primary system and the political dynamics it invites.

Eroding Consent of the Governed

Madison listed "enabl[ing] the government to control the governed" as the first challenge of the new republic. He and his colleagues calculated that they could induce the consent of citizens through their belief in the fairness of elections and the legitimacy of transferring power according to a system of representation.

America's belief in the founding principles of democracy—political equality and popular consent—are fraying. Following Trump's term, two-thirds of Americans describe politicians as corrupt. This scathing assessment is extraordinary among democratic countries: it registered in the 20 percent to 40 percent range in France, Germany, and the United Kingdom.[68] Democracy is similarly disdained. Fifty-three percent of Americans are not satisfied with democracy's operations compared to 45 percent in France, 38 percent in the United Kingdom (after the contentious departure from the European Union), and 20 percent in Germany.[69] The dismal view of American democracy does not appear to be fading quickly. Half a year after Trump's departure, two thirds described it as "threatened" rather than secure.[70]

Partisanship fuels American distrust in the political system, producing a seesawing of political trust as control of the White House shifted. Sixty-six percent of Republicans expressed political trust in 2017 after Trump's victory, compared to 49 percent following the 2020 election; Democrats swung in the opposite direction from 42 percent in 2017 to 59 percent after Biden's win.[71]

This erosion is neither new, nor are its sources singularly tied to primaries. Nonetheless, primaries intensify real-world conflicts, partisan polarization, and other such trends by creating a platform to blitz Americans with reports of corruption, rigged elections, and unequal treatment. Primaries invite cycles of recrimination in which candidates lacerate the process for its lack of democracy. Sanders and, more so, Trump savaged the party primaries as corrupt. A reform that was intended to promote democracy is now habitually flogged for its absence.

Trust in democratic institutions and their authority to conduct elections fairly have lost their footing as a foundational element of America's civic culture. With primaries sharpening the edge of partisans, elections are now seen as rigged instead of neutral and trusted processes. During Trump's term in office, political trust in the fairness of elections seesawed as control of the White House changed: in the period from fall 2019 to August 2020, 67 percent up to over 80 percent of Republicans expressed confidence that votes would be counted correctly in the 2020 election. Two months after Biden's inauguration, however, Republican confidence in the correct counting of ballots for the next election fell to 36 percent. Seventy-two percent of Trump voters concluded that there was enough fraud to change the outcome. By contrast, the pattern flipped for Democrats, with confidence in vote counting jumping thirteen points from fall 2019 to March 2021.[72]

Fraying Restraints on Political Elites

Madison's knowledge of the experiences of states after 1776 and world history left him alert to the "violence of faction," demagogues skilled at exploiting divisions, and the risks that fractious colonists might resist the peaceful transfer of power. The Constitution's response, in part, was to specify rules and procedures for deciding elections to facilitate the peaceful transition of power.[73] George Washington left office in 1796 troubled that the "baneful effects" of factions could "burs[t] into a flame." One of the surprises of early American history, however, was the taking hold of regular transitions following the peaceful (though bitter) departure of John Adams after losing his rematch with Jefferson in 1801. Subsequent generations accepted the peaceful transfer of power and built candidate nomination processes that filtered out demagogues who might defy this tradition.

Primaries have bypassed the check on the advancement of candidates who shun the Constitution and rule of law. The result is that Republican leaders were powerless to bar Trump from joining televised debates that projected his message to many millions, gaining access to primary ballots, and securing the nomination. Primaries stripped them of the institutional position to stop Trump and his disdain for the Constitution and rule of law.

Trump's threat to the peaceful transfer of power was a veritable checklist of Madisonian horrors. His fomenting of racial antagonism and demagoguing of election fraud whipped Republicans into a modern-day mob to support his challenges to democratic institutions by bending the rules and acting outside the law.[74] He used this following to breach the much-touted system of checks and balances by corrupting Republican lawmakers to fall in line. Party loyalty became a covenant that produced support for Trump's mutinous actions.[75]

American Narrowing and European Broadening

America's reliance on primaries is exceptional. While more countries and parties use primary elections, the scope and influence of the primary in the United States stands out.[76] The comparatively peripheral role of primaries abroad is reflected in its status as a party decision and not as legally binding.

The US reliance on primaries reflects broader differences in the nature of political conflict. Where the US primary channels political conflict *within* each political party, the structure of European political party competition focuses on broad disputes *between* distinct parties.[77] The orientation to inter- rather than intraparty struggles put a premium on the encompassing organizations of mass-oriented political parties and trade unions to mobilize everyday citizens, including those who might otherwise be inactive. By contrast, the primary rewards factions and narrowly based political groupings. The result in the United States is that the "mobilization to politics is more likely to bring in people who would otherwise be active, not those who would be otherwise inactive."[78]

America's Loss

Where is America's much praised civic culture, anchored in acceptance of the Constitution and the rule of law? The January 6 insurrection and support for a renegade president who encouraged it are glaring signs that polarization and the rising fury over political inequality, racial disparities, and political distrust pose a dire threat to American democracy. America's much vaunted system of checks and balances lays in shambles.

How can the clear and present danger to American democracy be fought off?

7

Renewing American Democracy and Restraining Political Elites

Preserving American democracy depends on a fundamental rethinking of political representation. The old idea is that elected officials beneficently "speak for" citizens and that citizens should defer to them.[1] A new and disturbing conclusion is unavoidable: the record of America's governing elite is scarred by avoidable mishaps and the instigating of insurrection.

If American democracy is going to better approach its founding principles of political equality and popular consent, we need to revitalize citizens and reorient elite competition to restrain ambition and reward service to the common good. Restraining elites to check their abuse does not preclude their essential role in the democratic governance of complex societies. Busy work and private lives distract citizens from following many public issues, investing in skillful consultation and negotiations in a diverse society, and participating in public decision making that requires intensive preparation. At a practical level, political representation relies on accountable "doers" who act. This requires divisions of labor, delegations of authority, and professional specialists with technical expertise to inform authoritative decision makers and citizens. Experts are also an important source of innovative policy proposals and evaluations of government policies to identify their effectiveness.[2]

Moving toward a well-functioning representative democracy requires fortifying its formal rules and procedures and designing institutional reforms to invite and then channel "strategic action by elites" that enhances political equality.[3] Equal political participation by citizens is a starting point for revitalizing American democracy: political activity through voting, community organizing, and speech is what governing elites observe. With properly designed institutions, equal activity fuses the motivations of elected officials with responsiveness to broad publics.[4]

This chapter identifies the strains and breakdowns in the current political system that create opportunities to stabilize and invigorate American democracy. It begins by linking reform strategies to political and institutional constraints. It then identifies two imperatives for a strategically guided effort at reform—restraining elites and designing in broader and more inclusive and organized citizen participation.

Thinking Strategically about Reform

The threats to American democracy and the thirst for renewal have generated a plethora of reform proposals.[5] While many are thoughtful and well meaning, some of the proposals are ineffective, or worse, contribute to political inequality. We need strategically conceived reforms that strengthen political representation as a fundamental component of democracy, restrain governing elites, and cultivate political equality.[6]

Get Real

Revitalizing American democracy by turning the clock back to an earlier period or adopting alluring but risky efforts at transformation is neither feasible nor advisable.

Protecting Turf

The institutional pattern of primaries to select nominations defines the expectations, operations, and power of government officials, party activists, organized groups, and donors. Each one will intensely oppose efforts at transformational change as threats to its institutional position and power.

Even reforms of the organizational biases of primaries face an uphill climb against America's misconceived notion of democracy—one that fosters political inequality and unresponsiveness. It is indicative of the faded legitimacy of American democracy that 73 percent agree that it was important for the national government to allow citizens to vote directly to decide key issues in place of legislators. This exceeds the sentiment in the largest Western European countries and reflects a Don Quixote syndrome—the enduring wish since the Declaration of Independence for thoroughgoing and never obtainable power by the people.

America's Quixotic pursuit of real democracy is on full display in the headlong rush to transform elections by adopting rank choice voting (RCV), which allows citizens to rank multiple candidates until the weakest are removed, their votes reassigned, and a majority-winner declared. It is attractive for eliminating primaries and fostering civility among candidates to avoid losing support from voters whose most preferred candidate is eliminated. As in the past, however, the enthusiasm for RCV may unintentionally further degrade American democracy by elevating political inequality. My research with Joanne Miller suggests that RCV in the 2013 elections in Minneapolis produced a pattern of higher political participation by those with higher income and education. This pattern is familiar to scholars of citizen political participation.[7]

Promising Approaches to Reform

A long line of political observers and academics has conducted a kind of parlor game of imagining epic reforms to cure the ills of American democracy. The election—and near-election—of presidents who lose the popular vote has led to generations of proposals to scrap the US Constitution's provision for an Electoral College.[8] Democrats and their allies have pressed to revisit the Constitution to "correct" its allotment of two senators to each state. Their grievance: Republicans wield outsized power by prevailing in small states.[9] Given the dense network of formidable opponents of change, the prospects of rewriting the Constitution are dim. Change is possible, but it must be strategically attuned to institutional patterns and organized constraints.

Reforms that tilt toward elite checking and equal voice will be most effective if they are designed to begin small to get started without provoking intense resistance. This will require both resources (money and organizational capacity for political engagement) and a new conception of democracy as engaging broad—rather than narrow—constituencies. Another key strategic objective is activating well-organized supporters across America's federated structures down to the community level. The history of democratic reform counsels modesty and patience instead of grandiosity and appreciation for "short-term half-way steps that can divide opponents enough to get policy balls rolling in new directions."[10] This pragmatic approach differs from the naïve Mugwump tradition of reformers who latch onto apolitical, idealized models in which power inequalities disappear and "the people" prevail.

The Opportunities of Elite Divisions and Citizen Renewal

The potential for strategically tailored reform exists. The history of democracy is one of conflict over political equality and democratic institutions as established arrangements collide with new forces, interests, and identities. The fight for voters by rival political factions has, at certain junctures, activated otherwise submerged conflicts, boosted citizen awareness of their stakes, lifted participation, and reconfigured the terms of elite competition.

Following Barack Obama's 2012 reelection, the Republican Party conducted an "autopsy" to explain its loss of the popular vote in five of the last six presidential elections—a streak that Trump extended to seven of the last eight contests. The sober party report traced its minority status to catering to its core constituencies and its failure to be "inclusive and welcoming" to women and Hispanics in order to "broade[n] the base of the Party and invit[e] as many voters as possible."[11]

The demographics change and reshuffled electoral constituencies have continued. Fifty-five percent of the white vote propelled Ronald Reagan to a landslide in 1980 but sent Mitt Romney to a decisive loss to Barack Obama. This shifting outcome is tied to the sharply declining proportion of the electorate that is white: it fell from nearly 90 percent in 1980 to 74 percent in 2008 and 67 percent in the 2020 presidential election. The rapid demographic change was starkly evident in the 2021 Georgia US Senate special election: In the heart of the Old South, Rev. Raphael Warnock won with 29 percent of the white electorate and 85 percent of the non-white vote.

The rising prominence of voters of color both presses against forms of political inequality (including primaries) and agitates white voters unnerved by change and provoked by politicians. The rush by Republican-controlled legislatures after the 2020 election to enact new voter restrictions repeats a recurring reactionary response, as does the resistance and conflict. Egalitarian change triggers the ideologies and practices associated with America's white supremacist order.[12]

Demography alone is unlikely to produce transformation.[13] Even with Trump's deeply set racial nationalism, he adjusted his 2020 presidential campaign to compete more effectively in 2020 than 2016 for Latino voters and African Americans. He increased his support among Latinos by eight points and blacks by seven points compared to 2016. In addition, congressional Republican candidates flipped several Democratic seats with the support of these constituencies.

Nonetheless, Democrats continue to enjoy large majority support from the fastest-growing segments of the electorate—Latinos (accounting for 52 percent of population growth from 2010 to 2019) and Asians, who nearly doubled in size in the 2010–2019 period. In addition, the national and state Republican strategy of erecting barriers that disproportionately hinder voters of color instigates voters of color, defying the GOP autopsy's recommendation. This is a dubious strategy in the face of significant voting rights laws (even after recent Supreme Court decisions) and a phalanx of organizations and donors that will turn out voters of color and go to court to overturn these laws.[14]

Political turbulence and change create opportunity. While most Americans are anchored by partisan loyalty, there is a broader unease. After a year that featured extraordinarily visceral racial tensions and President Trump's ungrounded charges of voter fraud, 65 percent of Americans report that the political system needs dramatic change, compared to 47 percent in the United Kingdom and 39 percent in Germany.[15]

The challenge for reformers seeking to restrain elites and foster political equality and popular consent is to navigate the strong inertial elements in American politics while exploiting the cracks in political coalitions and changing electoral constituencies.

Reforms to Restrain Elites

"In framing a government which is to be administered by men over men," James Madison counseled in 1788, "the great difficulty lies in this: you must first enable the government to control the governed; and in the next place oblige it to control itself."[16] American commentators since the eighteenth century have been preoccupied by fear of popular revolt, and yet it was Donald Trump—not agrarian populists, the protesters at the violent 1968 Chicago convention, or mourners of George Floyd—who bear responsibility for the storming of the US Capitol and incendiary demagoguery to overthrow the authority and legitimacy of democratic institutions.

Insufficient attention has been given to the second part of Madison's counsel: controlling governing elites.[17] Madison's warning from two centuries ago rings loud today: "Men of factious tempers . . . or of sinister designs, may [gain power] . . . and then betray the interests, of the people."[18] The Constitution's checks and balances have deadlocked Congress, but presidents now wield enormous unilateral powers to act, manipulate citizens, and cower their partisans in Congress.[19] The first step toward rejuvenating political representation is to mitigate the threat of governing elites.

Defending the Formal Rules and Procedures of Political Representation

The attacks on New York and the Pentagon on September 11, 2001, precipitated unilateral actions by President George W. Bush to conduct spying, torture, permanent detentions (including of US citizens), and more. By 2008, many of President Bush's policies were blunted. The source: a defense of the Constitution and law by lawyers and a panoply of civic organizations from advocates of civil liberties to humanitarian activists and religious groups. "The rule of law, seemingly so vulnerable in the [immediate aftermath of the 9/11 attacks], proved far more resilient," David Cole reports, because of the "loosely coordinated political actions of concerned individuals and groups . . . that took up the task of defending liberty [and the law]." "President Bush [who] . . . initially rejected the constraints of law . . . was forced to [retreat]" after citizens rose up intent on defending America's formal rules and procedures.[20]

A similar civic mobilization to defend the procedures and laws of fair elections is emerging and necessary. Under the frightful shadow of a pandemic that threatened the 2020 elections, tens of thousands of citizens volunteered as poll workers. When President Trump challenged Joe Biden's victories, the elaborate legal doctrine on elections was joined by a broad network of democracy advocates as well as campaign supporters.

Previously faceless election officials became the visible bulwark of the rigorous conducting of the elections and then the recounting of votes and verification of signatures. Prominent election administrators—such as Georgia's secretary of state Brad Raffensperger—set aside their partisan affiliations and preference for Trump to follow the law and established administrative procedure.

My team at the University of Minnesota started in 2009 to work with frontline election officials to support and advance the professionalization of election administration. The Certificate in Election Administration now offers the country's first full online curriculum for current election officials around the country who are seeking new skills as well as students interested in entering the profession.[21] The courses are taught by experienced, non-partisan, and admired leaders in election administration and train students in election law as well as best practices in administrative procedures, data management, and election security. As waves of students move through the program, it is adding to the dissemination of common concepts and standards of practice and offering an alternative to the ad hoc, word-of-mouth practices in some states. The national professionalization of elections meshes the federated structure of political representation with the growing administrative capacity of local, state, and national jurisdictions.

Election officials are the frontline defenders of democratic institutions, and 2020 demonstrated that civic groups and the judiciary count on them to be the trusted workers of democracy.

Defending democracy requires investment in the infrastructure of elections and protecting its formal rules and procedures.

Restoring Political Parties as Representative Institutions

Andrew Jackson and his strategist Martin Van Buren redefined political parties as integral to political representation and the filtering of public views in the selection of presidential candidates with appropriate character. Croly and other Progressive Era critics of La Follette similarly defended the party as a core component of the representative process.

It is time to disrupt the party's modern use as a pass-through for the factious preferences of activists, groups, and donors. Instead, we need to restore the representative function of political parties. This entails returning power in some form to party officials and allies who are focused on winning the support of majorities and mobilizing a broader spectrum of Americans, including marginalized groups.

Turning to political parties to revive democracy faces two challenges. First, surprisingly little new thinking has been devoted to designing new reforms of political party structures to advance political equality. The paucity of serious practical thinking about political parties as an integral institution of political representation extends even to those who emphasize the importance of democratic rules and procedures.[22] Second, antipathy to political parties is one of the constants in American political history. The imperfections of political parties are real and yet pale in comparison to the dire threats to democracy. The political party is an instrument for creating a "system of political control" that channels competition among candidates toward responding to majorities and filters out candidates that would undermine the Constitution.[23] Today's imperative is to equip the next set of party leaders to do what Republicans were unable in 2016: block the nomination of Donald Trump. Several party reforms can contribute to restoring political representation.

Fewer and More Important Elections

We have an election problem. Americans are called upon to enter the ballot box to elect 519,682 officials for national, state, and local offices—from president to township posts and school districts.[24] Primaries are a multiplier, inflating the number of elections. Many voters, for instance, cast ballots twice every two years for the US House of Representatives—first in the primary and then in the general election.

America's election mania is "not normal" compared to Western Europe.[25] Americans may be asked to vote in twenty to forty separate national, state, and local contests within a four-year period. By contrast, German voters cast ballots in as few as six to eight races during a four- or five-year stretch; some mayoral elections occur every six to eight years. Local elections in the United Kingdom boost the number of elections, but the tally is still considerably less than in the United States: twelve races at most in a four-year period, with most voters participating in fewer than ten races.[26]

The sheer number of elected offices is exacerbated by the frequency with which voters are called to cast ballots. Turning out several times a year is common; some parts of the country look to voters to cast ballots on four or five occasions a year. Adding to the burden is the complexity of tracking candidates, the separate locations and timing of elections, and the distinctive laws that govern contests across the country.[27]

America's glut of elections is another ill-conceived scheme hatched during the Progressive Era to achieve accountability. Insider advantages, outright corruption, and unresponsive government would be eliminated, reformers imagined, by putting more and more officials on the ballot and expecting citizens to turn out repeatedly and make discerning choices.[28]

But equating the proliferation of elections with genuine democracy is wrong. In practice, the Progressive Era reforms further truncated democracy into elections, sapping the capacity for other forms of citizen engagement and organizing.[29] Even on its own terms, more elections overload citizens: for each election, they need to divert time from work and family to physically cast a ballot, gather information to distinguish the many candidates on many ballots, and cast a meaningful vote. Overloaded citizens with little information skip elections.[30] Apart from the marquee presidential contests, majorities of people skip or ignore today's flood of elections, especially in races for local and certain state offices. Even in the important elections to Congress, a half or less of the voting-age population turns out for midterm contests. With many citizens opting out, the voters who turn up often come with an agenda or interest to promote, contradicting Progressive Era hopes of broad citizen participation.

Constant voting is not intrinsically democratic, as demonstrated in Europe and elsewhere.

Governments in parliamentary democracies commonly take four or five years to enact their agendas, simplifying the work of citizens to judge the performance of elected officials.[31]

Near the end of his life, Walter Mondale lucidly reflected on his conversations with Hubert Humphrey about the McGovern-Fraser reforms, which multiplied America's election mania. Mondale concluded that the decision in the 1970s to adopt primaries "pushed us off-track from the substantive debates between the parties." "It's healthier," he reasoned, "for our democracy to fight it out between the parties over the policy issues that are most important to the American people."[32]

Mondale returned to the advice of Progressive Era critics of primaries and Martin Van Buren: treat political parties as a "method of representation" and recoup their place in nominations and elections. Croly forcefully positioned political parties as the practical means by which "government by the people [worked] through their representatives" and gave priority to the national interest as opposed to the self-interests of party factions and stakeholders.[33]

The Mondale proposal for "fewer really good elections that matter more" would require a serious public conversation about the feasibility—and democratic payoff—of America's flood of elections. Taking seriously the costs to citizens might lead to a host of sensible decisions: retire defunct municipal and local elections that draw few candidates and voters; hold national, state, and local elections on the same dates; and consolidate primaries in states within a particular region. The aim should be concentrating the public mind and elevating public awareness and knowledge. These steps would move toward the conditions for democracy recommended by Progressive thinker John Dewey—designing institutions to "improve . . . the methods and conditions of debate, discussion, and persuasion."[34]

Strengthening the Institutional Attention to the Median Voter

Officials in properly reconstituted political parties are institutionally wired to pursue electoral success by selecting candidates with the best opportunities to win general elections.[35] The problem is that primaries distort these incentives by overweighting for the activists, groups, and donors who disproportionately influence nominations.

A targeted step to elevate consideration of the median voter is to continue and expand "superdelegates," party convention delegates selected because they are elected officials and senior party leaders. They introduce a kind of "peer review" to the nomination process that factors in governing experience, weeds out renegades, and incorporates the potential to win the small but decisive median voters needed to prevail in general elections.

Initially, the Democrats—and not the Republicans—created superdelegates after the landslide losses by George McGovern in 1972 and Jimmy Carter in 1980. They comprise about 15 percent of national convention delegates. In the Republican Party, "unpledged" delegates make up about half that proportion of national convention delegates.

Increasing the number of untethered delegates creates the potential to block unacceptable candidates by tipping the nomination.[36] Trump won more than the required simple majority of the delegates in 2016 because candidates dropped out. This is neither a surprise nor a prediction of a future with different rules: they departed once they saw no prospect of prevailing. But if the Republican Party had a robust body of unpledged delegates—along with a stronger push by party leaders to weed out hopeless candidates to provide a clear alternative—moderate candidates would have a reason to remain in the race.

Making the case for superdelegates collides with the mistaken equating of democracy with primaries and the weakening of parties. Indeed, the Democratic Party diminished superdelegates in the 2020 convention by limiting their participation during the first ballot. My counsel: Resist. The defense of the heavily biased system of primaries opened the door to Trump and Wallace and supports vast political inequality. Superdelegates are a buffer against dangerous candidates; the current level of unpledged and superdelegates is too low and too constrained to matter.

Arcing toward Political Equality

The future of democracy is tied to mobilizing a broader spectrum of citizens and incorporating the intermittent voters whom politicos skip as a "bad investment." Inclusively recruiting citizens is the path to improve political equality and enlarging the challenges to governing elites who discount large segments of citizens.

Progress will require going beyond hortatory appeals to redesigning institutions. Here are two reforms.

Let Them Fight It Out

The first invites broader participation in party nominations in order to (1) offset the control of activists and organized groups and (2) promote the selection of moderate candidates.[37] Reformers have pressed states to "open" participation in primaries to any registered voters instead of "closed" contests restricted to registered partisans. The hope is that open primaries will attract sufficient political independents and less extreme partisans who back moderate candidates to offset ideological party factions. While the concept of broadening participation to create countervailing pressures seems sensible, the initial results are mixed.[38]

Another reform to wire moderation into elections is the creation of a nonpartisan primary in which the top two finishers (even if in the same party) go on to face each other in the general election. California's nonpartisan primary (or "top-two system") has received particular attention. The results are not yet consistently delivering the desired impacts.[39]

The success of these reforms in counteracting narrow factions in controlling party nominations remains uncertain but worthy of continued experimentation. Nonetheless, neither reform poses significant risk of further accelerating polarization. Given the threats of the current primary system, the risks of leaving the current system in place appear higher than reforms to create open or nonpartisan primaries.

Crashing "the Room Where It Happens"

The Broadway musical *Hamilton* artfully captures political dealing in "The Room Where It Happens." Populated with the framers of America's Constitution, the showstopper dissects the bare-knuckled but effective negotiation of authoritative governing elites when "No one else was in the room": "No one really knows how the game is played / The art of the trade / How the sausage gets made / We just assume that it happens."

Hamilton supplies a toe-bouncing musical snapshot of America's habitual deference to the necessity of governing elites striking secret compacts: great music but a dangerous model for making decisions. Hamilton traded favors to create a national bank. He touted it as essential to spurring economic growth, but its secretive maneuvering later contributed to recurrent populist backlashes and Andrew Jackson's election on the pledge to end it.[40]

The activism of state politics in the 1780s revives another model for robust political representation: it pairs the broad organizing of citizens including the marginalized with an insider strategy to penetrate the "room where it happens" to influence the "art of the trade."[41] This form of governing challenges the contemporary insularity of American politics while still retaining the rules and procedures associated with political representation—the bedrock principles of equal political participation along with the practical work of negotiation and policy formulation.[42]

The model of the 1780s that marries grassroots organizing and the effective influencing of government policy making enjoys a long, varied, and continuing tradition. Associations of millions of volunteers in organizations like Kiwanis, the Temperance Society, and many others linked everyday people into substantive policy debates within local, state, and federal governments.[43] Contemporary grassroots organizing is committed to sustaining citizen activism and cultivating the necessary skills to penetrate the room where it happens, with a particular focus on marginalized communities that previously lacked power.[44] Organizers of public deliberations are focused on "connect[ing] the community with its government." The point of town hall meetings and organized community deliberations is not to "just talk" but also to motivate "powerful actors . . . to be encouraged, persuaded, or obliged to heed [citizens]."[45]

The pairing of robust citizen engagement with elite negotiation is receiving growing interest in the United States and globally. "Public budgeting" is wiring citizen assemblies into debates over government spending priorities and receiving attention.[46] Within the United States, government agencies have been required by statute and courts to solicit input from groups and individuals directly impacted by new policies. Reforms of the Chicago Policy Department and Chicago public schools "incorporat[ed] empowered participation and deliberation into their governance structures."[47] Bridgeport, Connecticut, and San Jose, California, are other examples of efforts to join citizens into the process of government decision making.[48]

The model of the 1780s departs from the contemporary focus on short-term transactional mobilization for a candidate by engaging in sustained organizing. It also differs from the assumption that protest and social disruption are the only models of change.

The search for steps to reinvigorate political representation is vital but requires caution born of experience. New innovations—from public budgeting to citizen engagement in policing—confront the familiar barriers of elite gaming and resistance.[49] Nor are these admirable experiments spared the risk that political activists (on both the left and right) will assume outsized influence.[50] Designing institutions for democratic governance is hard work; watching for unintended effects is as important as imagining the payoff of change.

The Fight for American Democracy

The dire challenges facing American democracy require a new politics. Life's sharply uneven circumstances have torn the social fabric. The civic culture rooted in the US Constitution and law that impressed observers since the nineteenth century has frayed. Political polarization has corrupted perceptions of reality and infused hatred into differences over policy and candidates.

Building democracy is hard work. Time to roll up our sleeves and join our neighbors in the noble work of our public lives.

Notes

Chapter 1

1. Adam Liptak, "Trump vs. the Constitution," *New York Times*, November 29, 2016, https://www.nytimes.com/interactive/2016/11/29/us/politics/trump-constitution.html.
2. Leigh Ann Caldwell, "These Republican Leaders Say Trump Should Not Be President," *NBC News*, October 8, 2016; David Graham, "Which Republicans Oppose Donald Trump?" *The Atlantic*, November 6, 2016.
3. David Montgomery, "The Abnormal Presidency," *Washington Post*, November 10, 2020, https://www.washingtonpost.com/graphics/2020/lifestyle/magazine/trump-presidential-norm-breaking-list/; Fact Checker, "Trump Claims," *Washington Post*, January 20, 2021, https://www.washingtonpost.com/graphics/politics/trump-claims-database/?itid=lk_inline_manual_4.
4. Kenneth Vogel and Nicholas Confessore, "Access, Influence and Pardons: How a Set of Allies Shaped Trump's Choices," *New York Times*, March 21, 2021.
5. Byron Shafer, *Quiet Revolution: The Struggle for the Democratic Party and the Shaping of Post-Reform Politics* (New York: Russell Sage Foundation, 1983).
6. Desmond King and Rogers Smith, "Racial Orders in American Political Development," *American Political Science Review* 99 (February 2005): 75–92; Rogers Smith, "Beyond Tocqueville, Myrdal, and Hartz: The Multiple Traditions in America," *American Political Science Review* 87 (September 1993): 549–66.
7. Academics and political observers tend to blame the damaging consequences of the direct primary reform on citizens and popular sovereignty. Bruce Cain, *Democracy More or Less: America's Political Reform Quandary* (New York: Cambridge University Press, 2014).
8. Nadia Urbinati, *Democracy Disfigured: Opinion, Truth, and the People* (Cambridge, MA: Harvard University Press, 2014); Maria Paula Saffon and Nadia Urbinati, "Procedural Democracy, the Bulwark of Equal Liberty," *Political Theory* 41 (June 2013): 441–81; Nadia Urbinati and Mark Warren, "The Concept of Representation in Contemporary Political Theory," *Annual Review of Political Science* 11 (2008): 387–412; Nadia

Urbinati, "Competing for Liberty: The Republican Critique of Democracy," *American Political Science Review* 106 (August 2012): 607–21; David Plotke, "Representation Is Democracy." *Constellations* 4 (1997): 19–34; Lisa Disch, "Democracy's 'Diarchy' and the Partnership of Legitimacy and Hegemony," *Contemporary Political Theory* 15 (2016): 220–25; Robert Dahl, *Democracy and Its Critics* (New Haven, CT: Yale University Press, 1989).

9. Sidney Verba, "Would the Dream of Political Equality Turn Out to Be a Nightmare?" *Perspectives on Politics* 1 (December 2003): 663–79, 663.

10. The term "eligible voters" refers to citizens who can legally cast a ballot; it excludes noncitizens and felons based on state law. This is a more restricted and accurate calculation than simply counting all individuals eighteen years of age and over.

11. Michael P. McDonald, "2016 Presidential Nomination Contest Turnout Rates," *United States Elections Project*, http://www.electproject.org/2016P; Michael P. McDonald, "2020 Presidential Nomination Contest Turnout Rates," *United States Elections Project*, http://www.electproject.org/2020P.

12. Bernard L. Fraga. "Candidates or Districts? Reevaluating the Role of Race in Voter Turnout," *American Journal of Political Science* 60, no. 1 (2016): 97–122.

13. E. E. Schattschneider, *The Semisovereign People* (New York: Holt, Rinehart and Winston, 1960).

14. Kay Schlozman, Henry Brady, and Sidney Verba, *Unequal and Unrepresented: Political Inequality and the People's Voice in the New Gilded Age* (Princeton, NJ: Princeton University Press, 2018).

15. Matt Grossman and David Hopkins, *Asymmetric Politics: Ideological Republicans and Group Interest Democrats* (New York: Oxford University Press, 2016); Nolan McCarty, Keith T. Poole, and Howard Rosenthal, *Polarized America: The Dance of Ideology and Unequal Riches* (Cambridge, MA: MIT Press, 2016).

16. Surveys of Democratic and Republican delegates to the national convention, Table 1-28 profile of national convention delegates, 1968–2008 (percent). In Harold W. Stanley and Richard G. Niemi, eds., *Vital Statistics on American Politics, 2013–2014* (Washington, DC: CQ Press, 2013), http://library.cqpress.com.ezp2.lib.umn.edu/elections/vsap13-1536-88566-2579791.

17. I discuss this transformation of the party nomination process and the rise of party activists in the first chapter of my book with Bob Shapiro. Lawrence R. Jacobs and Robert Y. Shapiro, *Politicians Don't Pander: Political Manipulation and the Loss of Democratic Responsiveness*

(Chicago: University of Chicago Press, 2000); see also John H. Aldrich, *Why Parties?: The Origin and Transformation of Political Parties in America* (Chicago: University of Chicago Press, 1995); John H. Aldrich, *Before the Convention: Strategies and Choices in Presidential Nomination Campaigns* (Chicago: University of Chicago Press, 1980); Nelson Polsby, *Consequences of Party Reform* (New York: Oxford University Press, 1983). Kathleen Bawn, Martin Cohen, David Karol, Seth Masket, Hans Noel and John Zaller, "A Theory of Political Parties: Groups, Policy Demands and Nominations in American Politics," *Perspectives on Politics* 10 (September 2012): 571–97.

18. Theodore White, *The Making of the President, 1972* (New York: Atheneum, 1973), 114–15.

19. I discuss the internal efforts of the Reagan campaign and White House to mobilize and sustain the New Right Coalition in *Who Governs?* with Jamie Druckman.

20. The impact of primaries in chasing out moderates and replacing them with more ideological candidates mostly occurred during the first few decades of the new system. Research on later periods finds less clear-cut effects. Chapter 6 presents research that demonstrates the effects of presidential primaries earlier in the new system.

21. Mead Gruver, "In Wyoming, Cheney Faces Blowback for Vote to Impeach Trump," Associated Press, January 28, 2021.

22. Geoffrey Skelley, "9 of the 10 House Republicans Who Voted for Impeachment Already Have Primary Challengers," FiveThirtyEight, March 17, 2021.

23. Barry Burden, "Candidate Positioning in US Congressional Elections," *British Journal of Political Science* 34 (2004): 211–27.

24. Reliable estimates of the voter eligible population (VEP) for congressional districts are unevenly available. The 12 to 15 percent VEP range is a reasonable estimate for the 2010 primaries. The Ocasio-Cortez turnout in 2018 is from the New York State Board of Elections. It is possible that the VEP turnout in Ocasio-Cortez's district may be 6.4 percent; the 29,778 voters in her district in the 2018 Democratic primary represent a low number compared to other primaries that year.

25. Morris P. Fiorina, Samuel J. Abrams, and Jeremy C. Pope, *Culture War? The Myth of a Polarized America* (New York: Longman, 2006), Chaps. 4–7; Stephen A. Jessee, "Partisan Bias, Political Information and Spatial Voting in the 2008 Presidential Election," *Journal of Politics* 72, no. 2 (2010): 327–40.

26. From 1972 to 2016, the GOP nominee attracted 47 percent on average by the time opposition stopped. Marty Cohen, David Karol, Hans Noel, and John Zaller, "Party versus Faction in the Reformed Presidential Nominating System," *PS: Political Science and Politics* 49 (October 2016): 701–8.

27. Racial resentment was a leading driver of support for Trump. In terms of aggregate support, exit polls report that Trump's 2016 campaign increased white support by 1 percent compared to 2012 and a seven- to eleven-point rise among Blacks, Latinos, and Asians. John Sides, Michael Tesler, and Lynn Vavreck, *Identity Crisis: The 2016 Presidential Campaign and the Battle for the Meaning of America* (Princeton, NJ: Princeton University Press, 2019); Marc Hooghe and Ruth Dassonneville, "Explaining the Trump Vote: The Effect of Racist Resentment and Anti-Immigrant Sentiments," *PS: Political Science and Politics* 51, no. 3 (July 2018): 528–34.

28. Schattschneider, *The Semisovereign People*.

29. Caleb Crain, "The Case against Democracy," *New Yorker*, November 7, 2016.

30. Joseph Schumpeter, *Capitalism, Socialism, and Democracy*, 2nd ed. (New York: Harper & Brothers, 1947), 262.

31. Jason Brennan, "Trump Won Because Voters Are Ignorant, Literally," *Foreign Policy*, November 10, 2016; Peter Beinart, "The Electoral College Was Meant to Stop Men Like Trump from Being President," *The Atlantic*, November 21, 2016; Timothy Egan, "We're with Stupid," *New York Times*, November 17, 2017.

32. Bruce Cain, *Democracy More or Less: America's Political Reform Quandary* (New York: Cambridge University Press, 2015), 77.

33. Michael Crozier, Samuel Huntington, and Joji Watanuki, *The Crisis of Democracy: Report on the Governability of Democracies to the Trilateral Commission* (New York: New York University Press, 1975).

34. Jason Brennan, *Against Democracy* (Princeton, NJ: Princeton University Press, 2016). Estlund makes the case for an "epistocracy" that would depend on knowledge. In contrast to Brennan, he hedges his enthusiasm in recognition of the limits of an epistocracy. David Estlund, *Democratic Authority: A Philosophical Framework* (Princeton, NJ: Princeton University Press, 2007); Brennan, *Against Democracy*; Cain, *Democracy More or Less*, 6–7, 77; Bruce Cain, "Populist Illusions and Pluralist Realities," *American Interest*, October 3, 2014, https://www.the-american-interest.com/2014/10/03/populist-illusions-and-pluralist-realities/.

35. Edmund Burke, "Speech to the Electors of Bristol," November 3, 1774, *The Works of the Right Honourable Edmund Burke* (London: Henry G. Bohn, 1854–1856); Schumpeter, *Capitalism, Socialism, and Democracy.*

36. Alan Blinder, "Is Government Too Political?" *Foreign Affairs* 76 (November–December 1997): 115–26.

37. Lawrence Jacobs and Desmond King, *Fed Power: How Finance Wins* (New York: Oxford University Press, 2016; 2nd ed., 2021).

38. Benjamin I. Page and Robert Y. Shapiro, *The Rational Public: Fifty Years of Trends in Americans' Policy Preferences* (Chicago: University of Chicago Press, 1992).

39. Samuel Popkin, *The Reasoning Voter* (Chicago: University of Chicago Press, 1991); Paul Sniderman, *The Democratic Faith* (New Haven, CT: Yale University Press, 2016); Arthur Lupia, *Uninformed: Why People Know So Little about Politics and What We Can Do about It* (New York: Oxford University Press, 2016).

40. Lawrence Jacobs, Fay Lomax Cook, and Michael Delli Carpini, *Talking Together: Public Deliberation in America and the Search for Community* (Chicago: University of Chicago Press, 2009).

41. Jacobs and Shapiro, *Politicians Don't Pander*; Druckman and Jacobs, *Who Governs?*.

42. Schattschneider, *The Semisovereign People*; Frances Fox Piven and Richard Cloward, *Regulating the Power: The Functions of Public Welfare*, updated version (New York: Vintage Press, 1993).

43. Kevin M. Esterling, Michael A. Neblo, and David M. J. Lazer, "Means, Motive, and Opportunity in Becoming Informed about Politics: A Deliberative Field Experiment with Members of Congress and Their Constituents," *Public Opinion Quarterly* 75 (2011): 483–503; Michael A. Neblo, Kevin M. Esterling, Ryan P. Kennedy, David M. J. Lazer, and Anand E. Sokhey, "Who Wants to Deliberate—and Why?," *American Political Science Review* 104 (2010): 566–83.

44. Robert Dahl, *A Preface to Democratic Theory* (Chicago: University of Chicago Press, 1956); Philip Tetlock, *Expert Political Judgment* (Princeton, NJ: Princeton University Press, 2006); Lawrence Brown and Lawrence Jacobs, *The Private Abuse of the Public Interest* (Chicago: University of Chicago Press, 2008).

45. National Commission on the Causes of the Financial and Economic Crisis in the United States, *The Financial Crisis Inquiry Report* (Washington, DC: US Government Printing Office, 2011), http://www.gpo.gov/fdsys/pkg/GPO-FCIC/pdf/GPO-FCIC.pdf; Jacobs and King, *Fed Power*; 9/11 Commission,

Final Report of the National Commission on Terrorist Attacks Upon the United States (Washington, DC: US Government Printing Office, 2004), https://9-11commission.gov/report/; Diane Vaughan, *Challenger Launch Decision: Risky Technology, Culture, and Deviance at NASA* (Chicago: University of Chicago Press, 1997); Scott Sagan, Sagan, Scott. "Review Symposium," *Administrative Science Quarterly* 42 (June 1997): 401–05.

46. Michael Gordon and Bernard E. Trainor, *The Endgame: The Inside Story of the Struggle for Iraq, from George W. Bush to Barack Obama* (New York: Pantheon, 2012); Thomas Ricks, *Fiasco: The American Military Adventure in Iraq* (New York: Penguin, 2006).

47. William Hanage, Christian Testa, Jarvis Chen, et al., "COVID-19: US Federal Accountability for Entry, Spread, and Inequities—Lessons for the Future," *European Journal of Epidemiology* 35 (2020): 995–1006.

48. Woodrow Wilson, *Congressional Government* (Boston: Houghton Mifflin, 1885); Schattschneider, *The Semisovereign People*; Grant McConnell, *Private Power and American Democracy* (New York: Knopf, 1966); Theodore Lowi, *The End of Liberalism: Ideology, Policy, and the Crisis of Public Authority* (New York: Norton, 1969); Schlozman, Brady, and Verba, *Unequal and Unrepresented*.

49. My emphasis on a procedural conception of political representation draws on Urbinati and is motivated by the threats to the bedrock of democratic civil society and government. Urbinati *Disfigured Democracy;* Saffon and Urbinati, "Procedural Democracy."

50. My emphasis on a procedural conception of political representation draws on Urbinati and is motivated by the threats to the bedrock of democratic civil society and government. Urbinati *Disfigured Democracy;* Saffon and Urbinati, "Procedural Democracy."

51. Max Weber, Guenther Roth, and Claus Wittich, *Economy and Society: An Outline of Interpretive Sociology* (Berkeley: University of California Press.

52. Tyler Reny, Loren Collingwood, and Ali Valenzuela, "Vote Switching in the 2016 Election: How Racial and Immigration Attitudes, Not Economics, Explain Shifts in White Voting," *Public Opinion Quarterly* 83 (Spring 2019): 91–113; Matthew Fowler, Vladimir Medenica, and Cathy Cohen, "Why 41 Percent of White Millennials Voted for Trump," *Washington Post*, December 15, 2017; John Sides, Michael Tesler and Lynn Vavreck, "Hunting Where the Ducks Are: Activating Support for Donald Trump in the 2016 Republican Primary," *Journal of Elections, Parties and Public Opinion* 28 (2018): 135–56.

53. Channel 12 Richmond, "KKK Leader Disavows Violent Past, Declares Trump 'Best' for President," April 16, 2016, https://www.nbc12.com/story/31846257/kkk-leader-disavows-violent-past-declares-trump-best-for-president/; Daniel Marans and Kim Bellware, "Meet the Members of Donald Trump's White Supremacist Fan Club," *Huffington Post*, August 25, 2015, https://www.huffpost.com/entry/donald-trump-white-supremacists_n_55dce43ee4b08cd3359dc41a; Sam Stein, "Donald Trump Declines Three Chances to Disavow David Duke," *Huffington Post*, February 28, 2016, https://www.huffpost.com/entry/donald-trump-racist-examples_n_56d47177e4b03260bf777e83.

54. Reny, Collingwood, and Valenzuela, "Vote Switching in the 2016 Election";; Fowler, Medenica, and Cohen, "Why 41 Percent of White Millennials Voted for Trump"; Sides, Tesler, and Vavreck, "Hunting Where the Ducks Are."

55. Gordon Wood, *The Creation of the American Republic, 1776–1787* (Chapel Hill: University of North Carolina Press, 1998); Gordon Wood, *The Radicalism of the American Revolution* (New York: Knopf, 1991); Benjamin Barber, *Strong Democracy: Participatory Politics for a New Age* (Berkeley: University of California Press, 1984); Hahrie Han, *How Organizations Develop Activists: Civic Associations and Leadership in the 21st Century* (New York: Oxford University Press, 2014).

56. Theda Skocpol, *States and Social Revolutions* (New York: Cambridge University Press, 1979), and *Protecting Soldiers and Mothers* (Cambridge, MA: Harvard University Press, 1992); Stephen Skowronek, *Building a New American State: The Expansion of National Administrative Capacities, 1877–1920* (Cambridge: Cambridge University Press, 1982); Karen Oren and Stephen Skowronek, *The Search for American Political Development* (New York: Cambridge University Press, 2004).

57. Oren and Skowronek, *The Search for American Political Development*, 82–85.

58. Theda Skocpol, "Thinking Strategically about Policy Feedbacks," September 2018, unpublished manuscript (in author's possession); Suzanne Mettler and Joe Soss, "The Consequences of Public Policy for Democratic Citizenship: Bridging Policy Studies and Mass Politics," *Perspectives on Politics* 2 (2004): 55–73.

59. For Madison and early American state builders, the term "republican" specifies government based on representation and does not refer to today's GOP.

60. The methods of middle-level generalizing and macrohistorical research are discussed here: Giovanni Sartori, "Concept Misformation in Comparative Politics," *American Political Science Review* 64 (December 1970): 1033–53; Theda Skocpol, "Why I Am an Historical Institutionalist," *Polity* 28 (Autumn 1995): 103–6; Theda Skocpol, *Vision and Method in Historical Sociology* (New York: Cambridge University Press, 1984).

61. Gary Gerstle, *American Crucible: Race and Nation in the Twentieth Century* (Princeton, NJ: Princeton University Press, 2017); Michael Kazin, "Trump and American Populism: Old Whine, New Bottles," *Foreign Affairs*, October 6, 2016); King and Smith, "Racial Orders in American Political Development;" Michael Hanchard, *The Spectre of Race: How Discrimination Haunts Western Democracy* (Princeton, NJ: Princeton University Press, 2018)

Chapter 2

1. Joseph Ellis, *The Quartet: Orchestrating the Second American Revolution, 1783–1789* (New York: Penguin, 2015).

2. Mancur Olson, *The Logic of Collective Action; Public Goods and the Theory of Groups* (Cambridge, MA: Harvard University Press, 1965).

3. Barber, *Strong Democracy*; Han, *How Organizations Develop Activists*; Urbinati, *Disfigured Democracy*; Urbinati, "Competing for Liberty."

4. Quoted in Michael Klarman, *The Framers' Coup: The Making of the United States Constitution* (New York: Oxford University Press, 2016), 178–79.

5. Quoted in Sean Wilentz, *The Rise of American Democracy: Jefferson to Lincoln* (New York: W.W. Norton & Company, 2005), 33.

6. George Van Cleve, *A Slaveholders' Union: Slavery, Politics, and the Constitution in the Early Republic* (Chicago: University of Chicago Press, 2010).

7. King and Smith, "Racial Orders in American Political Development."

8. Alexis de Tocqueville, *Democracy in America*, ed. J. P. Mayer (New York: Anchor Books, 1969); Moisei Ostrogorski, *Democracy and the Organization of Political Parties* (New York: Macmillan, 1902).

9. Gordon Wood, *Revolutionary Characters: What Made the Founders Different* (New York: Penguin Books, 2006), 7–10.

10. Wood, *Revolutionary Characters*, 4–11.

11. Madison's itemization of structural limitations appeared in his "Vices of the Political System of the United States, April 1787," *Founders Online*, National Archives, last modified June 13, 2018, http://founders.archives. gov/documents/Madison/01-09-02-0187. [Original source: *The Papers of*

James Madison, vol. 9, *9 April 1786–24 May 1787 and Supplement 1781–1784*, ed. Robert A. Rutland and William M. E. Rachal (Chicago: University of Chicago Press, 1975), 345–58.]

12. Richard Brookhiser, *James Madison* (New York: Basic Books, 2011); Ellis, *The Quartet*.

13. The flaws of the Constitution's framers have long drawn attention. Critics have flagged their "political depravity" in using "frauds and tricks" to ratify the Constitution (McMaster writing in 1896) and their dim-witted arrogance (Woodward). More recent research reveals their ownership and sexual abuse of slaves (Gordon-Reed). John Bach McMaster, *The Political Depravity of the Founding Fathers*, Studies in the History of the United States (New York: Noonday Press, 1964); William Woodward, *George Washington: The Image and the Man* (New York: Boni and Liveright, 1926); Annette Gordon-Reed, *The Hemingses of Monticello: An American Family* (New York: W. W. Norton, 2008).

14. Wood, *Revolutionary Characters*, 117, 123.

15. Klarman, *The Framers' Coup*, 244, 208–9. The quotes are from Elbridge Gerry and Edmund Randolph.

16. Wood, *The Radicalism of the American Revolution*, 27.

17. Charles Sydnor, *Gentleman Freeholders: Political Practices in Washington's Virginia* (Chapel Hill: University of North Carolina Press, 1952).

18. Quoted in Wood, *The Radicalism of the American Revolution*, 254.

19. Wood, *The Radicalism of the American Revolution*, 82–91.

20. Wood, *The Radicalism of the American Revolution*, 86–87.

21. Quoted in Wilentz, *The Rise of American Democracy*, 14.

22. Wilentz, *The Rise of American Democracy*, 9.

23. Jackson Turner Main, "Government by the People: The American Revolution and the Democratization of the Legislatures," *William and Mary Quarterly* 23 (1966): 391–407; Jackson Turner Main, *Political Parties before the Constitution* (Chapel Hill: University of North Carolina Press, 1973); Calvin Johnson, *Righteous Anger at the Wicked States: The Meaning of the Founders' Constitution* (New York: Cambridge University Press, 2005); Wood, *The Creation of the American Republic*.

24. Wood, *The Radicalism of the American Revolution*, 244–45, 250, 259; Wilentz, *The Rise of American Democracy*, 17.

25. Wood, *The Radicalism of the American Revolution*, 232–42; Hugh Swinton Legare quoted in Wood, *The Radicalism of the American Revolution*, 232.

26. Wood, *The Creation of the American Republic*, 422, 478.

27. Wood, *The Creation of the American Republic*, 507.

28. Madison, "Vices of the Political System of the United States," 345–58; Wood, *The Creation of the American Republic*, 180, 398; Jack Rakove, *James Madison and the Creation of the American Republic,* ed. Mark C. Carnes (New York: Pearson Scott Foresman, 2007), 22 .

29. Wood, *The Creation of the American Republic*, 195; Madison, "Vices of the Political System of the United States."

30. Wood, *The Creation of the American Republic*, 195, 397, 477.

31. Wood, *The Radicalism of the American Revolution*, 251; Ellis, *The Quartet*, 133–34.

32. Ron Chernow, *Alexander Hamilton* (New York: Penguin Books, 2004), 171.

33. Wood, *The Creation of the American Republic,* 473–74.

34. Wood, *The Radicalism of the American Revolution*, 254; Ellis, *The Quartet*, 133–34.

35. Ralph Ketcham, *James Madison: A Biography* (Charlottesville: University of Virginia Press, 1990), 77.

36. Wood, *The Creation of the American Republic*, 195; Wilentz, *The Rise of American Democracy.*

37. The following sections build on research by Theda Skocpol, *Diminished Democracy* (Norman: University of Oklahoma Press, 2003), and Han, *How Organizations Develop Activists*, on voluntary associations and citizen organizing as well as Barber's discussion of "strong democracy" and its practical translation into the practice of politics. Benjamin Barber, *Strong Democracy: Participatory Politics for a New Age,* 20th ann. ed. (Berkeley: University of California Press 2004), Preface.

38. The importance of organizational resources to start and sustain collective action is discussed by Doug McAdam, *Political Process and the Development of Black Insurgency, 1930–1970* (Chicago: University of Chicago Press, 1982); Doug McAdam, John D. McCarthy, and Mayer N. Zald, *Comparative Perspectives on Social Movements: Political Opportunities, Mobilizing Structures, and Cultural Framings* (Cambridge: Cambridge University Press, 1996); John D. McCarthy and Mayer N. Zald, *The Trend of Social Movements in America: Professionalization and Resource Mobilization* (Morristown, NJ: General Learning Press, 1973).

39. Wood, *The Radicalism of the American Revolution*, 244–45, 259.

40. Benjamin Warford-Johnston, "American Colonial Committees of Correspondence: Encountering Oppression, Exploring Unity, and Exchanging Visions of the Future," *History Teacher* 50 (November 2016): 83–128.

41. Unless otherwise noted, the discussion of the Shays' Rebellion draws particularly on Klarman, *The Framers' Coup*, 88–99.

42. Wood, *The Radicalism of the American Revolution*, 82–91; Wood, *The Creation of the American Republic*, 325–26.

43. Wilentz, *The Rise of American Democracy*, 18.

44. Klarman, *The Framers' Coup*, 88–101.

45. Ellis, *The Quartet*, 101.

46. This dynamic echoes prior research that collective action may be triggered by new political opportunities that create new incentives as well as by tangible outcomes that confirm the payback from participation. Sidney Tarrow, *Power in Movement: Social Movements and Contentious Politics* (Cambridge: Cambridge University Press, 1998); Charles Tilly, *Social Movements, 1768–2004* (Boulder, CO: Paradigm, 2004).

47. Wood, *The Radicalism of the American Revolution*, 244–45, 259; Wilentz, *The Rise of American Democracy*, 30.

48. Wood, *The Creation of the American Republic*, 191, 365–68.

49. Wilentz, *The Rise of American Democracy*, 344.

50. Wood, *The Creation of the American Republic*, 379–80.

51. Wood, *The Radicalism of the American Revolution*, 255.

52. Letter from Madison to Thomas Jefferson, April 23, 1787. https://founders.archives.gov/documents/Jefferson/01-11-02-0299

53. Quoted in Klarman, *The Framers' Coup*, 97 (emphasis added).

54. William Gamson, "The Social Psychology of Collective Action," in *Frontiers in Social Movement Theory*, ed. Aldon Morris and Carol McClurg Mueller (New Haven, CT: Yale University Press, 1992), 53-76.; Mallory SoRelle, *Democracy Declined: The Failed Politics of Consumer Financial Protection* (Chicago: University of Chicago Press, 2020).

55. Wilentz, *The Rise of American Democracy*, 20–27.

56. Wood, *The Creation of the American Republic*, 251–55, 365, 366, 368; Gamson, "The Social Psychology of Collective Action."

57. Gamson, "The Social Psychology of Collective Action."

58. Wood, *The Creation of the American Republic*; Klarman, *The Framers' Coup*.

59. Isaac Kramnick, "Republican Revisionism Revisited," *American Historical Review* 87 (1982): 629–64; Craig Calhoun, ed., *Habermas and the Public Sphere* (Cambridge, MA: MIT Press, 1992).

60. Wood, *The Radicalism of the American Revolution*; Wood, *The Creation of the American Republic*.

61. Charles Beard, *An Economic Interpretation of the Constitution of the United States* (New York: Macmillan, 1913). See also Woody Holton,

Unruly Americans and the Origins of the Constitution (New York: Hill and Wang, 2007).

62. Klarman, *The Framers' Coup*, 615.

63. Brookhiser, *James Madison*.

64. As he waited for the Constitutional Convention to assemble, Madison designed the "Virginia Plan" to serve as a starting point for its deliberations—seizing the initiative and setting a fulsome agenda. It sharply broke from the Articles of Confederation by proposing a national government complete with three national branches of government: legislative, executive, and judicial. Quoted in Donald Dewey and Barbara Peterson, *James Madison: Defender of the American Republic* (New York: Nova Science, 2011), 45; Brookhiser, James Madison.

65. Ellis, *The Quartet,* 132; Klarman, *The Framers' Coup*.

66. During 1786, Madison completed two significant studies to pinpoint what he saw as the flaws of confederations. "Of Ancient & Modern Confederacies" studied Greece, the Holy Roman Empire, Sweden, and Holland, and "Vices of the Political System of the United States" catalogued the inadequacies at home. Brookhiser, *James Madison.*

67. Klarman, *The Framers' Coup*, xi; Ellis, *The Quartet*.

68. Wood, *The Creation of the American Republic*, 476.

69. Letter from James Madison to Thomas Jefferson, October 24, 1787, in *The Papers of James Madison*, vol. 10, 205–20; Ellis, *The Quartet*, 133–34; Wood, *The Creation of the American Republic*, 370–71.

70. Klarman, *The Framers' Coup*.

71. Quoted in Klarman, *The Framers' Coup*, 208–9.

72. Klarman, *The Framers' Coup*, 178–81.

73. Allan Lichtman, *The Embattled Vote in America* (Cambridge, MA: Harvard University Press, 2018).

74. Klarman, *The Framers' Coup*, 213, 228–37.

75. See Hamilton's defense of George Washington's 1793 Neutrality Proclamation. Hamilton's argument for "energy" in the executive and carving out of implied presidential power laid the groundwork for the unilateral actions of contemporary presidents of both political parties. Harold Koh, *The National Security Constitution* (New Haven, CT: Yale University Press, 1990); Charlie Savage, "Trump and His Lawyers Embrace a Vision of Vast Executive Power," *New York Times*, June 4, 2018, https://nyti.ms/30yw 7vT; Lawrence Jacobs, "Trump Wields the Imperial Presidency," presented at "A Republic, If We Can Keep It" conference, Cornell University, Ithaca, New York, April 12–13, 2018.

76. Klarman, *The Framers' Coup*, 208–9.

77. James Madison's letter to Jefferson of October 24, 1787, and in numbers 10 and 51 of *The Federalist*; Boyd, *Papers of Jefferson*, vol. 12, 276–79; *The Federalist*, 63–65, 351–53.

78. Wood, *Revolutionary Characters*, 48–49.

79. Jon Meacham, *Thomas Jefferson: The Art of Power* (New York: Random House, 2012), 260.

80. Quoted in Klarman, *The Framers' Coup*, 607.

81. Klarman, *The Framers' Coup*, 231.

82. Klarman, *The Framers' Coup*, 255.

83. Wood, *The Creation of the American Republic*, 473.

84. Quoted in Klarman, *The Framers' Coup*, 170.

85. Klarman, *The Framers' Coup*, 178–81.

86. Quoted in Klarman, *The Framers' Coup*, 256.

87. King and Smith, "Racial Orders in American Political Development."

88. Van Cleve, *A Slaveholders' Union*; Klarman, *The Framers' Coup*, 303–4.

89. Klarman, *The Framers' Coup*, 257–304; Van Cleve, *A Slaveholders' Union*.

90. Jeffrey Tulis and Nicole Mellow, *Legacies of Losing in American Politics* (Chicago: University of Chicago Press, 2018).

91. Holton, *Unruly Americans*.

92. The views of the Constitution's critics were expressed in state ratifying conventions as well as in articles and letters in state and community publications. Herbert Storing has assembled these disparate presentations into one coherent volume: *The Complete Anti-Federalist*, v (Chicago: University of Chicago Press, 1975), 212.

93. Pauline Maier, *Ratification: The People Debate the Constitution, 1787–1788* (New York: Simon & Schuster, 2010).

94. Klarman, *The Framers' Coup*.

95. Storing, *The Complete Anti-Federalist*, 211–21.

96. Brutus Junior, *New-York Journal*, November 8, 1787, 137. *The Anti-Federalist Papers*, ed. Bill Bailey, https://www.thefederalistpapers.org/wp-content/uploads/2012/11/The-Anti-Federalist-Papers-Special-Edition.pdf.

97. Meacham, *Thomas Jefferson: The Art of Power*, 213.

98. Holton, *Unruly Americans*.

99. Richard Henry Lee quoted in Klarman, *The Framers' Coup*, 371.

100. Storing, *The Complete Anti-Federalist*, 212–19.

101. Storing, *The Complete Anti-Federalist*, 39–40.

102. In Storing, *The Complete Anti-Federalist*, 44–47.

103. Storing, *The Complete Anti-Federalist*, 208–29.

104. *The Anti-Federalist Papers, 190-192.*

105. In Storing, *The Complete Anti-Federalist*, 113–17. The Anti-Federalist "Letters of Cato" were published in newspapers in the hotly contested ratification state of New York. Historians suspect they were written by prominent politician George Clinton, who was New York governor during the ratification debate and later served as vice president of the United States during 1805-1809 under President Thomas Jefferson and during 1809-1812 under President James Madison.

106. Quoted in Klarman, *The Framers' Coup*, 367.

107. Letters of Cato quoted in Storing, *The Complete Anti-Federalist*, 228–29.

108. Holton, *Unruly Americans*.

109. Luther Martin (section 2.4.42), Patrick Henry (section 5.16.2), and Letters of Cato (Storing, *The Complete Anti-Federalist*, 112); Wood, *The Radicalism of the American Revolution*, 255.

110. *The Anti-Federalist Papers, 143-44.*

111. Klarman, *The Framers' Coup*, 386–95.

112. William Grayson quoted in Klarman, *The Framers' Coup*, 371; Patrick Henry and Letters of Cato, Storing, *The Complete Anti-Federalist*, 117, 222.

113. *The Anti-Federalist Papers, 136-7.*

114. Storing, *The Complete Anti-Federalist*, 114–16.

115. *The Anti-Federalist Papers, 275.*

116. Quoted in Klarman, *The Framers' Coup*, 367.

117. Klarman, *The Framers' Coup*.

118. Ellis, *The Quartet*.

119. Maier, *Ratification: The People Debate*.

120. Klarman, *The Framers' Coup*, 287–88.

121. Wood, *Revolutionary Characters*, 48–49.

122. Storing, *The Complete Anti-Federalist*, 215.

123. Hannah Pitkin, *The Concept of Representation* (Berkeley: University of California Press, 1967); Jane Mansbridge, "Rethinking Representation," *American Political Science Review* 97 (2003): 515–28; Lisa Disch, "Toward a Mobilization Conception of Democratic Representation," *American Political Science Review* 105 (2011): 100–114.

124. Elizabeth McKenna, Hahrie Han, and Michelle Oyakawa, *Prisms of the People: Power and Organizing in Twenty-First-Century America* (Chicago: University of Chicago Press, 2021).

Chapter 3

1. The appraisal of Jefferson was offered by Supreme Court Justice John Marshall (an estranged second cousin); that of Jackson was offered by Supreme Court Justice Joseph Story. Wilentz, *The Rise of American Democracy*, 99, 248; Robert Remini, *Andrew Jackson and the Course of American Empire, 1767–1821* (New York: Harper and Row, 1977); Robert Remini, *Andrew Jackson and the Course of American Freedom* (New York: Harper and Row, 1981).

2. Quoted in James Ceaser, "Political Parties and Presidential Ambition," *Journal of Politics* 40 (August 1978): 708–39, 724.

3. Wilentz, *The Rise of American Democracy*, 40; Wood, *The Radicalism of the American Revolution*, 348.

4. Wilentz, *The Rise of American Democracy*, 27–28, 50–51.

5. Wood, *The Radicalism of the American Revolution*, 362–64.

6. Wilentz, *The Rise of American Democracy*, 18.

7. Wilentz, *The Rise of American Democracy*, 138.

8. Philip Foner, ed., *The Democratic-Republican Societies, 1790–1800: A Documentary Sourcebook of Constitutions, Declarations, Addresses, Resolutions, and Toasts* (Westport, CT: Greenwood Press, 1976).

9. Quoted in Wilentz, *The Rise of American Democracy*, 69; see 40–41, 66–69.

10. Foner, *The Democratic-Republican Societies*, 109.

11. Wilenz, 47; Marco Sioli, "The Democratic-Republican Societies at the End of the Eighteenth Century: The Western Pennsylvania Experience," *Pennsylvania History* 60 (1993): 288–304.

12. As part of the cluster of laws passed in 1798, it became harder for immigrants to become citizens and easier for the president to deport noncitizens designated as dangerous or coming from hostile countries—a power that remains intact.

13. Wilentz, *The Rise of American Democracy*, 72–73.

14. Wilentz, *The Rise of American Democracy*, 90, 96–97.

15. US Election Project, "National General Election VEP Turnout Rates, 1789–Present," http://www.electproject.org/national-1789-present.

16. Alexander Keyssar, *The Right to Vote: The Contested History of Democracy in the United States* (New York: Basic Books, 2009), 2.

17. Wilentz, *The Rise of American Democracy*, 116–22.

18. Max Edling, *A Revolution in Favor of Government* (New York: Oxford University Press, 2003).

19. Richard McCormick, *The Presidential Game: The Origins of American Presidential Politics* (New York: Oxford University Press, 1982); Sidney Milkis, *The President and the Parties: The Transformation of the American Party System since the New Deal* (New York: Oxford University Press, 1993).

20. Wilentz, *The Rise of American Democracy*, 75–90.

21. This brief discussion of populism draws on the vibrant analysis of its history and conceptual definition. We return to this discussion in later chapters. Michael Kazin, *The Populist Persuasion: An American History* (Ithaca, NY: Cornell University Press, 1995). See also Margaret Canovan, "Trust the People! Populism and the Two Faces of Democracy," *Political Studies* 47 (1999): 2–16.

22. Wilentz, *The Rise of American Democracy*, 96-97.

23. Wilentz, *The Rise of American Democracy*, 75, 120.

24. Wilentz, *The Rise of American Democracy*, 60–61, 70–73, 97.

25. Wood, *The Radicalism of the American Revolution*; Wilentz, *The Rise of American Democracy*.

26. Wilentz, *The Rise of American Democracy*, 176–80.

27. Wilentz, *The Rise of American Democracy,* 93–94.

28. Ostrogorski, *Democracy and the Organization of Political Parties.*

29. Quoted in Wilentz, *The Rise of American Democracy*, 97.

30. Jefferson campaigned against Hamilton's expansion of executive power but arguably did more to widen it. Most significantly, he asserted the prerogative—not enumerated in the Constitution—to purchase Louisiana from Napoleon and double the country's size. He also claimed the authority in Article II of the Constitution and its reference to the executive's position as commander-in-chief to launch war against the Barbary States. Moreover, he claimed the executive power to resist the judicial and legislative branches and assert presidential authority. John Yoo, "Jefferson and Executive Power," *Boston University Law Review* 88, no. 2 (2008): 421–57; but cf. David Mayer, *The Constitutional Thought of Thomas Jefferson* (Charlottesville: University Press of Virginia, 1994).

31. Quoted in Wilentz, *The Rise of American Democracy*, 97.

32. Although the end of the war was greeted joyously, there have been sharp criticisms of its costs, inept leadership, hardships on the most vulnerable, and opportunism by New England merchants. Wilentz, *The Rise of American Democracy*, 176–77.

33. Quoted in Wilentz, *The Rise of American Democracy*, 253.

34. Wilentz, *The Rise of American Democracy*, 116–17, 121, 183–87, 201–202.

35. Wilentz, *The Rise of American Democracy*, 347.

36. The 1819 downturn's severity was amplified by risky speculation in public land and debt as well as mistaken actions by the Second Bank of the US, which is alternatively blamed for precipitating the crisis by its excessive use of monetary policy (Rothbard) or prolonging the crisis due to its inadequate response once it broke out. Clyde Haulman, "Virginia Commodity Prices during the Panic of 1819," *Journal of the Early Republic* 22 (2002): 675–88; Murray Rothbard, *The Panic of 1819: Reactions and Policies* (New York: Columbia University Press, 1962).

37. Clay received 47,217 votes and 37 electoral votes. After the House selected Adams, Clay was appointed as secretary of state, which was then considered a powerhouse position. Although there is no smoking gun of a deal, Clay's appointment has long been considered payback for lobbying state House delegations to support Adams even in states where voters had favored Jackson. Adams cut other deals to secure an Electoral College majority; for example, he promised Daniel Webster not to remove Federalists from the administration, and one delegate bargained to secure his brother's judgeship. Remini, *Andrew Jackson and the Course of American Freedom*, 85–89, 94.

38. Remini, *Andrew Jackson and the Course of American Freedom*, 87, 94.

39. Wilentz, *The Rise of American Democracy*, 28.

40. James Chase, *Emergence of the Presidential Nominating Convention: 1789–1832* (Urbana: University of Illinois Press, 1973), 110–11.

41. Quoted in Remini, *Andrew Jackson and the Course of American Freedom*, 30–31.

42. Quoted in Ceaser, "Political Parties and Presidential Ambition," 723–24.

43. Although Jackson flirted with the antiparty mood that prevailed after the War of 1812, Van Buren coaxed him to embrace party goals instead of his personal preferences (Chase, *Emergence of the Presidential Nominating Convention*, 99–101).

44. Ceaser, "Political Parties and Presidential Ambition," 624–29.

45. Major Wilson, "Republicanism and the Idea of Party in the Jacksonian Period," *Journal of the Early Republic* 8 (1988): 419–42, 419–20, 440; Ceaser, "Political Parties and Presidential Ambition," 728.

46. Van Buren's contributions to building Jackson's party organization borrowed from his earlier role in developing a disciplined and networked organization of New York State politicians who were linked by policy, power, and patronage. In New York State, Van Buren started his political career as a county official in his mid-twenties, then became a state

senator and attorney general. By the time he was elected to the US Senate in 1820, he had built a formidable organization known as Albany Regency that coalesced state politicians who shared views and wielded power over nominations and patronage. Once in Washington, DC, Jackson relied on him as his primary political adviser and rewarded him with positions as secretary of state (1829–1831), vice president (1833–1837), and presidential nominee in 1836.

Nineteenth-century reformers criticized Van Buren's approach to building political parties as corrupt. Patronage, in his view, was a pragmatic compromise to secure the greater good of permanent party competition: Politicians rewarded voter loyalty and worked in the party organization with the intense reward of jobs.

47. Daniel Feller, "Politics and Society: Toward a Jacksonian Synthesis," *Journal of the Early Republic* 10 (Summer 1990): 135–61, 156–58; Wilson, "Republicanism and the Idea of Party in the Jacksonian Period," 419–42, 419–20; Richard Hofstadter, *The Idea of a Party System: The Rise of Legitimate Opposition in the United States, 1780–1840* (Berkeley: University of California Press, 1969); Remini, *Andrew Jackson and the Course of American Freedom*, 37.

48. Jeffrey Tulis, *The Rhetorical Presidency* (Princeton, NJ: Princeton University Press, 1987).

49. Wilentz, *The Rise of American Democracy*, 369–73.

50. Wilentz, *The Rise of American Democracy*, 282–92, 307–9; Chase, *Emergence of the Presidential Nominating Convention*, 99–100.

51. Wilentz, *The Rise of American Democracy*, 301–5.

52. Edling, *A Revolution in Favor of Government*.

53. Frank Freidel, "The Old Populism and the New," *Proceedings of the Massachusetts Historical Society* 85 (1973): 78–90; Kazin, *The Populist Persuasion*, 17–18.

54. Quoted in Wilentz, *The Rise of American Democracy*, 281; Wilson, "Republicanism and the Idea of Party in the Jacksonian Period," 429–34.

55. Wilentz, *The Rise of American Democracy*, 252–53, 281, 307–8; Remini, *Andrew Jackson and the Course of American Freedom*, 12–15, 30–31.

56. Lawrence Jacobs and Desmond King, *Fed Power: How Finance Wins* (New York: Oxford University Press, 2016; 2nd ed., 2021).

57. Richard Hofstadter, *Great Issues in American History: From the Revolution to the Civil War, 1765–1865* (New York: Vintage Books, 1958), 60–61; Bray Hammond, *Banks and Politics in America, from the Revolution to the Civil War* (Princeton, NJ: Princeton University Press, 1957), 102.

58. Andrew Jackson, "Veto Message Regarding the Bank of the United States," July 10, 1832, http://avalon.law.yale.edu/19th_century/ajveto01.asp.

59. Wilentz, *The Rise of American Democracy*, 361, 370. Jackson blamed banks for bankrupting him after he endorsed loans by a business associate who later was forced out of business and, in so doing, wiped out Jackson's finances.

60. Remini, *Andrew Jackson and the Course of American Freedom*, 30; Letter from Andrew Jackson to John Donelson, February 9, 1824, in James Parton, *Life of Andrew Jackson*, vol. 3 (New York: Mason Brothers, 1861), 40.

61. H. W. Brands, *Andrew Jackson: His Life and Times* (New York: Anchor Books, 2005), 379, 282; letter from Andrew Jackson to John Donelson, February 9, 1824 in Parton, *Life of Andrew Jackson*, 40; Remini, *Andrew Jackson and the Course of American Empire*, 63.

The caucus's violation of the Constitution's separation of powers was a primary criticism. By equipping the legislative branch to control the selection of the chief executive, the caucus fused what the Constitution aimed to separate. The effect, as John Quincy Adams put it, was to "plac[e] the President in a state of undue subserviency to the members of the legislature." Indeed, a plausible case for presidential catering to the legislature occurred during the lead-up to the presidential nomination in 1812 when Madison came to accept congressional pressure to prepare for the War of 1812. Wilentz, *The Rise of American Democracy*, 190–92.

62. Quoted in Wilentz, *The Rise of American Democracy*, 4.

63. Wilentz, *The Rise of American Democracy*, 369–73.

64. Remini, *Andrew Jackson and the Course of American Freedom*, 99, 138–39, 224.

65. Chase, *Emergence of the Presidential Nominating Convention*, 110–11; Wilentz, *The Rise of American Democracy*, 455; Remini, *Andrew Jackson and the Course of American Freedom*, 62.

66. Kazin, *The Populist Persuasion*, 17–18; Wilentz, *The Rise of American Democracy*, 182.

67. Richard D. Brown, "Modernization and the Modern Personality in Early America, 1680–1865: A Sketch of a Synthesis," *Journal of Interdisciplinary History* 2 (1972): 214–20, 217–18.

68. Remini, *Andrew Jackson and the Course of American Freedom*, 147.

69. The Anti-Masonic candidate William Wirth garnered 7.78 percent of the vote, and a smattering of other candidates received the remaining

0.55 percent. David Leip, Atlas of U.S. Presidential Elections, https://usel ectionatlas.org/RESULTS/.

70. Wilentz, *The Rise of American Democracy*, 361–74.

71. Wilentz, *The Rise of American Democracy*, 251–53.

72. Wilentz, *The Rise of American Democracy*.

73. McCormick, *The Presidential Game*, 197.

74. Chase, *Emergence of the Presidential Nominating Convention*, 41.

75. McCormick, *The Presidential Game*, 135.

76. Party conventions were not adopted by the Democrats at the national level until 1832 and more fully in 1836, but state party conventions were held in a dozen states prior to selecting candidates and Jackson electors for the 1828 elections.

77. Jackson's incumbency ensured him renomination in 1832, but the Democrats used the national convention to replace the sitting vice president (Jackson rival John C. Calhoun) with Jackson's close political ally Van Buren. In 1836, the Democrats relied on a national convention to select its presidential and vice presidential candidates, and the process gradually developed and became routinized over time.

78. Stan Haynes, *The First American Political Conventions: Transforming Presidential Nominations, 1832–1872* (Jefferson, NC: McFarland & Company, 2012), 40–41.

79. Richard B. Latner, *The Presidency of Andrew Jackson: White House Politics, 1829–1837* (Athens: University of Georgia Press, 1979), 136–37.

80. Letter from Andrew Jackson to John Donelson, February 9, 1824, in Parton, *Life of Andrew Jackson*, 40; Haynes, *The First American Political Conventions*, 40–41.

81. Latner, *The Presidency of Andrew Jackson*, 128.

82. Wood, *The Creation of the American Republic*, 366–69.

83. Quoted in Wilentz, *The Rise of American Democracy*, 4.

84. Quoted in Frederick Marryat, *A Diary in America, With Remarks on Its Institutions*, ed. Sydney W. Jackman (New York: Knopf, 1962).

85. Wilentz, *The Rise of American Democracy*, 248, 307–8.

86. Jaffrey Pasley, "Minnows, Spies, and Aristocrats: The Social Crisis of Congress in the Age of Martin Van Buren," *Journal of the Early Republic* 27 (Winter 2007): 599–653.

87. Quoted in William J. Cooper, *The Lost Founding Father: John Quincy Adams and the Transformation of American Politics* (New York: Liveright, 2017).

88. Wilentz, *The Rise of American Democracy*, 189–97.

89. Quoted in Wilentz, *The Rise of American Democracy*, 187–88.

90. Wilentz, *The Rise of American Democracy*, 425.

91. Wilentz, *The Rise of American Democracy*, 3.

92. Marryat, *A Diary in America*.

93. Van Buren letter to Ritchie, January 13, 1827 quoted in Chase, *Emergence of the Presidential Nominating Convention*, 99–101; Donald Cole, *Martin Van Buren and the American Political System* (Princeton, NJ: Princeton University Press, 1984); Wilson, "Republicanism and the Idea of Party in the Jacksonian Period."

94. Chase, *Emergence of the Presidential Nominating Convention*, 99–101.

95. Van Buren letter to Ritchie, January 13, 1827 quoted in Chase, *Emergence of the Presidential Nominating Convention*, 99–101.

96. Ceaser, "Political Parties and Presidential Ambition," 624–29; Cole, *Martin Van Buren and the American Political System*; Wilson, "Republicanism and the Idea of Party in the Jacksonian Period."

97. Schattschneider, *The Semisovereign People*.

98. King and Smith, "Racial Orders in American Political Development"; Smith, "Beyond Tocqueville, Myrdal, and Hartz"; Rogers Smith, *Civic Ideals: Conflicting Visions of Citizenship in U.S. History* (New Haven, CT: Yale University Press, 1997).

99. Gordon-Reed, *The Hemingses of Monticello*; Annette Gordon-Reed, *Thomas Jefferson and Sally Hemings: An American Controversy* (Charlottesville: University of Virginia Press, 1997); Sean Wilentz, "The Details of Greatness," *New Republic*, March 29, 2004, 27–35; Sean Wilentz, "Life, Liberty, and the Pursuit of Thomas Jefferson," *New Republic*, March 10, 1997, 32–42.

100. Wilentz, *The Rise of American Democracy*, 183–97; Keyssar, *The Right to Vote*, 45–46.

101. Wilentz, *The Rise of American Democracy*, 312–14, 341–45.

102. The blending of racial, gender, and class exclusions with the expansion of white male enfranchisement is consistent with the masterful historical research by Sean Wilentz (*The Rise of American Democracy*) and King and Smith ("Racial Orders in American Political Development"). The attention to racial orders and their contradictions offers a more nuanced account than those that compare the scope of citizenship in the early nineteenth century to the twentieth century and find it wanting (Edward Pessen, "The Egalitarian Myth and the American Social Reality: Wealth, Mobility, and Equality in the 'Era of the Common Man,'" *American Historical Review* 76 [1971]: 989–1084).

103. Wilentz, *The Rise of American Democracy*, 135–38; King and Smith, "Racial Orders in American Political Development."

104. Alexander Keyssar, *The Right to Vote: The Contested History of Democracy in the United States* (New York: Basic Books, 2009), 43–63.

105. Wilson, "Republicanism and the Idea of Party in the Jacksonian Period," 427.

Chapter 4

1. Belle Case La Follette and Fola La Follette, *Robert M. La Follette* (New York: Macmillan, 1953).

2. Nancy Unger, *Fighting Bob La Follette: The Righteous Reformer* (Chapel Hill: University of North Carolina Press, 2000), 239; Richard Drake, *The Education of an Anti-Imperialist: Robert La Follette and U.S. Expansion* (Madison: University of Wisconsin Press, 2013), 181–82.

3. La Follette and La Follette, *Robert M. La Follette*, 616–19; Unger, *Fighting Bob La Follette*, 244–46.

4. The form of the direct primaries varied when they were first introduced. They were mostly contests among delegates seeking to attend the party conference as contrasted with the contemporary "candidate primary" that features the name of the candidate. The implementation of the "delegate primary" varied; it sometimes occurred with voters knowing the candidate preference or a preference poll binding the delegates.

5. Cain, "Populist Illusions and Pluralist Realities"; Shigeo Hirano and James Snyder, *Primary Elections in the United States* (New York: Cambridge University Press, 2019).

6. Cain, "Populist Illusions and Pluralist Realities"; Hirano and Snyder, *Primary Elections in the United States*.

7. Gerald McFarland, *Mugwumps, Morals, and Politics, 1884–1920* (Amherst: University of Massachusetts Press, 1975).

8. Lawrence Goodwyn, *Democratic Promise: The Populist Moment in America* (Cambridge: Cambridge University Press, 1976); Kazin, *The Populist Persuasion*; Michael Kazin, "Democracy Betrayed and Redeemed: Populist Traditions in the United States," *Constellations* 5, no. 1 (1998): 75–84; Elizabeth Sanders, *Roots of Reform: Farmers, Workers, and the American State, 1877–1917* (Chicago: University of Chicago Press, 1999); Gary Gerstle, *American Crucible: Race and Nation in the Twentieth Century* (Princeton, NJ: Princeton University Press,

2002); Martin Ridge, "Populism Revolt: John D. Hicks and The Populist Revolt," *Reviews in American History* 13 (March 1985): 142–54.

9. Robert La Follette, *La Follette's Autobiography: A Personal Narrative of Political Experiences* (Getzville, NY: William S. Hein & Company, 1960), 86.

10. Herbert Croly, *The Promise of American Life* (New York: Macmillan, 1911), 144.

11. Unger, *Fighting Bob La Follette*, 12, 21, 26; David P. Thelen, *Robert M. La Follette and the Insurgent Spirit* (Boston: Little, Brown and Company, 1976).

12. Unger, *Fighting Bob La Follette*, 108–9.

13. La Follette, *La Follette's Autobiography*, 21.

14. La Follette, *La Follette's Autobiography*, 5–7, 11, 21, 29; Unger, *Fighting Bob La Follette*, 112.

15. La Follette, *La Follette's Autobiography*, 82.

16. The reported sum of bribes was $8,300 in the late nineteenth century. La Follette, *La Follette's Autobiography*, 95.

17. La Follette, *La Follette's Autobiography*, 89.

18. Unger, *Fighting Bob La Follette*, 110, 131.

19. Quoted in William Nester, *Theodore Roosevelt and the Art of American Power: An American for All Time* (Lanham, MD: Lexington Books, 2019), 255.

20. Quoted in Jeremy Bailey, "The Progressives and Presidential Representation," in *The Idea of Presidential Representation: An Intellectual and Political History* (Lawrence: University Press of Kansas, 2019), 104.

21. Unger, *Fighting Bob La Follette*, 121–s2, 135, 226.

22. Nathan Miller, *Theodore Roosevelt: A Life* (New York: William Morrow & Co., 1992).

23. La Follette and his supporters founded the National Republican League in 1911 as a platform for the Wisconsinite's presidential run in 1912. These Progressives and others skeptically observed TR's change of heart in 1912 toward reform—notably direct primaries—as opportunistically serving his political aggrandizement. Where TR once criticized La Follette as a "radical" for promoting these reforms and appeased the regular Republican Party regulars, he now strove to seize that mantel as an alternative to Taft and Wilson. Sidney Milkis and Daniel Tichenor, "'Direct Democracy' and Social Justice: The Progressive Party Campaign of 1912," *Studies in American Political Development* 8 (Fall 1994): 282–340.

24. La Follette's hostility to TR was mutual. La Follette's devotion to political reform for decades prior to 1912 was mocked as unrealistic by TR, who supported party regulars in the Republican Party until it served TR's political interests to oppose them. Later in 1917, when La Follette took the lead in opposing America's entry into the First World War and absorbed harsh attacks, TR energetically joined the critics. He publicly endorsed the Wisconsinite's expulsion from the US Senate and denounced him as a "sinister enemy of democracy," a "shadow hun," and "the most dangerous political leader [of domestic subversion]." Unger, *Fighting Bob La Follette*, 255.

25. Frank Norris, *The Octopus: a Story of California* (New York: Doubleday, Page & Co., 1901), 25.

26. Michael McGerr, *A Fierce Discontent: The Rise and Fall of the Progressive Movement in America, 1870–1920* (New York: Oxford University Press, 2005); Richard White, *The Republic for Which It Stands* (New York: Oxford University Press, 2017).

27. Quoted in Unger, *Fighting Bob La Follette*, 144, 272.

28. La Follette, *La Follette's Autobiography*, 34.

29. La Follette, *La Follette's Autobiography*, 321, emphasis in original.

30. La Follette, *La Follette's Autobiography*, 11; Robert La Follette, "The Danger Threatening Representative Government," speech at Mineral Point, Wisconsin, August 28, 1897, Wisconsin Historical Society; Unger, *Fighting Bob La Follette*, 102.

31. La Follette, "The Danger Threatening Representative Government"; Robert La Follette, *The Political Philosophy of Robert M. La Follette as Revealed in His Speeches and Writings*, comp. Ellen Torelle (Westport, CT: Hyperion Press, 1975).

32. Herbert Croly, *Progressive Democracy* (New York: Macmillan), 145–48.

33. Quoted in Milkis, *The President and the Parties*, 22.

34. John Dewey, *The Public and Its Problems* (New York: Holt, 1927); Milkis, *The President and the Parties*.

35. Tulis, *The Rhetorical Presidency*.

36. Quoted in Milkis, *The President and the Parties*, 27–28.

37. La Follette, "The Danger Threatening Representative Government."

38. Urbinati, *Disfigured Democracy*; Richard Hofstadtler, *The Age of Reform* (New York: Knopf, 1955); Jan-Werner Muller, *What Is Populism?* (Philadelphia: University of Pennsylvania Press, 2016).

39. Urbinati, *Disfigured Democracy*; Benjamin Arditi, "Populism as a Spectre of Democracy," *Political Studies* 52 (2004): 135–43.

40. Muller, *What Is Populism?*, 6.

41. Richard Hofstadter, *The Paranoid Style in American Politics* (New York: Alfred A. Knopf, 1964); but cf. Goodwyn, *Democratic Promise*.

42. Canovan, "Trust the People!"; Arditi, "Populism as a Spectre of Democracy," 137.

43. But see discussion of populism and Latin America. Scott Mainwaring, Timothy Scully, and Jorge Vargas Cullell, "Measuring Success in Democratic Governance," in Mainwaring and Scully, eds., *Democratic Governance in Latin America* (Stanford, CA: Stanford University Press, 2010), 11–51.

44. Address at Ann Arbor, Michigan, March 12, 1898, in La Follette, *The Political Philosophy of Robert M. La Follette*, 29; La Follette, "The Danger Threatening Representative Government."

45. Drake, *The Education of an Anti-Imperialist*, 184.

46. La Follette, "The Danger Threatening Representative Government."

47. Message to the Legislature, 1901, in La Follette, *The Political Philosophy of Robert M. La Follette*, 38–39.

48. La Follette, *The Political Philosophy of Robert M. La Follette*, 48–49. La Follette's reference to "trustee" is a subtle but significant reference: it implicitly acknowledges Madison's framework in which citizens elected representatives who do the deciding. The alternative concept is that elected officials are "delegates" who follow the instructions of citizens, as was the case in the 1780s.

49. Address at Ann Arbor, Michigan, March 12, 1898, in La Follette, *The Political Philosophy of Robert M. La Follette*, 30–31.

50. Von Nostitiz and Sandri, "State Funding and Party Primaries"; William Cross, Ofer Kenig, Scott Pruysers, and Gideon Rahat, *The Promise and Challenge of Party Primary Elections: A Comparative Perspective* (Quebec: McGill- Queen's University Press, 2016).

51. Primaries were used in fourteen of forty-five states by 1896 but mostly in some counties and for limited purposes. Alan Ware, *The American Direct Primary: Party Institutionalization and Transformation in the North* (Cambridge: Cambridge University Press, 2002) .

52. La Follette, *La Follette's Autobiography*, 84–86; Paul H. Giddens, "The Origin of the Direct Primary: The Crawford County System," *Western Pennsylvania History* 60, no. 2 (1977): 145–58.

53. Quoted in La Follette, *The Political Philosophy of Robert M. La Follette*, 36–37.

54. Quoted in La Follette, *The Political Philosophy of Robert M. La Follette,* 29–31; La Follette, "The Danger Threatening Representative Government."

55. Quoted in Unger, *Fighting Bob La Follette,* 113.

56. Cain, "Populist Illusions and Pluralist Realities," 10–14; Hirano and Snyder, *Primary Elections in the United States.*

57. Charles Merriam and Louise Overacker, *Primary Elections,* rev. ed. (Chicago: University of Chicago Press, 1928).

58. In comparison to presidential primaries, states adopted primaries for other offices more widely (all but two states adopted primaries by 1939) and were more apt to change them. Louise Overacker, "Direct Primary Legislation, 1936–1939," *American Political Science Review* 3, no. 3 (1940): 499–506; Louise Overacker, "Direct Primary Legislation in 1930–31," *American Political Science Review* 26, no. 2 (1932): 294–300; Louise Overacker, "The Presidential Primary since 1924," *American Political Science Review* 22, no. 1 (1928): 108–9.

59. Louise Overarcker, *The Presidential Primary* (New York: Macmillan, 1926), 22; Overacker "The Presidential Primary since 1924," 109.

60. James Davis, *U.S. Presidential Primaries and the Caucus-Convention System* (Westport, CT: Greenwood Press, 1997); Ware, *The American Direct Primary.*

61. "The Future of the Direct Primary," *Editorial Research Reports,* vol. 3 (Washington, DC: CQ Press, 1926), http://library.cqpress.com/cqresearcher/cqresrre1926091100; Charles Mee, *The Ohio Gang: The World of Warren G. Harding* (New York: M. Evans and Co., 1981).

62. Roy O. West quoted in "Minutes of the National Conference on Practical Reform of Primaries," January 20–21, 1898, New York City, (Chicago: Wm. C. Hollister & Bros., Printers), 97.

63. Hyman Feldman, "The Direct Primary in New York State," *American Political Science Review* 11, no. 3 (1917): 494–518; H. W. Dodds, "Removable Obstacles to the Success of the Direct Primary," *Annals of the American Academy of Political and Social Sciences* 106, no. 1 (1923): 18–21.

64. James Woodburn, *Political Parties and Party Problems in the United States* (New York: G. P. Putnam's Sons, 1906), 19.

65. Roy O. West quoted in "Minutes of the National Conference on Practical Reform of Primaries," 97.

66. Feldman, "The Direct Primary in New York State."

67. Herbert Marguiles, "The Decline of the Progressive Movement in Wisconsin, 1890–1920," State Historical Society of Wisconsin, 1968.

68. Unger, *Fighting Bob La Follette,* 125.

69. J. David Alvis and Jason Jividen, *Statesmanship and Progressive Reform: An Assessment of Herbert Croly's Abraham Lincoln* (New York: Palgrave Macmillan, 2013), 17.

70. Ceaser, "Political Parties and Presidential Ambition."

71. Henry Jones Ford, "The Direct Primary," *North American Review* 190, no. 644 (1909): 1–14, 12–14.

72. West quoted in "Minutes of the National Conference on Practical Reform of Primaries," 96.

73. Thomas L. Johnson, quoted in "Minutes of the National Conference on Practical Reform of Primaries," 99.

74. Ernest C. Meyer, *Nominating Systems: Direct Primaries versus Conventions in the United States* (Madison, Wisconsin, 1902); Feldman, "The Direct Primary in New York State," 908–9.

75. Woodburn, *Political Parties and Party Problems*, 291; Feldman, "The Direct Primary in New York State"; Dodds, "Removable Obstacles to the Success of the Direct Primary."

76. Herbert Croly, *The Promise of American Life* (New York: Macmillan, 1911), 69, 282–83, 324, 331.

77. Quoted in *Eric Goldman, Rendezvous with Destiny* (New York: Alfred A. Knopf, 1952), 315–43.

78. Ford, "The Direct Primary," 4, 12–14.

79. Johnson, quoted in "Minutes of the National Conference on Practical Reform of Primaries," 99.

80. West quoted in "Minutes of the National Conference on Practical Reform of Primaries," 96.

81. While FDR's strategy to unseat conservative Democrats and realign the party failed, his efforts may have contributed to reelecting liberals faced with hostile challengers and widening congressional support for his agenda. Sean Savage, *Roosevelt: The Party Leader, 1932–1945* (Lexington: University Press of Kentucky, 1991).

82. Quoted in Susan Dunn, *Roosevelt's Purge: How FDR Fought to Change the Democratic Party* (Cambridge, MA: Harvard University Press, 2010), 23. Milkis, *The President and the Parties.*

83. Croly and Lippmann shared a commitment to expanding the national government's interventions in the economy and the country's development. They both turned to Alexander Hamilton's ambition of building a strong national government in the Washington administration as an inspiration and a necessary weapon to fend off the new corporation. Kevin O'Leary, "Herbert Croly and Progressive Democracy," *Polity* 26 (Summer 1994): 533–52; Milkis, *The President and the Parties.*

84. Croly, *The Promise of American Life*, 23, 125.

85. Walter Lippmann, *The Phantom Public* (New York: Harcourt, Brace and Company, 1925).

86. Johnson, quoted in "Minutes of the National Conference on Practical Reform of Primaries," 99; Woodburn, *Political Parties and Party Problems*, 292.

87. Croly, *The Promise of American Life*, 120.

88. Croly, *The Promise of American Life*, 69, 324, 331, 342–43 (emphasis added).

89. Croly embraced Jefferson's democratic values, even as he rejected his affinity for local agrarian community and opposition to Hamilton's nationalism as, in effect, ceding power to corporations and monopolies. O'Leary, "Herbert Croly and Progressive Democracy"; Milkis, *The President and the Parties*.

90. Croly, *The Promise of American Life*, 69, 324, 331.

91. Ford, "The Direct Primary," 4, 12–14.

92. Croly, *The Promise of American Life*, 282–83; Croly, *Progressive Democracy*, 359.

93. Croly, *Progressive Democracy*, 284.

94. Ford, "The Direct Primary," 4, 12–14.

95. Croly quoted in Goldman, *Rendezvous with Destiny*, 315–43.

96. Croly, *The Promise of American Life*, 199.

97. Keyssar, *The Right to Vote*, 45, 63, 138.

98. Matthew Jacobson, *Barbarian Virtues: The United States Encounters Foreign Peoples at Home and Abroad, 1876–1917* (New York: Hill & Wang, 2000); Nancy MacLean, *Behind the Mask of Chivalry: The Making of the Second Ku Klux Klan* (New York: Oxford University Press, 1995); Desmond King, *Making Americans: Immigration, Race, and the Origins of the Diverse Democracy* (Cambridge, MA: Harvard University Press, 2000).

99. Drake, *The Education of an Anti-Imperialist*, 282–83.

100. J. Morgan Kousser, *The Shaping of Southern Politics: Suffrage Restriction and the Establishment of the One-Party South, 1880–1910* (New Haven, CT: Yale University Press, 1974).

101. Quoted in Drake, *The Education of an Anti-Imperialist*, 282–83.

102. Drake, *The Education of an Anti-Imperialist*, 11–13, 282–83; Unger, *Fighting Bob La Follette*, 120–21, 228; *Robert M. La Follette and the Insurgent Spirit*, 187–88.

103. Milkis and Tichenos, " 'Direct Democracy' and Social Justice," 315–20.

104. McGerr, *A Fierce Discontent*, 183, 190.

105. King and Smith, "Racial Orders in American Political Development," 64.

106. Quoted in Kousser, *The Shaping of Southern Politics*, 76.

107. Kousser, *The Shaping of Southern Politics*; Robert G. Boatright, *Congressional Primary Elections* (New York: Routledge, 2014).

108. King and Smith, "Racial Orders in American Political Development"; V. O. Key, *Southern Politics in State and Nation* (New York: A. A. Knopf, 1949); Boatright, *Congressional Primary Elections*.

109. George E. Mowry, *The California Progressives* (Berkeley: University of California Press, 1951); George E. Mowry, *Theodore Roosevelt and the Progressive Movement* (Madison: University of Wisconsin Press, 1946); Richard Hofstadter, *The American Political Tradition and the Men Who Made It* (New York: A. A. Knopf, 1948).

110. Martin Sklar, *The Corporate Reconstruction of American Capitalism, 1890–1916* (Cambridge: Cambridge University Press, 1988); Gabriel Kolko, *The Triumph of Conservatism: A Reinterpretation of American History, 1900–1916* (New York: Free Press of Glencoe, 1963).

111. Quoted in Jeff Taylor, *Politics on a Human Scale: The American Tradition of Decentralism* (Lanham, MD: Lexington Books, 2013), 105–6.

112. Kazin, *The Populist Persuasion*; Goodwyn, *Democratic Promise*.

113. Goodwyn, *Democratic Promise*.

114. Stephen Skowronek, *Building a New American State: The Expansion of National Administrative Capacities, 1877–1920* (Cambridge: Cambridge University Press, 1982), 78.

115. Stephen Skowronek and Stephen Engel, "Introduction: The Progressives' Century," in *The Progressives' Century: Political Reform, Constitutional Government, and the Modern American State*, ed. Stephen Skowronek, Stephen M. Engel, and Bruce Ackerman (New Haven, CT: Yale University Press, 2016), 1–15.

116. Cain, *Democracy More or Less*, 71, 95.

117. West, quoted in "Minutes of the National Conference on Practical Reform of Primaries," 97.

118. Sanders, *Roots of Reform*.

Chapter 5

1. Much of this discussion is based on an interview with Barbara Mikulski, July 16, 2020.

2. William J. Crotty, *Decision for the Democrats: Reforming the Party Structure* (Baltimore: Johns Hopkins University Press, 1978), 49.

3. Allen Matusow, *The Unraveling of America: A History of Liberalism in the 1960s* (New York: Harper & Row, 1984).

4. John Morton Blum, *Years of Discord: American Politics and Society, 1961–1974* (New York: W. W. Norton & Company, 1991), 6.

5. Paul Krugman, "For Richer," *New York Times*, October 20, 2002, https://www.nytimes.com/2002/10/20/magazine/for-richer.html.

6. Matusow, *The Unraveling of America*; Blum, *Years of Discord*.

7. Norman Mailer, "Superman Comes to the Supermarket," *Esquire*, November 1960.

8. Robert Caro, *The Years of Lyndon Johnson*, vol. 4: *The Passage of Power* (New York: Knopf, 2012), 2.

9. Blum, *Years of Discord*, 288.

10. Blum, *Years of Discord*; Matusow, *The Unraveling of America*.

11. Matusow, *The Unraveling of America*, 277.

12. Lawrence Jacobs and Robert Y. Shapiro, "Lyndon Johnson, Vietnam, and Public Opinion: Rethinking Realists' Theory of Leadership," *Presidential Studies Quarterly* 29 (September 1999): 592–616.

13. Fifty-seven percent of white respondents indicated that the Johnson administration was pushing too fast on civil rights; only 7 percent said that it was not going fast enough. See information on the Gallup polls in Hazel Erskine, "The Polls: Speed of Racial Integration," *Public Opinion Quarterly* 32, no. 3 (1968): 513–24.

14. Lawrence Jacobs and Robert Y. Shapiro, "Issues, Candidate Image, and Priming: The Use of Private Polls in Kennedy's 1960 Presidential Campaign," *American Political Science Review* 88 (September 1994): 527–40.

15. Blum, *Years of Discord*.

16. David Broder, "The Democrats Dilemma," *The Atlantic*, March 1974, 32-33.

17. Harvey Zeidenstein, "Presidential Primaries—Reflections of 'The People's Choice'?," *Journal of Politics* 32 (1970): 856–74.

18. Theodore H. White, *The Making of the President, 1968* (New York: Atheneum, 1969); William Crotty and John Jackson, *Presidential Primaries and Nominations* (Washington, DC: CQ Press, 1985); Elaine C. Kamarck, *Primary Politics: Everything You Need to Know about How America Nominates Its Presidential Candidates*, 3rd ed. (Washington, DC: Brookings Institution Press, 2018), 13.

19. Kamarck, *Primary Politics*, 8–10.

20. Humphrey failed to beat Kennedy in a single primary they both entered and trailed his vote total by more than 1.2 million votes.

21. Phone interview, Walter Mondale, July 2, 2020.

22. White, *The Making of the President, 1968*, 316–17, 326.

23. Phone interview, Walter Mondale, March 5, 2021.

24. Memorandum from Vice President Humphrey to President Johnson, February 17, 1965, https://history.state.gov/historicaldocuments/frus1 964-68v02/d134.

25. White, *The Making of the President, 1968*, 315–19.

26. *Time*, "Political Notes: Off & On," January 26, 1968.

27. Although McCarthy entered the race in November 1967 to challenge Johnson and not Humphrey, who did not start running until April 27, 1968, the strain between the two Minnesotans was sufficiently deep-seated in the state that it endured more than a half a century.

28. "McCarthy Applauded," *Daily Collegian* (University Park, Pennsylvania), January 13, 1968, 6; "Politics: A Voice for Dissent," *Time*, December 8, 1967 .

29. "Unforeseen Eugene," *Time*, March 22, 1968.

30. White, *The Making of the President, 1968*, 193, 204–7.

31. Matusow, *The Unraveling of America*; White, *The Making of the President, 1968*.

32. "Mark Hatfield Fails to Convince," *Eugene Register-Guard,* June 27, 1968.

33. Kennedy won 2.3 million votes (31 percent) in the primaries he entered. White, *The Making of the President, 1968*, 313.

34. Carl Ogelsby quoted in Frank Kusch, *Battleground Chicago: The Police and the 1968 Democratic National Convention* (Chicago: University of Chicago Press, 2004), 44.

35. Polsby, *Consequences of Party Reform*, 27; Crotty and Jackson, *Presidential Primaries and Nominations*, 30.

36. Polsby, *Consequences of Party Reform*; Crotty, *Decision for the Democrats*.

37. Party members have recently become more present in UK and Germany parties.

38. David Farber, *Chicago'68* (Chicago: University of Chicago Press, 1988), 48, 78, 168, 229.

39. Kusch, *Battleground Chicago*, 98, 110.

40. Farber, *Chicago'68*, 89, 185–87; Kusch, *Battleground Chicago*, 78–83, 97–100.

41. Kusch, *Battleground Chicago*, 90, 96.

42. Farber, *Chicago'68*, 151.

43. Kusch, *Battleground Chicago*.

44. White, *The Making of the President, 1968*, 334.

45. Kusch, *Battleground Chicago*, 78–79, 89, 100, 105.

46. Kusch, *Battleground Chicago*, 99.

47. Farber, *Chicago'68*, 185; Kusch, *Battleground Chicago*, 78.

48. Kusch, *Battleground Chicago*, 102.

49. Kusch, *Battleground Chicago*, 111.

50. Polsby, *Consequences of Party Reform*.

51. White, *The Making of the President, 1968*, 352–53.

52. Commission on the Democratic Presidential Nominees, *The Democratic Choice*, August 1968.

53. Shafer, *Quiet Revolution*, 25–36.

54. Shafer, *Quiet Revolution*, 44–45.

55. The *New York Times* stood out for covering the DNC's approval of a commission and anticipating its potential impact. Although its reporter Max Frankel appreciated the hurdles, he did anticipate the potential of "stripping the power of backroom brokers and opening the gates to popular participation." Max Frankel, "Delegate Fights Transform Party," *New York Times*, August 28, 1968.

56. David Leip, Atlas of US Presidential Elections, https://uselectionatlas.org/RESULTS/.

57. Shafer, *Quiet Revolution*, 48–50.

58. Phone interview, Walter Mondale, November 9, 2018.

59. Crotty, *Decision for the Democrats*, 103; Shafer, *Quiet Revolution*, 148.

60. Shafer, *Quiet Revolution*, 50–51.

61. Shafer, *Quiet Revolution*, 156–57.

62. Mondale interview, July 2, 2020.

63. Shafer, *Quiet Revolution* 57–59, 210; Kusch, *Battleground Chicago*, 89.

64. Shafer, *Quiet Revolution*, 127.

65. They convened for a March 1969 session, first consideration of its recommendations in September 1969, and voted to accept the report in November 1969.

66. Eli Segal quoted in Shafer, *Quiet Revolution*, 203–4.

67. Crotty, *Decision for the Democrats*, 36–37, 145.

68. Shafer, *Quiet Revolution*, 57–59, 210.

69. Shafer, *Quiet Revolution*, 125–26, 153–55, 210.

70. Shafer, *Quiet Revolution*, 155.

71. Crotty, *Decision for the Democrats*, 42–48.

72. *Congressional Record*, 92nd Congress, First Session, vol. 117, part 25 (Washington, DC: US Government Printing Office, 1971), 32909.

73. Quoted in Shafer, *Quiet Revolution*, 146–47.

74. *Congressional Record*, 92nd Congress, 32909–18.

75. Shafer, *Quiet Revolution*, 195, 222–25; Crotty, *Decision for the Democrats*; *Congressional Record*, 92nd Congress, 32909.

76. Broad, organized opposition to the commission's reforms did develop days before the 1972 convention but it was moot: the commission's recommendations had been largely implemented and were difficult for states to reverse even if they favored that option. Crotty, *Decision for the Democrats*, 145; David B. Truman, "Party Reform, Party Atrophy, and Constitutional Change: Some Reflections," *Political Science Quarterly* 99, no. 4 (1984): 637–55, 639.

77. The commission took aim at additional tools that state parties used to choose delegates, exclude rank-and-file Democrats, and reap the rewards of steering support toward particular presidential candidates. State party leaders were stripped of the power to select delegates to serve as their proxies; barred from imposing "unit voting" that bound the entire state delegation to follow the majority's decision; and required making party meetings accessible by publicizing them, holding them on a regular schedule, and needing a quorum of at least 40 percent.

78. Truman, "Party Reform," 641–42; Davis, *U.S. Presidential Primaries and the Caucus-Convention System*, 252–53.

79. Crotty, *Decision for the Democrats*, 145; Shafer, *Quiet Revolution*, 22.

80. Kamarck, *Primary Politics*, 21.

81. The percentage of delegates chosen by primaries in 2020 was 97 percent for Democrats (3 percent by caucus) and 79 percent by Republicans (5 percent by caucus). As of 2020, the Democratic National Convention no longer counts superdelegates unless no candidate wins a clear majority on the first ballot; this boosted the 2020 percentage of delegates chosen by primaries.

82. Keyssar, *The Right to Vote*, 179.

83. Shafer, *Quiet Revolution*.

84. *Congressional Record*, 92nd Congress, 32909–18.

85. Shafer, *Quiet Revolution*.

86. Jeffrey Pressman and Denis Sullivan, "Convention Reform and Conventional Wisdom: An Empirical Assessment of Democratic Party Reforms," *Political Science Quarterly* 89, no. 3 (1974): 540..

87. *New York Times*, "Democrats Vote to Modify Quotas," October 8, 1973, https://nyti.ms/3uM0gG8; Broder, "The Democrats Dilemma"; Robert DiClerico and James Davis, *Choosing Our Choices: Debating the Presidential Nominating Process* (Lanham, MD: Rowan and Littlefield, 2000).

88. Shafer, *Quiet Revolution*, 489.

89. Sidney Tarrow, "Social Protest and Policy Reform," *Comparative Political Studies* 8 (June 2010): 529–42. Tarrow's formulation in this article that protest is a "necessary but not sufficient conditions for extraordinary policymaking" overstates the tangible impact of Chicago's riots on the DNC's decisions.

90. Is it possible that the agenda of the New Left and 1968 protesters was fulfilled by the commission's reforms in 1969–1970 even if later consequences proved disappointing? This may seem plausible, but the commission's direction (channeling political engagement into the bowels of political party administration) was fundamentally at odds with the New Left agenda of democratic participation outside what they considered the stultifying confines of party organization and mobilizing for elections.

91. There is a complicated normative issue related to the protest account. Crediting protesters with the adoption of primaries plays into the hands of democracy's critics, who make a similar point in order to denigrate citizen agency. Cain, *Democracy More or Less*.

92. Mondale interviews, July 2, 2020, and October 1, 2020.

93. Austin Ranney, *Curing the Mischiefs of Faction: Party Reform in America* (Berkeley: University of California Press, 1975).

94. Mondale interview, July 2, 2020.

95. Mondale interview, July 2, 2020.

Chapter 6

1. Edward Foley, "Sorry, President Trump. January 6 Is Not an Election Do-Over," *Washington Post*, December 29, 2020.

2. FiveThirtyEight, "Our Way-Too-Early 2024 Republican President Primary Draft," March 10, 2021, https://53eig.ht/3de9Vip; Alia Slisco, "De Santis and Mike Pence Lead Latest Poll for 2024 Republican Presidential Candidate," *Newsweek*, March 24, 2021, https://bit.ly/3wRMiUq.

3. Dan Carter, *The Politics of Rage: George Wallace, The Origins of the New Conservatism, and the Transformation of American Politics*, 2nd ed. (Baton Rouge: Louisiana State University Press, 2000).

4. Lawrence Meyer, "George Wallace's Message to the Establishment," *Washington Post, ,* May 21, 1972; "Wallace Views the Vote," *New York Times,* March 14, 1972; Eleanor Randolph and Peggy Vlerebome, "St. Petersburg Speech," *St. Petersburg Times,* February 13, 1972, https://www.tampabay.com/news/politics/elections/looking-backto-1972-george-wallace-vs-the-lying-media/2339941/ .

5. Pressman and Sullivan, "Convention Reform and Conventional Wisdom."

6. Gerstle, *American Crucible*; Kazin, "Trump and American Populism."

7. Jeff Stein, "Text of Bernie Sanders's Iowa Speech," Vox, February 2, 2016, https://www.vox.com/2016/2/2/10892752/bernie-sanders-iowa-speech; "Text of Bernie Sanders' Wall Street and Economy Speech," Market Watch, January 5, 2016, https://www.marketwatch.com/story/text-of-bernie-sanders-wall-street-and-economy-speech-2016-01-05; Bernie Sanders, *Our Revolution: A Future to Believe In* (New York: Thomas Dunne Books, 2016).

8. Speech in Rochester, New York, April 10, 2016, https://factba.se/transcript/donald-trump-speech-rochester-ny-april-10-2016; speech in Wilmington, Ohio, January 16, 2016, https://factba.se/transcript/donald-trump-speech-wilmington-oh-january-16-2016; speech in Richmond County, New York, April 17, 2016, https://factba.se/transcript/donald-trump-speech-richmond-county-ny-april-17-2016; acceptance speech, Republican National Convention, Cleveland, Ohio, July 21, 2016, https://www.politico.com/story/2016/07/full-transcript-donald-trump-nomination-acceptance-speech-at-rnc-225974.

9. Verba, "Would the Dream of Political Equality Turn Out to Be a Nightmare?," 663.

10. Before turning his fire on the "good guys" in the Republican Party, Ornstein had—with his coauthor Tom Mann—eviscerated the Republican Party as extreme in two searing books: Thomas Mann and Norman Ornstein, *The Broken Branch: How Congress Is Failing America and How to Get It Back on Track* (New York: Oxford University Press, 2008), and *It's Even Worse Than It Looks: How the American Constitutional System Collided with the New Politics of Extremism* (New York: Basic Books, 2012).

11. Norm Ornstein, "If Republicans Won't Risk Defeat to Tell the Truth, Trump Will Own Their Party," *Washington Post,* January 29, 2021, https://www.washingtonpost.com/outlook/trump-mcconnell-portman-toomey-kinzinger-republicans/2021/01/29/a71efed4-60f0-11eb-9061-07abcc1f9229_story.html.

12. Bawn, Cohen, Karol, Masket, Noel, and Zaller, "A Theory of Political Parties."

13. David T. Canon, *Race, Redistricting, and Representation: The Unintended Consequences of Black Majority Districts* (Chicago: University of Chicago Press, 1999), 3.

14. Gary Jacobson, *The Politics of Congressional Elections*, 6th ed. (New York: Pearson, 2004), 16.

15. Boatright, *Congressional Primary Elections*; Burden, "Candidate Positioning in US Congressional Elections."

16. This section draws on: Seth Masket, *Learning from Loss: The Democrats, 2016–2020* (Cambridge: Cambridge University Press, 2020); and Byron Shafer and Elizabeth Sawyer, "Factions, Constituencies, and Candidates: The Democrats," in *Eternal Bandwagon: The Politics of Presidential Selection (The Evolving American Presidency)*(Cham: Palgrave Macmillan, 2021), 85–120..

17. Masket, *Learning from Loss*; Arthur Hadley, *The Invisible Primary* (Englewood Cliffs, NJ: Prentice-Hall, 1976); Hans Noel, "Is the Party Deciding," *Mischief of Factions*, March 4, 2020; Cohen et al., "Party versus Faction in the Reformed Presidential Nominating System"; Wayne Steger, "Conditional Arbiters: The Limits of Political Party Influence in Presidential Nominations," *PS: Politics and Political Science* (October 2016); Grossman and Hopkins, *Asymmetric Politics.*

18. Grossman and Hopkins, *Asymmetric Politics.*

19. John Sides, "An Expert on Congressional Primaries Weighs In on Cantor's Loss," *Monkey Cage*, June 12, 2014, https://www.washingtonp ost.com/news/monkey-cage/wp/2014/06/12/the-expert-on-congressio nal-primaries-weighs-in-on-cantors-loss/?utm_term=.bae31dd6e25d; Robert Boatright, "No, Primaries Aren't Destroying Politics," Politico, February 18, 2014, https://www.politico.com/magazine/story/2014/02/ primaries-arent-destroying-american-politics-103633

20. Burke, "Speech to the Electors of Bristol."

21. Cain, *Democracy More or Less*, 11; Cain, "Populist Illusions and Pluralist Realities."

22. Meyer, *Nominating Systems*, 280; Feldman, "The Direct Primary in New York State," 908–9.

23. Jason Stanley, *How Fascism Works: The Politics of Us and Them* (New York: Random House, 2018).

24. Austin Ranney, "The Democratic Party's Delegate Selection Reforms, 1968–76," *America in the Seventies*, ed. Allan P. Sindler (Boston: Little, Brown and Company, 1977); Pressman and Sullivan, "Convention Reform and Conventional Wisdom," 545; Shafer, *Quiet Revolution*, 117, 199.

25. The roster of reasons for party polarization include—deep breath—the shift of white voters from the Democratic to the Republican Party after the passage of civil rights legislation, economic inequality, increased Hispanic immigration, residential shifts of whites from urban areas to suburbs and concentration of people of color in urban areas, redistricting maps that created more safe seats, and legislative leader initiatives to force votes that split the parties and unify their members. Aldrich, *Why Parties*; Gary W. Cox and Mathew D. McCubbins, *Setting the Agenda: Responsible Party Government in the US House of Representatives* (New York: Cambridge University Press, 2005); McCarty, Poole, and Rosenthal, *Polarized America*; Jeffrey M. Stonecash, Mark D. Brewer, and Mack D. Mariani, *Diverging Parties: Social Change, Realignment, and Party Polarization. Transforming American Politics* (Boulder, CO: Westview Press, 2003); Frances E. Lee, *Beyond Ideology: Politics, Principles, and Partisanship in the U.S. Senate* (Chicago: University of Chicago Press, 2009); Jamie L. Carson, Erik J. Engstrom, and Jason M. Roberts, "Candidate Quality, the Personal Vote, and the Incumbency Advantage in Congress," *American Political Science Review* 101, no. 2 (2007): 289–301; Sean M. Theriault, *Party Polarization in Congress* (Cambridge: Cambridge University Press 2008).

26. Edward Carmines and James Stimson, *Issue Evolution: Race and the Transformation of American Politics* (Princeton, NJ: Princeton University Press, 1989); Joseph Bafumi and Robert Shapiro, "A New Partisan Voter," *Journal of Politics* 71 (January 2009): 1–24.

27. Bawn, Cohen, Karol, Masket, Noel, and Zaller, "A Theory of Political Parties."

28. Geoffrey Layman, Thomas Carsey, John Green, Richard Herrera, and Rosalyn Cooperman, "Activists and Conflict Extension in American Party Politics," *American Political Science Review* 104 (May 2010): 324–46.

29. Bafumi and Shapiro, "A New Partisan Voter."

30. Alan Abramowitz, *The Disappearing Center* (New Haven, CT: Yale University Press, 2010); Matthew Levendusky, *The Partisan Sort* (Chicago: University of Chicago Press, 2009).

31. Noel Hans, *Political Ideologies and Political Parties in America* (New York: Cambridge University Press, 2013).

32. We collected data from 1952 to 2000 on our dependent variable of presidential polarization and through 1996 for our independent variables—state primaries and the four conditions used in previous research. Our dependent variable is the left-right ideology of presidents in their issue positions during the 1952–2000 period, which we used to create net

polarization scores based on the absolute distance between the mean of liberalism across all years from the mean measure of liberalism for each four-year presidential term. To study the impact of presidential primaries, we measured whether a primary was held (coded "1") for both parties in each state for each presidential election year. In addition, we studied potential competing influences on polarization that might neutralize or condition the effects of primaries: the design of state primaries ("open" or "closed," which was scored "1"), primary turnout for both parties in each state for each presidential election year, higher competition based on the strength of state-level victories, and James Stimson's public mood measure to track the public's ideological leanings at the national level.

Our analysis is of the impact of primaries on presidential polarization; research is needed to consider legislative primaries and polarization that encompasses the period before and after the 1970s.

33. We study the over-time impacts of primaries both in the short term (the effect of 1976 presidential primaries on President Carter's polarization score for 1977 to 1980) and in the longer term (the effect of the 1972 presidential primaries on President Reagan's polarization scores during his two terms in office). We utilize single-equation general error correction models (ECM) to analyze both effects of primary elections on presidential polarization. Specifically, we regress the polarization score of an elected president averaged across his four years in office following a given election year on whether or not there is a direct primary in that election year along with the four factors: size of voter turnout, closed primaries, competitiveness, and public mood.

34. Prior research on the potential effect of primaries on polarization started well after their start in 1972 and may have missed their impact as a result. Our research design of examining this potential effect both before the McGovern-Fraser recommendations and after is unique and creates analytic leverage in studying whether a change took place once presidential primaries proliferated in 1972.

35. Prior research on the potential effects of primaries on polarization identified as influences the following: voter turnout only registered large, significant results in the odd circumstances of an exceptional surge in voter turnout; neither open primaries nor competitiveness mattered at all. Eric McGhee, Seth Masket, Boris Shor, Steven Rogers, and Nolan McCarty, "A Primary Cause of Partisanship? Nomination Systems and Legislator Ideology," *American Journal of Political Science* 58, no. 2 (April 2014): 337–51; Douglas J. Ahler, Jack Citrin, and Gabriel S. Lenz, "Do Open Primaries

Improve Representation? An Experimental Test of California's 2012 Top-Two Primary," *Legislative Studies Quarterly* 41, no. 2 (May 2016): 237–68.

36. In 2017, the US House and Senate passed and Trump signed legislation to allow states to block Title X funding for Planned Parenthood in the Family Planning Program. By comparison, public opinion polls showed that between 62 percent and 75 percent of Americans supported the continued funding of Planned Parenthood. https://www.kff.org/health-costs/poll-finding/kaiser-health-tracking-poll-aca-replacement-plans-womens-health/; Sarah Pulliam Bailey, "Poll: Most Americans Oppose Defunding Planned Parenthood," *Washington Post,* January 27, 2017, https://www.washingtonpost.com/local/2017/live-updates/acts-of-faith/live-coverage-of-the-march-for-life/poll-most-americans-oppose-defunding-planned-parenthood/.

37. Bailey, "Poll."

38. Although the better sorting of voters into ideological parties have increased their polarization, the divisions among everyday Americans are less sharp than among political elites. The degree and breadth of public polarization remain a topic of debate among researchers. Fiorina, Abrams, and Pope, "Polarization in the American Public."

39. Abramowitz, *The Disappearing Center*; Levendusky, *The Partisan Sort.*

40. Marc Hetherington and Thomas Rudolph, *Why Washington Won't Work* (Chicago: University of Chicago Press, 2015).

41. Rogers Smith and Desmond King, "White Protectionism in America," *Perspectives on Politics,* May 2020; Sides, Tesler, and Vavreck, "Hunting Where the Ducks Are."

42. John Rawls, *A Theory of Justice* (Cambridge, MA: Harvard University Press, 1971), 360–61.

43. Schattschneider, *The Semisovereign People*; Lowi, *The End of Liberalism*; McConnell, *Private Power and American Democracy.* For research on the embracing of community and civic republicanism, see Isaac Kramnick, "Republican Revisionism Revisited," *American Historical Review* 87 (1982): 629–64; Craig Calhoun, ed., *Habermas and the Public Sphere* (Cambridge, MA: MIT Press, 1992).

44. Anthony Downs, *An Economic Theory of Democracy* (Boston: Addison Wesley, 1957); Duncan Black, *The Theory of Committees and Elections* (Cambridge: Cambridge University Press, 1958).

45. There isample and growing evidence of the US government's low and declining responsiveness to public opinion using different data and methods. Lawrence Jacobs and Benjamin Page, "Who Influences

U.S. Foreign Policy?" *American Political Science Review* 99 (February 2005): 107–24; Larry Bartels, *Unequal Democracy: The Political Economy of the New Gilded Age* (Princeton, NJ: Princeton University Press, 2008); Martin Gilens and Benjamin I. Page, "Testing Theories of American Politics: Elites, Interest Groups, and Average Citizens," *Perspectives on Politics* 12 (2014): 564–81; Dan B. Wood, *The Myth of Presidential Representation* (New York: Cambridge University Press, 2009).

46. Richard Wike, Laura Silver, Shannon Schumacher, and Aidan Connaughton, "Many in US, Western Europe Say Their Political System Needs Major Reform," Pew Research Center, March 31, 2021. Surveys were conducted in the United States (November 20–December 7, 2020) and in France, Germany, and the United Kingdom between November 10 and December 23, 2020. https://pewrsr.ch/2S4PI6y. Findings for American public opinion mirror those found in surveys by the Gallup organization and the American National Election Studies.

47. Paola Chavez and Veronica Stracqualursi, "Donald Trump on GOP Primary: 'This Is Not Democracy,'" ABC News, April 12, 2016, https://abcnews.go.com/Politics/donald-trump-gop-primary-democracy/story?id=38341901.

48. R. Douglas Arnold, *Logic of Congressional Action* (New Haven, CT: Yale University Press, 1990); Suzanne Mettler, *The Submerged State: How Invisible Government Policies Undermine American Democracy* (Chicago: University of Chicago Press, 2011).

49. Jacobs and Shapiro, *Politicians Don't Pander*; Lawrence Jacobs and Robert Y. Shapiro, "Lyndon Johnson, Vietnam, and Public Opinion: Rethinking Realists' Theory of Leadership"; Druckman and Jacobs, *Who Governs?*; Disch, "Toward a Mobilization Conception." The strategies of consultants is masterfully covered by Adam Sheingate, *Building a Business of Politics: The Rise of Political Consulting and the Transformation of American Democracy* (New York: Oxford University Press, 2016).

50. Zachary B. Wolf, Curt Merrill, and Daniel Wolfe, "How Voters Shifted during Four Years of Trump," CNN, updated December 14, 2020.

51. Druckman and Jacobs, *Who Governs?*

52. James Morone, *The Democratic Wish: Popular Participation and the Limits of American Government* (New York: Basic Books, 1990); Elizabeth Sanders, *Roots of Reform*.

53. Trump received support from "peripheral voters," but they did not make the difference in his nomination. Shane Goldmacher, "Donald Trump Is Not Expanding the GOP," Politico, May 17, 2016, https://www.politico.

com/magazine/story/2016/05/donald-trump-2016-polling-turnout-early-voting-data-213897/.

In Iowa, for instance, Cruz won the caucus and received nearly a quarter of the new voters compared to Trump's 30 percent. In New Hampshire, Trump won the lion's share of new voters but they comprised only 15 percent of the primary electorate and did not impact the race: Trump won by twenty points over his closest rival and would have readily prevailed without the new voters.

54. Reuven Hazan and Gideon Rahat, *Democracy within Parties: Candidate Selection Methods and Their Political Consequences* (Oxford: Oxford University Press, 2010).

55. Data on Sanders's 2020 and 2018 fundraising come from the Center for Responsive Politics. https://www.opensecrets.org/2020-presidential-race/bernie-sanders/candidate?id=N00000528; https://www.opensecrets.org/pres16/candidate?id=N00000528.

56. King and Smith, "Racial Orders in American Political Development."

57. Cain, "Populist Illusions and Pluralist Realities," 6–7.

58. Larry Bartels, "Ethnic Antagonism Erodes Republicans' Commitment to Democracy," *Proceedings of the National Academy of Sciences* (September 2020): 22752–59.

59. Reny, Collingwood, and Valenzuela, "Vote Switching in the 2016 Election"; Fowler, Medenica, and Cohen, "Why 41 Percent of White Millennials Voted for Trump"; Sides, Tesler and Vavreck, "Hunting Where the Ducks Are."

60. Regina P. Branton, "The Importance of Race and Ethnicity in Congressional Primary Elections," *Political Research Quarterly* 62, no. 3 (2009): 459–73; Canon, *Race, Redistricting, and Representation*. Researchers vary in whether they are describing districts with Black voters alone or districts with Hispanics, indigenous people, and other people of color. When I am referring to the former, I specifically mention that.

61. David Lublin, Lisa Handley, Thomas L. Brunell, and Bernard Grofman, "Minority Success in Non-Majority Minority Districts: Finding the 'Sweet Spot,'" *Journal of Race, Ethnicity and Politics* 5, no. 2 (2020): 275–98.

62. Calculated based on census data from the American Community Surveys, https://www.census.gov/programs-surveys/acs/data.html.

63. Jennifer L. Lawless, *Becoming a Candidate: Political Ambition and the Decision to Run for Office* (New York: Cambridge University Press, 2012).

64. Branton, "The Importance of Race and Ethnicity in Congressional Primary Elections."

65. Matthew Schousen, David T. Canon, and Patrick J. Sellers, "Representation and Ambition in the New African-American Congressional Districts: Supply-Side Effects," in *Race and Redistricting in the 1990s*, ed. Bernard Grofman (Bronx, NY: Algora, 1998).

66. Canon, *Race, Redistricting, and Representation*; Janai S. Nelson, "White Challengers, Black Majorities: Reconciling Competition in Majority-Minority Districts with the Promise of the Voting Rights Act," *Georgetown Law Journal* 95, no. 4 (2007): 1287–312.

67. Boatwright, *Congressional Primary Elections*.

68. Wike et al., "Many in US, Western Europe Say Their Political System Needs Major Reform." The distrust of political parties and the party system is not new. Christian Collett, "The Polls: Trends, Third Parties, and the Two-Party System," *Public Opinion Quarterly* 60 (1996): 431–49.

69. Wike et al., "Many in US, Western Europe Say Their Political System Needs Major Reform."

70. Anthony Salvanto et al., "CBS News Poll: Still More to Learn about January 6, Most Americans Say," CBS News, July 20, 2021, https://www.cbsnews.com/news/january-6-opinion-poll/.

71. Wike et al., "Many in US, Western Europe Say Their Political System Needs Major Reform."

72. Grinnell College National Poll, "Most Americans Agree on Foundation of Democracy, but Execution of Those Ideals Receives Failing Grades," March 31, 2021, https://www.grinnell.edu/news/poll-broken-democracy.

    This pattern of seesawing partisan perception of fairness is found in data collected by the American National Elections Studies (ANES) starting in 2004. The differences between Democrats and Republicans are not, however, as large in the ANES data.

73. The framers narrowed disputes from global challenges to more nested questions by establishing the constitutional authority of Congress to regulate US House and US Senate elections (Article I, section 4) and specifying the conduct of the Electoral College (Article II, section 1, and the Twelfth Amendment). For instance, the intense early-nineteenth-century disputes over presidential electors and the role of the House of Representatives were addressed by reforms of an existing structure without razing the republic.

74. Larry Bartels, "Ethnic Antagonism Erodes Republicans' Commitment to Democracy," *Proceedings of the National Academy of Sciences* (September 2020): 22752–59.

75. Matthew Graham and Milan Svolik, "Democracy in America? Partisanship, Polarization, and the Robustness of Support for Democracy in the United States," *American Political Science Review* 114 (2020): 392–409.

76. Felix-Christopher Von Nostitiz and Giulia Sandri, "State Funding and Party Primaries," in *Handbook of Political Party Funding*, ed. Jonathan Mendilow and Éric Phélippeau (Northampton, MA: Edward Elgar, 2018), 203–21; William Cross et al, *The Promise and Challenge of Party Primary Elections: A Comparative Perspective*.

77. Reuven Y. Hazan and Gideon Rahat, *Democracy within Parties: Candidate Selection Methods and Their Political Consequences* (Oxford: Oxford University Press, 2010).

78. Verba, "Would the Dream of Political Equality?," 675–66; Schlozman, Brady, and Verba, *Unequal and Unrepresented*.

Chapter 7

1. Schumpeter, *Capitalism, Socialism, and Democracy*, but cf. Hannah Pitkin, *The Concept of Representation* (Berkeley: University of California Press, 1967).

2. Mark Warren, "Deliberative Democracy and Authority," *American Political Science Review* 90 (March 1996): 46–60; Frank Fischer, *Democracy and Expertise: Reorienting Policy Inquiry* (Oxford: Oxford University Press, 2009).

3. Lisa Disch, "Toward a Mobilization Conception of Democratic Representation," *American Political Science Review* 105 (2011): 100–114; Urbinati, *Disfigured Democracy*; Saffon and Urbinati, "Procedural Democracy, the Bulwark of Equal Liberty."

4. Verba, "Would the Dream of Political Equality Turn Out to Be a Nightmare?"

5. For an outstanding compilation of such proposals, see American Academy of Arts and Sciences, "Our Common Purpose: Reinventing American Democracy for the 21st Century," Cambridge, Massachusetts, 2020.

6. Urbinati and Warren, "The Concept of Representation in Contemporary Political Theory."

7. We found that voters who were white and more affluent turned out at a higher rate, completed their ballots more accurately, and were more likely to use all three opportunities to rank their most preferred candidates compared to voters living in low-income neighborhoods and

in communities of color. Our analysis relied on data from two sources. First, we used census information on Minneapolis neighborhoods to identify wards with most and least residents of color and the most and least residents living below the poverty line. Second, we used data provided by the city clerk to examine racial and income differentials for undervoting (i.e., use of all three possible choices or just one or two choices) and spoiled ballots. Lawrence Jacobs and Joanne Miller, "Rank Choice Voting and the 2013 Minneapolis Elections," manuscript, February 2014, https://bit.ly/3vq9K9V.

Additional research also finds a socioeconomic status (SES) gradient. See, for instance, Jason A. McDaniel, "Writing the Rules to Rank the Candidates: Examining the Impact of Instant-Runoff Voting on Racial Group Turnout in San Francisco Mayoral Elections," *Journal of Urban Affairs* 38 (2016): 387–408.

Several studies found no or limited effects,[QY: word missing here] but the research designs raise questions. One study relies on self-reported understanding, which leaves open the possibility that voters were unable to fill out the ballot successfully without problems of over/under voting. In addition, it set the reference categories as females who were interested in the race; it would have been more effective to separate out those who were interested versus those not interested. Todd Donovan, Caroline Tolbert, and Kellen Gracey, "Self-Reported Understanding of Ranked-Choice Voting," *Social Science Quarterly* 100, no. 5 (2019): 1768–76.

Another study focuses on two elections without examining the potential of uncontrolled differences in each year or between them: David C. Kimball and Joseph Anthony, "Voter Participation with Ranked Choice Voting in the United States," presented at the *Annual Meeting of the American Political Science Association* (2016), https://www.umsl.edu/~kimballd/KimballRCV.pdf.

For prior research on the social, economic, and status skew of political participation, see Schlozman, Verba, and Brady, *The Unheavenly Chorus*; Schlozman, Brady, and Verba, *Unequal and Unrepresented*.

8. National Archives, Electoral College. https://www.archives.gov/electoral-college/faq#changes.

One clever proposal is inching forward. It calls for a national compact among states to award all of their electoral votes to the presidential candidate who wins the overall popular vote in the country. The National Popular Vote Interstate Compact has been adopted in fifteen states, representing 36 percent of Electoral College votes and 72 percent of the

270 votes needed to win the presidency and trigger the compact. While advocates insist that state approval of the compact would circumvent the Constitution, critics have raised objections that may find favor with a conservative Supreme Court. Thomas Neale and Andrew Nolan, "The National Popular Vote (NPV) Initiative: Direct Election of the President by Interstate Compact," *Congressional Research Service*, October 28, 2019. https://crsreports.congress.gov/product/pdf/R/R43823/9; Norman Williams, "Why the National Popular Vote Compact Is Unconstitutional," *BYU Law Review* 5 (2012): 1523–80.

9. With Democrats and Republicans each having fifty US senators in 2021–2022, the Democrats represent a population that is about a quarter larger, amounting to more than 41 million votes. For instance, Wyoming has the same number of US senators as the large state of California even though the latter has sixty-eight times the population. Ian Millhiser, "America's Anti-Democratic Senate," Vox, November 6, 2021, https://www.vox.com/2020/11/6/21550979/senate-malapportionment-20-million-democrats-republicans-supreme-court

10. Skocpol, "Thinking Strategically about Policy Feedbacks."

11. Republican National Committee, "Growth and Opportunity Project," March 2013, https://online.wsj.com/public/resources/documents/RNC report03182013.pdf.

12. King and Smith, "Racial Orders in American Political Development"; Rogers Smith, "Beyond Tocqueville, Please! Response," *American Political Science Review* 89 (December 1995): 987–995.

13. Racial diversity is altering the electorate, but its impact in boosting the prospects of Democrats and an agenda to offset racial disparities may be muted by redistricting and Republican support among voters of color in red states. Nate Cohn, "Why Rising Diversity Might Not Help Democrats as Much as They Hope," *New York Times*, May 4, 2021.

14. Research finding that Republican restrictions may not be effective because of the backlash and countermobilization include Enrico Cantoni and Vincent Pons, "Strict ID Laws Don't Stop Voters: Evidence from a U.S. Nationwide Panel, 2008–2018," *National Bureau of Economic Research*, Working Paper 25522, February 2019, https://www-nber-org.ezp2.lib.umn.edu/papers/w25522. Summary discussion is offered by David Bateman, "Voter Suppression Started Way before Jim Crow. It's a Longstanding American Tradition," Monkey Cage, March 29, 2021, https://www.washingtonpost.com/politics/2021/03/29/voter-suppression-started-way-before-jim-crow-its-longstanding-american-tradition/.

While this research suggests the limits of voter suppression legislation, their focus is only on immediate effects. If the state legislation remains in place, the longer-term impacts may be most damaging to the participation of voters of color.

15. Pew Research Center, March 31, 2021.

16. James Madison, The Federalist 51, in *The Federalist,* ed. Jacob Ernest Cooke (Middletown, CT: Wesleyan University Press, 1982).

17. Robert Dahl, "James Madison: Republican or Democrat?," *Perspectives on Politics* 3 (September 2005): 439–48.

18. Madison, The Federalist 10, in *The Federalist.*

19. Harold Koh, *The National Security Constitution* (New Haven, CT: Yale University Press, 1990); Charlie Savage, "Trump and His Lawyers Embrace a Vision of Vast Executive Power," *New York Times,* June 4, 2018, https://nyti.ms/30yw7vT; Jacobs, "Trump Wields the Imperial Presidency."

20. David Cole, "After September 11: What We Still Don't Know," *New York Review of Books,* September 29, 2011, and Cole, *Engines of Liberty: The Power of Citizen Activists to Make Constitutional Law* (New York: Basic Books, 2016).

21. https://www.hhh.umn.edu/certificate-programs/certificate-election-administration.

22. Nancy Rosenblum, *On the Side of the Angels: An Appreciation of Parties and Partisanship* (Princeton, NJ: Princeton University Press, 2008); Urbinati, *Disfigured Democracy.*

23. Robert Dahl, "What Political Institutions Does Large-Scale Democracy Require?," *Political Science Quarterly* 120 (Summer 2005): 193; Dahl, *A Preface to Democratic Theory* (Chicago: University of Chicago Press, 1956), no, *Polyarchy: Participation and Opposition* (New Haven, CT: Yale University Press, 1971).

24. Jennifer Lawless, *Becoming a Candidate: Political Ambition and the Decision to Run for Office* (New York: Cambridge University Press, 2012), 33.

25. Richard Pildes, "In Nearly All Other Democracies, This Is Not Normal." *New York Times,* July 21, 2021; Matthew Streb, *Rethinking American Electoral Democracy,* Controversies in Electoral Democracy and Representation (New York: Routledge, 2008); Ivor Crewe, "Electoral Participation" in *Democracy at the Polls: A Comparative Study of Competitive National Elections,* ed. David Butler, Howard R. Penniman, and Austin Ranney (Washington, DC: American Enterprise Institute for Public Policy Research, 1981), 216-63.

26. Hubert Heinelt, Eran Razin, and Karsten Zimmermann, *Metropolitan Governance: Different Paths in Contrasting Contexts: Germany and Israel* (Frankfurt: Campus Verlag, 2011); Pitrová Miroslava, "Municipalities in the Federal Republic of Germany—Progress and Current Situation," *Politics in Central Europe* 4 (2008): 59–74; Hellmut Wollmann, "The Directly Elected Executive Mayor in German Local Government," in *Transforming Local Political Leadership* (London: Palgrave Macmillan, 2005), 29–41; Mark Sanford, *Local Government in England: Structures*, House of Commons Briefing Paper Number 07104, November 20, 2020, https://researchbriefings.files.parliament.uk/documents/SN07104/SN07104.pdf.

27. Streb, *Rethinking American Electoral Democracy*.

28. Streb, *Rethinking American Electoral Democracy*, Chapter 3.

29. Han, *How Organizations Develop Activists*.

30. Martin Wattenberg, Ian McAllister, and Anthony Salvanto, "How Voting Is Like Taking an SAT Test: An Analysis of American Voter Rolloff," *American Politics Quarterly* 28 (2000): 234–50.

31. Pildes, "In Nearly All Other Democracies, This Is Not Normal."

32. Phone interviews with Walter Mondale, March 30 and July 2, 2020.

33. Croly, *The Promise of American Life*, 282–23; Woodburn, *Political Parties and Party Problems in the United States*, 292.

34. John Dewey, "The People and Its Problems," in *The Later Works*, vol. 2, ed. Jo Ann Boydston and Bridget Walsh (Carbondale: Southern Illinois University Press, 2008), 365.

35. Dahl, "What Political Institutions Does Large-Scale Democracy Require?"; Dahl, *A Preface to Democratic Theory*; Dahl, *Polyarchy*.

36. The one case when superdelegates mattered was the Democratic Party's 1984 nomination of Walter Mondale over Gary Hart; it did not have the intended impact.

37. Marty Cohen, David Karol, Hans Noel, and John Zaller, "Party versus Faction in the Reformed Presidential Nominating System," *PS: Political Science and Politics*, 49 (October 2016): 701–8, http://ow.ly/g4ai30jA9Ls.

38. Some research suggests that "closed" systems are linked to rising polarization. Elizabeth Gerber and Rebecca Morton, "Primary Election Systems and Representation," *Journal of Law, Economics, and Organization* 14 (1998): 304–24; Karen Kaufmann, James Gimpel, and Adam Hoffman, "A Promise Fulfilled? Open Primaries and Representation," *Journal of Politics* 65 (May 2003): 457–76.

Other studies fail to find this effect. Still more research indicates that open primaries are not associated with rising polarization; they fail to affect the ideology of lawmakers elected to the House of Representatives or to state legislatures. Todd Cherry and Stephan Kroll, "Crashing the Party: An Experimental Investigation of Strategic Voting in Primary Elections," *Public Choice* 114 (March 2003): 387–420; Eric McGhee, Seth Masket, Boris Shor, Steven Rogers, and Nolan McCarty, "A Primary Cause of Partisanship? Nomination Systems and Legislator Ideology," *American Journal of Political Science* 58 (2014): 337–51; Jon Rogowski and Stephanie Langella, "Primary Systems and Candidate Ideology: Evidence from Federal and State Legislative Elections," *American Politics Research* 43 (2014): 846–71. In addition, one study reports that voters lack enough information to identify moderate candidates and end up choosing more ideologically distant candidates. Douglas Ahler, Jack Citrin, and Gabriel Lenz, "Do Open Primaries Improve Representation? An Experimental Test of California's 2012 Top-Two Primary," *Legislative Studies Quarterly* 41 (2016): 237–68.

39. Research reports no effects of California's nonpartisan primaries on the ideological positioning of candidates, a slight moderation of winning candidates, and greater partisan polarization. Kristin Kanthak and Rebecca Morton, "The Effects of Primary Systems on Congressional Elections," in *Congressional Primaries and the Politics of Representation*, ed. Peter Galderisis and Mike Lyons (Lanham, MD: Rowman and Littlefield, 2001), 116-31; Elisabeth Gerber and Rebecca B. Morton, "Primary Election Systems and Representation," *Journal of Law, Economics & Organization* 14 (1998): 304–24; McGhee, Masket, Shor, Rogers, and McCarty, "A Primary Cause of Partisanship?"; Thad Kousser, Justin Phillips, and Boris Shor, "Reform and Representation: Assessing California's Top-Two Primary and Redistricting Commission," presented at the annual conference of the Midwest Political Science Association in Chicago, Illinois, 2013.

40. Hamilton's deal-making and Jackson's assaults branded the US national bank with a stigma that continues to scar the latter-day version—the Federal Reserve System. Jacobs and King, *Fed Power*.

41. McKenna, Han, and Oyakawa, *Prisms of the People*.

42. Pitkin, *The Concept of Representation*; Disch, "Toward a Mobilization Conception"; Saffon and Urbinati, "Procedural Democracy."

43. Skocpol, *Diminished Democracy*.

44. Han, *How Organizations Develop Activists*; McKenna, Han, and Oyakawa, *Prisms of the People*.

45. Jacobs, Cook, and Carpini, *Talking Together*; John Gastil, *By Popular Demand* (Berkeley: University of California Press, 2000), 7.Peter Levine, Archon Fung, and John Gastil, "Future Directions for Public Deliberation," in *The Deliberative Democracy Handbook: Strategies for Effective Civic Engagement in the Twenty-First Century* ed. John Gastil and Peter Levine (San Francisco: Jossey-Bass, 2005), 276.

46. Organisation for Economic Co-operation and Development, "Innovative Citizen Participation and New Democratic Institutions," June 2020, https://bit.ly/3fo8U7k; Carole Pateman, "Participatory Democracy Revisited," *Perspectives on Politics* 10 (2012): 7–19.

47. Archon Fung, *Empowered Participation Reinventing Urban Democracy* (Princeton, NJ: Princeton University Press, 2004).

48. Elena Fagotto, "Embedded Deliberation: Moving from Deliberation to Action," presentation at the National Conference on Dialogue and Deliberation, San Francisco, California, August 3–6, 2006.

49. Resistance in the Chicago Police Department stymied the public voice but it also spurned further changes that produced a significant shift toward civilian police oversight. Fran Spielman, "City Council Approves Civilian Police Oversight Ordinance," *Chicago Sun Times*, July 21, 2021, https://chicago.suntimes.com/2021/7/21/22586897/chicago-police-cpd-civilian-oversight-board-city-council-union-fop-lightfoot-catanzara-contract.

50. Citizen organizing to influence policy has drawn attention, challenged the established agendas, and spawned initiatives. But the impact remains uneven. Public budgeting, for instance, has influenced policy priorities but consistently faced stultifying resistance by established powers. Even its public forums on budgets have struggled to gain broad public awareness and tended to underrepresent marginalized groups.

Index

For the benefit of digital users, indexed terms that span two pages (e.g., 52–53) may, on occasion, appear on only one of those pages.